Beyond Modernity

Ex Oriente Lux

New Perspectives on Russian
Religious Philosophers

SERIES

VOL. 1

Edited by Artur Mrówczyński-Van Allen,
Teresa Obolevitch, and Paweł Rojek

This book is the first in the series *Ex Oriente Lux*, and provides an introduction to the context of the subsequent volumes.

We believe that the Russian religious philosophy of the nineteenth and twentieth centuries has great importance for Christian theology and philosophy. Russian thinkers, rooted in the tradition of the Church Fathers, avoided the theological dualism that so deeply penetrates Western thought. Such philosophers and theologians as Peter Chaadaev, Alexei Khomiakov, Vladimir Soloviev, Evgeni Trubetskoy, Pavel Florensky, Sergey Bulgakov, Nikolai Berdyaev, Georges Florovsky, and Aleksei Losev developed unique views on the relationships between religion and culture, science, philosophy, and social life, which, unfortunately, are missing from contemporary Western debate. The pressing task is to include their legacy in the context of contemporary philosophical and theological dialogue.

The series *Ex Oriente Lux* aims to meet this need. It serves as a way to bring Eastern Christian intuitions into the contemporary post-secular philosophical and theological context. Each subsequent volume will focus on one Russian thinker and include a selection of essays on his main ideas in historical and contemporary perspectives. The books in the series are prepared by both Western and Russian scholars, creating a space for discussion.

The books in the *Ex Oriente Lux* series come out of research connected with the annual conferences on Russian religious philosophy held in Krakow, Poland. The "Krakow Meetings" are organized jointly by the Pontifical University of John Paul II in Krakow, Poland, the Institute of Philosophy *Edith Stein* in Granada, Spain, and the International Center for the Study of the Christian Orient in Granada, Spain.

The Next Volumes in the Series

Peter Chaadaev: Between the Love of Fatherland and the Love of Truth
Alexei Khomiakov: We Are Sobornost'
Evgeni Trubetskoy: Icon and Philosophy

Beyond Modernity

*Russian Religious Philosophy
and Post-Secularism*

EDITED BY

Artur Mrówczyński-Van Allen,
Teresa Obolevitch,
and Paweł Rojek

☙PICKWICK *Publications* • Eugene, Oregon

BEYOND MODERNITY
Russian Religious Philosophy and Post-Secularism

Ex Oriente Lux 1

Copyright © 2016 Wipf and Stock Publishers. All rights reserved. Except for brief quotations in critical publications or reviews, no part of this book may be reproduced in any manner without prior written permission from the publisher. Write: Permissions, Wipf and Stock Publishers, 199 W. 8th Ave., Suite 3, Eugene, OR 97401.

Pickwick Publications
An Imprint of Wipf and Stock Publishers
199 W. 8th Ave., Suite 3
Eugene, OR 97401

www.wipfandstock.com

PAPERBACK ISBN: 978-1-4982-3977-6
HARDCOVER ISBN: 978-1-4982-3979-0
EBOOK ISBN: 978-1-4982-3978-3

Cataloguing-in-Publication data:

Names: Mrówczyński-Van Allen, Artur, 1968–, editor. | Obolevitch, Teresa, 1974–, editor. | Rojek, Paweł, 1981–, editor.

Title: Beyond modernity : Russian religious philosophy and post-secularism / edited by Artur Mrówczyński-Van Allen, Teresa Obolevitch, and Paweł Rojek.

Description: Eugene, OR : Pickwick Publications, 2016 | Ex Oriente Lux 1 | Includes bibliographical references.

Identifiers: ISBN 978-1-4982-3977-6 (paperback) | ISBN 978-1-4982-3979-0 (hardcover) | ISBN 978-1-4982-3978-3 (ebook)

Subjects: LSCH: Russians—Intellectual life—20th century. | Russians—Intellectual life—19th century. | Postmodernism—Religious aspects—Christianity. | Christianity and culture—Russia. | Religion and culture—Russia. | Christian philosophy—Russia. | Religious thought—Russia.

Classification: BR932 .B43 2016 (print) | BR932 .B43 (ebook)

Manufactured in the U.S.A.   10/10/16

Contents

Contributors | ix

Introduction: "Abel, where is your Brother Cain?" The Russian Way of Overcoming Modernity—Artur Mrówczyński-Van Allen, Teresa Obolevitch, Paweł Rojek | 1

Part I: General Overview

1 *Aspects of the Russian Tradition of Philosophical-Theological Synthesis in the Post-Secular Context: Georges Florovsky, Sergey Bulgakov, Alain Badiou, and the "Theology Dwarf"*—Artur Mrówczyński-Van Allen, Sebastián Monticl Gómez | 13

2 *"Secularisation" and "Post-Secular" in Russian Religious Thought: Main Features*—Konstantin Antonov | 25

3 *Post-Secularity vs. All-Unity*—Grigory Gutner | 39

4 *Post-Secularism: A Preliminary Outline of the Issue with a Certain Ancient Russian Context*—Janusz Dobieszewski | 49

Part II: Systematic Studies

5   *Eleusa: Secularism, Post-Secularism, and Russian Sophiology*
    —Aaron Riches | 59

6   *Russian Sophiology and the Problem of the Subject in Modern Philosophy*—Natalia Vaganova | 86

7   *Post-Secular Metaphysics: Georges Florovsky's Project of Theological Philosophy*
    —Paweł Rojek | 97

8   *Sergey Bulgakov's Trinitarian Anthropology: Meaning, Hope, and Evangelizing in a Post-Secular Society*—Walter Sisto | 136

Part III: Historical Focuses

9   *Friedrich Nietzsche as a Christian Thinker: The Philosophy of Nietzsche in the Context of the Russian Religious Philosophy of the Nineteenth and Twentieth Centuries*—Igor Evlampiev | 147

10 *Eschatology or Progress? Vladimir Soloviev and his Criticism of St. Philaret of Moscow's Ecclesiology*—Fr. Pavel Khondzinskiy | 160

11 *Christianity in the Times of Postmodernism? A Reconstruction of Answers by Sergey Bulgakov and Nikolai Berdyaev*
    —Katharina Anna Breckner | 168

12 *Towards a New Understanding of Immanence and Transcendence: The Concept of Kairos in the Writings of Nikolai Berdyaev and Paul Tillich*—Monika Woźniak | 175

13 *Religion in Public Life according to Nikolai Berdyaev*
    —Halina Rarot | 186

14 *Religious Revival and Post-Secular Society according to Pavel Florensky*—Nikolai Pavliuchenkov | 199

15 *The Philosophy of Culture of Semen Frank and its Significance for the Post-Secular World*—Teresa Obolevitch | 210

16 The Way *Journal (1925–1941) and the Question of Freedom in the Context of European Post-Secular Culture*—Olga Tabatadze | 225

17 *Overcoming the Secular: Viktor Nesmelov's Teaching on Personhood as the Justification of the Radical Theological Commitment in the Dialogue between Faith and Reason*—Alexei Nesteruk | 238

18 *The Crisis of the Classical Anthropological Model: The Anthropological Mission of Post-Secularism according to Sergey Horujy*—Roman Turowski | 253

19 *Christian Philosophical Mysticism in the Poetry of "Leningrad's Underground" as a Challenge to Soviet Secularism*—Zhanna Sizova | 264

Contributors

Konstantin Antonov, Professor at St. Tikhon's Orthodox University, Moscow, Russia.

Katharina Anna Breckner (1962–2015), Independent scholar, Hamburg, Germany.

Janusz Dobieszewski, Professor at University of Warsaw, Warsaw, Poland.

Igor Evlampiev, Professor at Saint Petersburg State University, Saint Petersburg, Russia.

Grigory Gutner, Professor at the Institute of Philosophy of the Russian Academy of Science, Moscow, Russia.

Fr. Pavel Khondzinskiy, Professor at St. Tikhon's Orthodox University, Moscow, Russia.

Sebastián Montiel Gómez, Professor at the University of Granada, Granada, Spain.

Artur Mrówczyński-Van Allen, Professor at the International Center for the Study of the Christian Orient and Institut of Philosophy "Edith Stein," Granada, Spain.

Alexei Nesteruk, Professor at the University of Portsmouth, Portsmouth, The United Kingdom.

Contributors

Teresa Obolevitch, Professor at the Pontifical University of John Paul II in Krakow, Poland.

Nikolai Pavliuchenkov, Assistant Professor at St. Tikhon's Orthodox University, Moscow, Russia.

Halina Rarot, Professor at the Lublin University of Technology, Lublin, Poland.

Aaron Riches, Assistant Professor at the Institut of Philosophy "Edith Stein," Granada, Spain.

Pawel Rojek, Assistant Professor at the Pontifical University of John Paul II in Krakow, Poland.

Walter Sisto, Assistant Professor at D'Youville College, Buffalo, NY, United States.

Zhanna Sizova, Editor of the *Voda Zhivaya* Journal, Saint Petersburg, Russia.

Olga Tabatadze, Assistant Lecturer at the International Center for the Study of the Christian Orient, Granada, Spain.

Roman Turowski, Doctoral Student at the Pontifical University of John Paul II in Krakow, Poland.

Natalia Vaganova, Professor at St. Tikhon's Orthodox University, Moscow, Russia.

Monika Woźniak, Doctoral Student at the University of Warsaw, Warsaw, Poland.

INTRODUCTION

"Abel, where is your Brother Cain?"

The Russian Way of Overcoming Modernity[1]

Artur Mrówczynski-Van Allen
Teresa Obolevitch
Paweł Rojek

Post-secularism is the fundamental element for the end of modernity. It is its final stage, in which modernity is waking up from Francisco Goya's dream and realizing that, although it thought that it was awake, it was producing monsters. Modernity becomes aware that the enlightened "awakening of reason" was nothing but an illusion, a nightmare that it tries to exorcise with a new magic formula: "post-secularism." How have the relationships between the post-secular consciousness that tries to defend its alleged position of neutrality towards religion and its ever more obvious dependence on the religious nature of mankind—or even its own religious, or better said, mythical, character—been articulated? How were the Russian thinkers of the nineteenth and twentieth century able to identify this aspect of modernity? We hope the reader will be able to find answers to these questions in the works gathered here.

The innermost characteristic of the secular is the alienation that devours time and space, the time and space of the most human experience, forgiveness-and-donation (*for-give, per-don*). This is the monster of the nightmares that are far worse than the ones imagined by the genius of the aforementioned Spanish painter. Reducing this for-give space-time to a mere ethical question and subordinating that question, in two well-separated

---

1. This publication is a result of research generously supported by a grant from the National Science Center, Poland, No. 2014/15/B/HS1/01620.

spheres (the private and the public), to the power, self-proclaimed as autonomous, of "justice" and of the "law," reveals the fundamental soteriological ambition of secular reason. The process of the separation of *seaculum* from the *aeternitas* is the process of the birth, growth, rule, and finally the fall of modernity. It is the history of the fragmentation of man's deepest identity and the destruction of his relationship with God and, by extension, of his relationships with others, with the world that surrounds us.

Beyond Secular Reason

It must be admitted that this drama of fragmentation also forms an essential part of the history of the church. It emerged in Western late medieval theology and continues to shape our theopolitical imagination nowadays. This is why, as Monsignor Javier Martínez writes,

> our circumstances are not determined principally by the difficulties put on the church from the outside, but rather by the fact that, faced with the world in general and its culture, and faced, furthermore, with that harassment, there does not seem to be a community capable of explaining its aims or why it lives the way it does.[2]

The problem is that the Christians understand ourselves in the alien categories of the dominant secular culture. The church has been somehow "domesticated" or "colonized" by the culture of modernity. This process undermines the very foundations of the Christian way of feeling, thinking, and acting. What is worse, this colonization is so deep that Christians are usually not even aware of it. As a result, in many cases a rash fight against secularism might even deepen its fatal consequences. What is the way out? As Javier Martínez insists, Christians

> have to do with the way we understand how the Christian experience—the encounter with the living Christ in the communion of his body, of the church—affects our view of and relationship with reality, that is, how it affects our understanding of the "self" and of all of reality, how it affects our understanding and exercise of reason, of freedom, and of affection, how it affects our perception of beauty, of good, and of truth.[3]

---

2. Martínez, *Más allá de la razón secular*, 10.
3. Ibid., 11.

It turns out therefore, that the intellectual and cultural categories in which we understand and describe ourselves have critical moral consequences. These categories might bind the Christian experience to the limits of the private sphere or, on the contrary, allow it—as it should be—to spread into the whole life of the living member of the Body of Christ. An urgent need is thus to find appropriate categories for Christian experience.

One promising source of such categories might be the Russian religious philosophy of the turn of nineteenth and twentieth century. We tried to explore that tradition in our previous edited book, *Apology of Culture: Religion and Culture in Russian Thought*.[4] For many reasons the Russian thought of that time remained unaffected by Western philosophical and theological dualism.[5] Whereas the *Apology,* being based on the paradigm of the Russian legacy, was devoted to general issue of the relation between Christianity and culture, the current volume, *Beyond Modernity: Russian Religious Philosophy and Post-Secularism*, focuses on more recent and particular discussions on secularity. After outlining an overview of the general context of relation between religion and culture we are now ready to focus our research on more specific aspects of the relationship between Christian experience and thought, between the secular and the post-secular world.

Recently in Europe and in United Sates we have been confronted with a great debate on the relationship between religion and the secular world. It seems that we are witnessing a true post-secular turn. Jürgen Habermas, in his famous speech in 2001, urged secular reason to profit from the remains of religion which had been retained in contemporary societies. Many other authors, including Jacques Derrida, Alain Badiou, Slavoj Žižek, and Giorgio Agamben quite surprisingly became interested in Christianity. On the other hand, the Radical Orthodoxy movement (John Milbank, Catherine Pickstock, Graham Word, and others) and authors such as Stanley Hauerwas, Steven Long, David Schindler, William Cavanaugh, or Archbishop Javier Martínez, tried to answer this interest from the Christian point of view. In the works written by these important figures in modern thought, signs of the interrelationship between the intellectual, cultural, and moral spheres, between the personal and the community, between the political and the sacred, between the secular and the transcendent, between the philosophical and the theological, appear with significant persistence, although often in an indirect way.

---

4. Mrówczyński-Van Allen, Obolevitch, Rojek, *Apology of Culture.*

5. See Mrówczyński-Van Allen, Obolevitch, Rojek. "Apology of Culture and Culture of Apology," 2–3, cf. Rojek, "The Trinity in History and Society."

Modernity rests on the assumption of the fundamental division between the old pre-modern religious societies and contemporary modern secular ones. Secularization was seen for a long time as an inherent component of the process of modernization. Nowadays, however, the assumption of a "great divide" between the religious and secular ages is being questioned more and more. The border between "the religious" and "the secular" turned out to be not so clear and distinct as it was believed. This state of affairs was recognized—after the events of September 11—even by such a skeptical and "non-religious" philosopher as Habermas who presently stresses the relevance of religion in different spheres of public life. Religion is seemingly no longer treated as just the domain of private convictions, but increasingly takes an important place in political, sociological and philosophical discourse. The general problem of the role of religion entails a number of more specific questions, such as the issue of religious toleration, ecumenical and interreligious dialogue, the presence and contribution of religious (including metaphysical, concerning the sphere of transcendence) foundations and aspects in a multicultural, pluralistic society as well as their possible limits, the democratization of the sphere of religion, the problem of religious language, etc. One also should mention the problem of the relationship between religion and science, or, more general, faith and reason: whereas Habermas insists on a strong division between them, other thinkers admit the possibility (or even necessity) of their interplay.[6]

The debate on post-secularism has also engaged contemporary Russian thinkers. In Russia and other post-communist countries the question of post-secularism has a peculiar character in view of the strong (and still influential) heritage of atheistic propaganda which created the so-called "Soviet type of secularization."[7] For this reason the shape of reflection on post-secular culture in Russian thought is quite different from that in Western society: it pays more attention not only to the "crisis" of religious consciousness, but also to the alleged "death of God." It is no surprise that the topic of post-secularism recently "has received attention in both popular and more elite intellectual Russian press and blogosphere,"[8] and Russia itself is considered as a "laboratory of post-secularism."[9]

It seems to us that modernity and the process of secularization, with its post-secular epilogue, can clearly be observed in the history of what

6. See Szerszynski, "Rethinking the Secular."

7. See Klimova and Molostova, "'Scientific Atheism' in Action," Kyrlezhev and Shishkov, "Postsecularism in Post-Atheist Russia," and Shishkov, "Nekotoryye aspekty desekulyarizatsii," 166–69.

8. Stroop, "The Russian Origins of the So-Called Post-Secular Moment," 63.

9. Uzlaner, "Rossiya—laboratoriya postsekulyarnosti."

is usually called "the modern state," as a specific product of modernity in which the processes proper thereto are concentrated—the processes that in trying to colonize and domesticate the intellectual, cultural, and moral spheres, consequently only offer modern man views and versions thereof that are fragmentary and condemned to death.[10] It is no coincidence that, from its inception, the process of the creation of the modern state—which is the same process as the sacralization of the state—bears the signature of the theologian as lawyer. *Corpus mysticum*, from the twelfth century onward, became *corpus iuridicum*, and this process extended to include the state, eventually leading to the state's sacralization and the development of new foundational ideologies.[11]

The process of the secularization and nationalization of Christian categories has been clearly identified by Russian thinkers. Once again, we would like to recall Gogol's words about the legal and juridical occupying the "vacuums" left by the culture of the Christian community.[12] Nikolai Berdyaev, in turn, locates the difference between a state and a people in the fundamental fact that the state was created by an act of violence in a world that refuses love.[13] We must keep in mind, as Berdyaev points out, that Celsus defended the empire and imperial power using with arguments very similar to those used to defend the totalitarian state in our own time. Moreover, Berdyaev observes,

> the so-called liberal democracies, which claimed to be neutral in regard to the realm of the Spirit, no longer exist: they have increasingly become dictatorships . . . where once the emperors said that they were called not only to rule the state, but to look out for the salvation of the souls of their subjects, the caesars of today are also concerned with saving souls, if only from religious superstitions. Caesar always and irresistibly tends toward demanding for himself not only that which is Caesar's, but that which is God's.[14]

The modern state is therefore based on the very offer of salvation. This offer, however, was not only limited to the conception of law as a repressive instrument. It also established the *legal* possibility—and for that reason

10. See Mrówczyński-Van Allen, *Between the Icon and the Idol*, cf. Rojek, "Theocracy and Apocalypse."
11. Kantorowicz, *The King's Two Bodies*, 206–07.
12. Zenkovskii, *Russian Thinkers and Europe*, 35, see also Mrówczyński-Van Allen, Obolevitch, Rojek. "Apology of Culture and Culture of Apology," 4–5.
13. Berdyaev, *The Realm of Spirit and the Realm of Caesar*, 77.
14. Ibid., 78.

justified—for the expulsion, isolation, and elimination of others—whether these others are Jews, the bourgeois, kulaks, enemies of the proletariat, enemies of progress, neighbors, brothers, sisters, the elderly, or fetuses. This offer of salvation characterizes all modern states. It includes the control of all aspects and levels of life, and it encourages the response to evil with counter-evil, that is, with the accusation.

As Jean-Luc Marion writes in *Prolegomena to Charity*:

> If I (passively) undergo evil, it is actively that I kindle a counter-evil. And if evil is universal, in me and around me—as, in fact, it clearly is—then the counter-evil of the accusation will have to become universal also. And, in fact, the accusation does become universal. For accusation, obviously, offers itself as the final weapon of those who do not have, or no longer have, any other. But truly, must one own a weapon?[15]

This first victory of evil is decisive, because it leads those who suffer to affirm their innocence through accusation, to perpetuate suffering by demanding the suffering of others. It entices them, in other words, to oppose evil with counter-evil. Marion continues:

> The triumph of the logic of evil within the very effort to be rid of it stands out markedly in the universal accusation. This phenomenon can take the following formulation: just because the cause of evil remains to me unknown, uncertain, and vague doesn't mean that I must give up trying to suppress it . . . In order to speak of such a cause, our time has invented expressions: "round up the usual suspects," but above all, "determine accountability."[16]

In order to fulfill this undertaking, the state offers us the guarantees of the *rule of law*, sustained by the structure of the *ministry of justice*. The ministry of justice stealthily usurps the place of the ministry of forgiveness, conquering us with the logic of the accusation and erecting its power upon the structure of institutionalized vengeance. The rule of law offers us a space in which the other is the one upon whom I unload my sufferings and my responsibilities. It perpetually returns us to the position of Cain and makes us participants in his question: "Am I my brother's keeper?" (Genesis 4:9). As Marion indicates, our response turns out to be

> Of course not! If someone is my brother's keeper, it would be anyone other than me! If, of the two of us, one has to be responsible,

---

15. Marion, *Prolegomena to Charity*, 5.
16. Ibid.

> it is my brother, who is responsible for my unhappiness by the simple fact that he remains happy when I no longer am.[17]

This is the response accepted by all, in the sense that the normalcy in which we live is the normalcy of Cain, where the solitude of alienation devours the space of donation.

In the face of this secular devouring, a response appears in the form of a question, a question that shows us an entirely different way, a question that can only be asked outside of the secular paradigm, outside of the space and time enclosed in the *saeculum*. A question that can only be asked from beyond the secular sphere and from beyond the post-secular sphere as well—that is, from beyond modernity. A question that, with the appearance of a moral issue, transfers its ontological, anthropological, and historiosophical charge to explode modernity from within: "Abel, where is your brother Cain?" This question collapses the innermost structures of modernity, exploding it (both the immanence of secularism and the pseudo-transcendences of post-secularism) with the subtlest implication of eternal mercy.

This shocking question was asked by two great figures of twentieth century Russian culture. Vasily Grossman showed in his works that the normalcy of evil—its terrible banality—cannot extinguish the normalcy we carry within ourselves, which is simply the freedom to love, namely donation. The logic of donation, which is the inverse of logic of accusation, and which defeats alienation, permits a new question to appear, which Grossman dares to formulate with a terrible honesty, "Abel, where is your brother Cain?"[18] To our mind, it is significant that the same question appears in Berdyaev's book, *The Destiny of Man*, published in Paris in 1931.[19] This fact not only suggests that Grossman might have been familiar with the book, but it also allows us to affirm that Grossman himself belonged to the best tradition of Russian thought—a tradition that refused to capitulate before the dominant secular (or post-secular), modern culture and that made possible the interpretation of the true reality of the modern societies, his culture, his laws, and his *states*.

This question, "Abel, where is your brother Cain?" seems to be a symbol of the power of the tradition proper to the Russian legacy of overcoming the colonization by, and enslavement to, modernity. The mere possibility of asking this question is revealed to us by the center of the Christian event: the Incarnation, the death and the Resurrection of the Son of God, the mystery

---

17. Ibid., 8.
18. Grossman, "Avel," 113–16.
19. Berdyaev, *The Destiny of Man*, 276–77.

and the reality of Jesus Christ God-and-man, the mystery and the reality that bring us to the reality and the mystery of the relational, Trinitarian *perichoresis* of God. This question—which is a *stumbling block* to secular reason and is *foolishness* to the post-secular mentality—can only be asked when we start from this center. This divine-human reality (Godmanhood), and man rescued thereby through *theosis*, essentially rests on the response to secular and post-secular modernity. Modernity always entails a more or less obvious type of idolatry, of (anti)theology, of religion.

This seems to be the profound context that was able to give birth to the particular strain of Russian Christian thought. Within it, our authors explore the ways to understand some of the most important aspects of the period defined as the post-secular: from the very nature of the secular and the post-secular, secularization, the principle of All-Unity, freedom and liberalism, to metaphysics, ascetics, anthropology, nihilism, progress, eschatology, immanence and transcendence, culture, mysticism, and sophiology. Thus, despite the broad range of questions, and with our attention focused on the topicality of the post-secular, we are convinced that the works presented here represent a significant step forward in the inclusion of the heritage of Russian religious philosophy to this contemporary debate. We are sure that Russian philosophers of nineteenth and twentieth centuries, such as Vladimir Soloviev, Pavel Florensky, Sergey Bulgakov, Nikolai Berdyaev, Georges Florovsky or Semen Frank, formulated unique views on the relation between Christianity and science, philosophy and social life, which are missing in contemporary western debate. On the one hand we hope to prove that Russian thought is surprisingly attractive and up to date and, on the other, we would like to supplement this crucial European debate. In this way our rather academic project nevertheless has importance for contemporary Christian culture in general.

Because, as Grossman intuited and Berdyaev expressed, "moral consciousness began with God's question: 'Cain, where is your brother Abel?' It will end with another question on the part of God: 'Abel, where is your brother Cain?'"[20] And this *other question* means a step forward and indicates the direction of the path that will take us beyond modernity.

---

20. Ibid., 277.

Bibliography

Berdyaev, Nicholas. *The Destiny of Man*. Translated by Natalie Duddington. London: Geoffrey Bles: The Centenary Press, 1937.

———. *The Realm of Spirit and the Realm of Caesar*. Translated by Donald A. Lowrie. New York: Harper & Brothers, 1952.

Grossman, Vasiliy S. "Avel." In *Izbrannoye. V gorode Berdicheve: rasskazy, povesti, svidetel'stva*, 113–16. Ekaterinburg: U-Faktoriya, 2005.

Kantorowicz, Ernst. *The King's Two Bodies*. Princeton: Princeton University Press, 1997.

Klimova, Svetlana, and Elena Molostova. "Scientific Atheism in Action: Soviet Sociology of Religion as an Agent of Marxist-Atheist Propaganda from the 1960s to the 1980s." *Forum Philosophicum* 2 (2013) 169–90.

Kyrlezhev, Alexander, and Andrej Shishkov. "Post-Secularism in Post-Atheist Russia." Faenza: Institute for East-Central Europe and the Balkans (University of Bologna), 2011. Online: http://www.pecob.eu/flex/cm/pages/ServeBLOB.php/L/EN/IDPagina/3100.

Marion, Jean-Luc. *Prolegomena to Charity*. Translated by Stephen E. Lewis. New York: Fordham University Press, 2002.

Martínez, Javier. *Más allá de la Razón secular. Beyond Secular Reason*. Granada: Editorial Nuevo Inicio, 2008.

Mrówczyński-Van Allen, Artur. *Between the Icon and the Idol. The Human Person and the Modern State in Russian Literature and Thought: Chaadayev, Soloviev, Grossman*. Translated by M. P. Whelan. Eugene, OR: Cascade, 2013.

———, Teresa Obolevitch, and Paweł Rojek. "Apology of Culture and Culture of Apology: Russian Religious Thought against Secular Reason." In *Apology of Culture. Religion and Culture in Russian Thought*, edited by Artur Mrówczyński-Van Allen, Teresa Obolevitch and Paweł Rojek, 1–12. Eugene, OR: Pickwick Publications, 2015.

———, Teresa Obolevitch, and Paweł Rojek, editors. *Apology of Culture. Religion and Culture in Russian Thought*. Eugene, OR: Pickwick Publications, 2015.

Rojek, Paweł. "Theocracy and Apocalypse. Political Theology of Artur Mrówczyński-Van Allen. *Radical Orthodoxy* 3/1 (2015) 104–22.

———. "The Trinity in History and Society: The Russian Idea, Polish Messianism, and the Post-Secular Reason." In *Apology of Culture: Religion and Culture in Russian Thought*, edited by Artur Mrówczyński-Van Allen, Teresa Obolevitch and Paweł Rojek, 24–42. Eugene, OR: Pickwick Publications, 2015.

Shishkov, Andrey. "Nekotoryye aspekty desekulyarizatsii v postsovetskoy Rossii." *Gosudarstvo. Religiya. Tserkov'* 2 (2012) 165–77.

Stroop, Christopher. "The Russian Origins of the So-Called Post-Secular Moment: Some Preliminary Observations." *State, Religion and Church* 1 (2014) 59–82.

Szerszynski, Bronisław. "Rethinking the Secular: Science, Technology, and Religion Today." *Zygon* 4 (2005) 813–22.

Uzlaner, "Rossiya—laboratoriya postsekulyarnosti." Online: http://www.pravmir.ru/dmitrij-uzlaner-rossiya-laboratoriya-postsekulyarnosti/.

Zenkovskii, Vasiliy. *Russian Thinkers and Europe*. Translated by Galia S. Bodde. Ann Arbor, MI: American Council of Learned Societies, 1953.

PART I

General Overview

1

Aspects of the Russian Tradition of Philosophical-Theological Synthesis in the Post-Secular Context

Georges Florovsky, Sergey Bulgakov, Alain Badiou, and the "Theology Dwarf"[1]

Artur Mrówczyński-Van Allen
Sebastián Montiel Gómez

In the famous first few paragraphs of his "Theses on the Philosophy of History," Walter Benjamin recalled the story that was told about a machine built to play chess in such a way that it was able to respond to every move made by an opponent with a countermove that would ensure it would win the game. It looked like a puppet in Turkish dress, holding a water pipe in its mouth and seated before the chessboard, which was placed on a large table. A system of mirrors gave spectators the illusion that this table was transparent from all sides. But in fact a hunchbacked dwarf who was an expert chess player sat inside, guiding the puppet's hands with strings. Benjamin concluded that we can conceive of a philosophical counterpart to this device. The puppet we call "historical materialism" is to win every time. It could easily be a match for anyone, if it enlists the services of theology, which today, as we know, is wizened and has to keep out of sight.[2]

In our opinion, this quote from Benjamin allows us to define the term "post-secular" in a very illustrative way. Here we will allow ourselves to

---

1. This publication is a result of research generously supported by a grant from the National Science Center, Poland, No. 2014/15/B/HS1/01620.

2. Benjamin, "Theses on the Philosophy of History," 253–64.

expand the meaning of the term somewhat, applying it not only to a type of philosophy but to the predominant school of thought characteristic of our era. We believe this will help us sketch out some features of the philosophical-theological synthesis that is paradigmatic for the Russian Orthodox tradition, and begin to appreciate the topicality thereof, as it offers important suggestions for articulating contemporary Christian thought. In so doing, we hope to contribute something new to the conversation that started a few years ago.[3]

To this end, we will discuss some elements of the proposal made by the most representative, in our opinion, post-secular thinker, Alain Badiou, as well as aspects of Fr. Sergey Bulgakov's and Fr. Georges Florovsky's thought. Finally, we hope to discover what role is played today by the "dwarf" described by Benjamin.

The Post-Secular

There is no need to provide a detailed explanation here of what the terms "secular" and "post-secular" are understood to mean in the Western and Russian spheres. Some years have already gone by since Aleksandr Kyrlezhev's and Aleksandr Zhuravskiy's articles were published in the journal *Kontinent*.[4] And in an interview granted to the newspaper *Izvestiya* in 2009, Patriarch Cyril commented in no uncertain terms that today's society is not called "post-secular" for nothing.[5] These two clear points illustrate the traditional attention with which the modern world is observed and analyzed from Russia. Given this attention, here we will only allow ourselves to briefly outline the concept of "post-secular" and the interpretation that we propose.

At the end of the twentieth century, "post-secular philosophy" was still spoken of as a branch of modern philosophy born out of the criticism and crisis of metaphysics that addressed questions about the relationship between religion (the religious realm) and philosophy, between the sacred and the secular. Some time later, Jürgen Habermas defined it as a type of theory in which one of the central problems was the issue of the presence of religion in modern Western societies, which he already called "post-secular."[6] In the twenties Frank Rosenzweig's insight had already pointed

---

3. See Mrovchinski-Van Allen, "Russkiye mysliteli i Evropa segodnya."

4. Kyrlezhev, "Postsekulyarnaya epokha," Zhuravskiy, "Religioznaya traditsiya v usloviyakh krizisa sekulyarizma."

5. Kirill, "Tserkovnaya zhizn."

6. Habermas, "Religion in the Public Sphere."

at this type of thought.[7] Debates on the relationship between philosophy and religion have clearly led the way forward; one example is the renowned debate that emerged from the famous conference on "Christian philosophy" that took place on March 21, 1931 in the Societé Française de Philosophie.[8] What became increasingly clear were the two essential questions that post-secular philosophy had to address, namely: "how to interpret modernity" and "what place does or should religion occupy in this modernity?" Thinkers with such varied positions as John Milbank, Catherine Pickstock, Jürgen Habermas, Charles Taylor, Jacques Derrida, and Alain Badiou are among the philosophers who have tried to tackle these questions. The debate central to the philosophy of the past few decades on the character of the secular in modernity shows us that the secularization has not been as total as we might imagine. For example, in his work *A Secular Age*, Charles Tayler presents an option for interpreting secularity in which secularization implies the establishment of new conditions for religious convictions.[9] This process necessarily entailed working out a specific way of thinking, the characteristics of which are described by Msgr. Javier Martínez in his essay *Beyond Secular Reason*.[10]

In our opinion, what differentiates the secular age from the post-secular one is that in the latter we have discovered that in the former, there were in fact certain theologies (or crypto-theologies) hidden behind all of the secular philosophies. That is to say, the post-secular era does not consist so much in an apparent recovery of the positions of the religions but in the recovery of the awareness that all thought is in some way theological.

Fr. Sergey Bulgakov

From the outset we want to note that sophiology is not among the aspects of Fr. Sergey Bulgakov's thought that we will discuss herein. This is due to the simple reason that we do not feel that we have enough knowledge of the issue to do so; however, we agree with the assessment made by Natalia Vaganova in the prologue to her exceptional book, namely, that it is possible that we simply have not discovered the extent to which we could find Fr. Bulgakov's sophiology necessary.[11]

    7. Franke, "Franz Rosenzweig and the Emergence of a Post-Secular Philosophy," 161–80.
    8. Borghesi, "Cristianismo y filosofía," 310–24.
    9. Taylor, *A Secular Age*, 20.
    10. Martínez, *Beyond Secular Reason*.
    11. Vaganova, *Sofiologiya protoiyereiya Sergeiya Bulgakova*, 11.

What we can affirm is that Bulgakov's sophiology was the result of an intense quest to respond to dualism. From the time he published his first texts critical of Marxism in 1904 (*From Marxism to Idealism*) through the period in which he returned to the Orthodox faith and was ordained as a priest, this question became one of the fundamental issues in his work, finding expression in the text *Unfading Light* (1916). According to Lev Zander, this work includes a sort of summary of philosophical problems drawn up in the light of the Bulgakov's characteristic religious-philosophical perspective.[12] In the first sentence of the prologue itself, Bulgakov writes, "In these miscellanies, I would like to display in philosophical thought or to incarnate in speculation some religious contemplations connected with a life in Orthodoxy,"[13] and over the course of the book he analyzes the way religion and its relationship with dogmas, miracles, philosophy, apophatic theology, anthropological questions, history, theocracy, and eschatology, are understood. Without a doubt, all of the elements of this work are held together by a clear rejection of dualism, of the separation between the natural and the supernatural, between the immanent and the transcendent, between God and creation. Thus experience appears as a central point in his philosophical-theological reflection, while at the same time, as Leonid Vasilienko explains in his *Introduction to Russian Religious Philosophy*, he clearly ties it to Tradition and dogmatics.[14] Vasilienko indicates that according to Fr. Bulgakov, faith needs dogma, as for him, "dogma is the formula of that which is identified by faith as transcendent existence."[15]

We can find the follow-up to these reflections in the work published in the year 1921 with the illustrative title "The tragedy of philosophy. Philosophy and dogma." For Fr. Bulgakov, the tragedy of philosophy lies, as Vasilienko notes, in the fact of philosophy's separation from its Christian roots.[16] He compares all true philosophers to Icarus, who must try to fly, to raise himself up to the sky, but who is always, inevitably condemned to fall[17]—because they do not know how to overcome the contradiction that forms the very basis of philosophy: the relationship between experience and rational thought. Still in *Unfading Light*, Bulgakov indicates that the fundamental philosophical issues, the questions of philosophical systems, are not invented or thought (*vydumannyye*), but rather are firstly experienced

12. Zander, *Bog i mir*, 40.
13. Bulgakov, *Unfading Light*, xxxvii.
14. Vasilenko, *Vvedeniye v russkuyu religioznuyu filosofiyu*, 193.
15. Bulgakov, *Unfading Light*, 54.
16. Vasilenko, *Vvedeniye v russkuyu religioznuyu filosofiyu*, 193.
17. Bulgakov, "Tragediya filosofii," 314.

and sensed, and that they have a supra-philosophic origin.[18] But philosophy does not end in experience; it is subjected to reason and this process changes the Truth of experience into theoretical veracity, separated like an element of theoretical speculation from the indivisible unity of the living truth.[19] Therefore, reason tends to choose only one of the elements of truth and to create a system on the basis thereof. This "spirit of the system" is nothing but the reduction of multiplicity to one, and the reverse, the development of multiplicity from the one,[20] which means that these philosophies ultimately always turn out to be monist. Consequently, philosophical systems constructed in this way (which Bulgakov divides into three fundamental groups: idealist, panlogical, and realist) are condemned to lead to a false, or at the very least, incomplete way of understanding the world. Thus, Bulgakov writes, Western philosophy finds itself trapped in a circle, the vicious circle of the heresies, and in this sense the history of philosophy can be presented and interpreted as religious heresiology.[21]

The way to avoid the trap of the "drama of philosophy," of the rupture in the relationship between experience and reason, is to recover the correct articulation of the relationship between philosophy and the experience of the church based on the Revelation and the Tradition set forth in the dogmas (in the Creed), which very clearly show us the path back to the experience of the church of the Apostolic age and the subsequent Patristic legacy. This is the path taken by Fr. Bulgakov, as clearly demonstrated by the example of two articles published in the journal *Put'* in 1930. Issue 20 and 21 of this journal open with the two parts of Bulgakov's article "The Eucharistic Dogma,"[22] in which we can see how he puts the conclusions drawn from his research into practice. From the outset he studies the relationship between the physical and the metaphysical within the specific experience of the faithful's participation in the Eucharist, eating and drinking the Body and Blood of Jesus Christ. This study is based on and carried out on the foundation of a deep knowledge of the Scriptures, of the Patristic sources.

Fr. Georges Florovsky

Despite the well-known differences, we also find this model of philosophical-theological reflection in the works of Fr. Georges Florovsky. We believe

18. Bulgakov, *Unfading Light*, 82.
19. Ibid., 81.
20. Bulgakov, "Tragediya filosofii," 312.
21. Ibid., 317.
22. Bulgakov, "The Eucharistic Dogma."

it can be said that both philosophers intended to remain loyal to dogma, and that the quest for this loyalty led them both to Patristic sources. It is no coincidence that Florovsky himself acknowledges that the decisive push that led him to devote himself to Patristic studies came from Bulgakov.[23]

The conviction that Christianity is not a theoretical construction, but rather the Revelation of God in history and man's response to this Revelation, has played a fundamental role in Florovsky's thought throughout his life.[24] In his article "The Cunning of Reason" he sets forth a critical view of Western thought trapped in philosophical rationalism (from Comte's scientism, Darwin's determinism, Marxism, Bergson's naturalism, and Husserl's anti-psychologism, to neo-Scholasticism and neo-Kantianism), accusing it of having lost the sense of contemplation, which ultimately brings it to the "monism of reason."[25] In the return to the Fathers, Florovsky finds the path towards recovering the possibility of saving theology from the influence of this "monism of reason," an influence that has entailed "the Western religious tragedy."[26]

In the year 1936, at the First Congress of Orthodox Theologians in Athens, he was already calling back the spirit of the Fathers. In the talk he presented there, "Patristics and Modern Theology," he noted the topicality of Patristic thought and the pressing importance of a return to the Fathers.[27] For Florovsky, the most important aspect of Patristic thought was its existential, non-theoretical, experience-based character. He recalls Gregory of Nazianzus's statement that the Fathers theologized not in the manner of Aristotle but in the manner of the Apostles, and he called this theology a "kerygmatic theology" because the kerygma of the Apostles made the dogma of the Fathers possible. He stressed that Patristic theology has never been a theoretical system, writing that "Patristic theology was existentially rooted in the decisive commitment of faith."[28] These "existential" roots, however, did not condition the expression of the truths of the faith, and the Fathers learned to express them in the language of philosophy: as Florovsky said in Athens, it is true that the Holy Fathers have created a new philosophy, different from Platonism and Aristotelianism.[29] With this statement, however, he was not denying the importance of Greek thought's contribution to the

---

23. Blane, "A Sketch of the Life of Georges Florovsky," 49.
24. Ibid., 17–25.
25. Florovsky, "The Cunning of Reason."
26. Florovsky, *Ways of Russian Theology*, 2.302.
27. "Patristics and Modern Theology."
28. Florovsky, *Bible, Church, Tradition*, 108.
29. Florovsky, "Patristics and Modern Theology."

Patristic tradition (he did not hesitate to affirm, in *Ways of Russian Theology*, for example, that Hellenism represents an eternal category in Christian existence)[30]; rather on the contrary, he only defends the autonomy of the *new philosophy*, which had to be established based on the Revelation and experience. This affirmation appears in his article published in Munich in 1931 under the title "Offenbarung, Philosophie und Theologie."[31] In this article, he writes that faith is the evidence of experience and dogma is a witness of experience. Dogma is the testimony of thought about what has been seen and revealed, about what has been contemplated in the experience of faith—and this testimony is expressed in concepts and definitions. Dogma is "an intellectual vision." That is to say: it is the logical image, a "logical icon" of divine reality. And one could simply say: in establishing dogmas, the church expressed the Revelation in the language of Greek philosophy. And he adds, "To state it more correctly—Christian dogmatics itself is the only true philosophical *system*."[32]

Alain Badiou

It seems that a modern thinker has come to a very similar conclusion. This thinker is Alain Badiou, and he is, in our opinion, the most important non-secular modern thinker.

He begins his first *opus magnum*, *Being and Event*, published in 1988, by posing the problem of the millennia: how is it possible to conceive of multiplicity when metaphysics has always held that "what is not *one* being is not a *being*" (Leibniz)? Despite his contempt for those he calls "contemporary sophists," he sets off on his way back to Plato by taking from them his central claim: "the multiple is and the One is not." He thinks of this non-being of the One as an "axiomatic decision"[33] allegedly required by the principle of non-contradiction, even though the precise way he chooses to escape this ancient dilemma between the being of the One and that of the multiple possesses, according to him, no "thinkable determination." In other words, Badiou acknowledges that, in the sense of scientific or philosophical rationality, there is no ultimate justification for the basic decision involved in his system. It follows from this "axiomatic decision" that ontology, understood as it has traditionally been defined since Aristotle, that is, as the science of being-qua-being, must be identified with mathematics, because set theory is

30. Florovsky, *Ways of Russian Theology*, 2.175.
31. Florovsky, "Revelation, Philosophy, and Theology."
32. Ibid., 33.
33. Badiou, *Being and Event*, 26.

the only "intellectual achievement" that has allowed human beings to conceive of a "pure doctrine of the multiple." Of course, there are many different set theories, depending essentially on how one wants to handle infinite sets. Badiou's preference for the Zermelo-Fraenkel set theory is not by any means an innocent choice, even though he presents this specific *axiomatic* theory as *the* standard one. In fact, this preference is nothing but a second (and now hidden) "axiomatic decision." In the Zermelo-Fraenkel theory, sets or multiplicities need not (must not) be defined. Definitions would link Being with the Word and would make the Word creator of Being, thus allowing for the possibility of self-references, the most famous generators of multiplicities that are too large, or, even worse, paradoxical, for example, the set consisting of all sets, and likewise the most famous generators of salvation, for example, "I am Who I am." It is worth noting that Georg Cantor, a Catholic, never had problems living in coexistence with all of these infinite multiplicities. It was the primacy of the non-contradiction principle over word and intuition, established by Gottlieb Frege, Bertrand Russell, and others, that led mathematicians to axiomatize set theory in order to make it possible to exclude intractable infinite sets.

Therefore, in the Zermelo-Fraenkel theory, we only work with ten (schemes of) axioms that govern the unique relationship among these undefined multiplicities: that of "belonging." This relationship does not logically distinguish between *sets* (the containers) and *elements* (the contents), and thus prohibits the establishment of ontological hierarchies. In other words, the *being-qua-being* is made up of multiplicities of multiplicities of multiplicities . . . and so on in an abyssal vortex whose depth could in principle be infinite. But it is not, because one of the axioms postulates the "existence" of the "empty set," which is the multiplicity of nothing. That is, set theory, or Badiou's meta-ontological interpretation thereof, authorizes us to count-as-one the void. In so doing we obtain a point at which to arrest the fall into the multiple of the multiple of the multiple . . . That is, at the bottom of the abyss of multiple being is the void. And so, as Badiou asserts, "the void is the proper name of Being." Contrary to Kant, Badiou considers that we always have access, a mathematical access, to this vertiginous emptiness of *being qua being*. But not only ontology is at stake in Badiou's work; so too are *appearance*, *event*, *truth*, and *subject*. We know that everything that is presented (or experienced) as *one* is not, because the one is not. This one that is not appears as one only as a result of the pre-subjective operation of *counting-as-one* the multiple being. In a certain sense, this operation conceals the multiplicity of the multiplicities that belong to the multiplicity that is counted-as-one. Yet let us not deceive ourselves! There is neither anyone nor anything that performs this operation, not even a kind of transcendental subject. So, then, who or what counts-as-one? Elementary: axioms! For good reason Badiou repeatedly insists that being and thought are identical. Here we are not speaking of the Aristotelian-Platonic mysterious proportion or identity between things as existing and things as known, because for Badiou, thought has nothing to do with either truth or subject. Indeed, for Badiou, *subjects*, thoughtless and empty, are created through a process of "fidelity" to a *truth*, which in turn is that which is radically indiscernible in an *event*, a multiplicity that cannot be counted-as-one. Thus, the event is that which is not being-qua-being and "ontology has nothing to say about the event" or the truth. This makes it impossible for anyone to hear the phrase "I am the Truth," in which subject, being, and truth are amalgamated.

In this way, Badiou returns to Heidegger's systematic metaphysics, substituting the *poem* for the *mathema*. Being-qua-being is mathematical and paradigmatically cognizable. Truth is indiscernible and is not Being, but modifies Being. Time is spatialized. Therefore, History does not exist. Finally, negating the contradiction entails secularizing the Infinite, and this is set theory's fundamental achievement.

The increasing popularity of Badiou's thought and that of the head of his "propaganda department," Slavoj Žižek, is no longer surprising. The fact that this type of thought is becoming one of the more influential of the first half of the twenty-first century necessarily brings us to reflect on how to respond to it, or, in principle, on where the critical points that we must address are to be found.

In the article by Bulgakov referred to previously, the center of the exposition of the dogma of the Eucharist is the question of the relationship between "corporality" and spirituality, between the divinity and the humanity of the Incarnate Word. But do not we find, Bulgakov asks, "an ontological contradiction"[34] in this dogmatic affirmation regarding the Eucharist?

In Badiou's ontology, *Logos* Creator is automatically excluded by Badiou's foundational "axiomatic decision," namely "the One is not," a decision to which he is brought due to his reverence for the logical principle of non-contradiction.

Here there is an invitation to assume that reality reveals itself as a contradictory mystery, to abandon our favorite old logical principle, and to adopt a new, "transfigured" non-contradiction principle, which could well be called the principle of Chalcedon. With the Incarnation of the Son, our only access to full reality is through the Body of Jesus Christ. Therefore, there are in fact "two natures without confusion, change, division, or

---

34. Bulgakov, "The Eucharistic Dogma," 127.

separation; the distinction between the natures was never abolished by their union, but rather the character proper to each of the two natures was preserved as they came together in one person and one hypostasis"; these two natures are the finite character of created things and their participation in the absolute Infinity of the Creator.

Given all of the above, we can ask ourselves the following questions: Might not the ontological debate that, as we have seen, appears in the background, in fact be a hidden Christological one? Might not Badiou be an "axiomatic" Arian?

The answer to these questions necessarily brings us to the conclusion that has been put forth in the West by, for example, Eric Voegelin, describing the renewed ascendancy of gnostic speculation[35] and taking inspiration from Hans Urs von Balthasar (who wrote that the gnosis does not cease to spring forth in each and every one of the seasons of the spiritual development of the West[36]); both cite Irenaeus of Lyons as a source of support.

So where is the theology dwarf described by Benjamin today?

Is he in Badiou's thought, in his crypto-theology that falls perfectly within the heresies pointed out by Fr. Bulgakov? We are convinced that yes, the axiomatic decision from which the rest of Badiou's thought stems is, first and foremost, a theological decision. And Badiou's theology dwarf no longer needs a puppet in Turkish dress but rather one in a Mao suit. It is important to note that all of the Christological controversies in the church have had significant political consequences. Alain Badiou was one of the clearest and most notorious supporters of the Khmer Rouge genocide led by Pol Pot in the seventies.

But on the other hand, it is our choice to, tricked by the apparent neutrality of the chessboard of secular reason, continue to try to hide our theology under the table in the name of an apparent dialogue with the secular world, to continue to turn it into an ugly dwarf who tries to keep himself out of the view of others. The experience of the Russian philosophical-theological synthesis is very important in preventing us from doing so. We must accept as normal that the separation between theology and philosophy is superficial, because the question "is one?" is a philosophical question par excellence, but its answer will always be theological. And the Christian answer par excellence to this question is the answer that overcomes the ontological contradiction; it is the answer given by the dogma of Chalcedon. This necessary assertion makes the development of Christian thought in the post-secular context possible—a development in the direction defined

---

35. Voegelin, *Renaissance and Reformation*, 178.
36. Balthasar, *Ireneo de Lyon*, 13.

by Fr. Florovsky as the "new Christian philosophy," which must grow with strong roots in the experience of faith and its dogmatic expression.[37] It is only this type of philosophy that can free us from the curse of the "theology dwarf," of the not-so-modern heresies, and freely leave the apparently neutral gaming table in order to return to its primary vocation of being the doxology of the History of Salvation, to being the story of the Icon.

The post-secular context highlights the topicality of the philosophical-religious synthesis of Russian Christian thought. It confirms Florovsky's affirmation that our times have once again been called to theology.[38] Now that, as we have set forth in our main analysis, we are no longer trying at all costs to cover up the crypto-theologies (or counter-theologies, as Florovsky wrote[39]) that mark the history of the post-secular world, a world of new-old heresies, we must urgently rediscover that, as Fr. Florovsky taught, there is nothing neutral after the Incarnation, Crucifixion, and Resurrection, and that is why all of history, even "this desperate history of the world" appears now in the perspective of the ultimate eschatological contradiction.[40]

Bibliography

Badiou, Alan. *Being and Event*. New York: Continuum, 2007.
Balthasar, Hans Urs Von, editor. *Ireneo de Lyon, Geduld des Reifens. Die christliche Antwort auf den gnostischen Mythos im zweiten Jahrhundert*. Klosterberg: Benno Schwabe, 1943.
Benjamin, Walter. "Theses on the Philosophy of History." In *Illuminations: Essays and Reflections*, edited by Hannah Arendt, 253–64. Translated by Harry Zohn. New York: Schocken, 1969.
Blane, Andrew. "A Sketch of the Life of Georges Florovsky." In *Georges Florovsky. Russian Intellectual and Orthodox Churchman*, edited by Andrew Blane, 11–217. Crestwood, NY: St. Vladimir's Seminary Press, 1993.
Borghesi, Massimo. "Cristianismo y filosofía, entre modernidad y posmodernidad." *Revista Católica Internacional Communio* 3 (1999) 311–24.
Bulgakov, Sergey. "The Eucharistic Dogma." In *The Holy Grail and the Eucharist*. Translated by Boris Jakim, 63–138. Hudson, NY: Lindisfarne, 1997.
———. "Tragediya filosofii." In *Sochineniya v dvukh tomakh*. Vol. 1, *Filosofiya khozyaystva. Tragediya filosofii*, 309–518. Moscow: Nauka, 1993.
———. *Unfading Light*. Translated by Thomas Allan Smith. Grand Rapids, MI: Eerdmans, 2012.
Florovskiy, Georgiy. *Dogmat i istoriya*. Moscow: Izdatel'stvo Svyato-Vladimirskogo Bratstva, 1998.

---

37. Florovsky, "Revelation, Philosophy, and Theology."
38. Florovsky, *Ways of Russian Theology*, 2.305.
39. Ibid., 2.306.
40. Florovskiy, *Dogmat i istoriya*, 76.

Florovsky, Georges. "The Cunning of Reason." In *Exodus to the East: Forebodings and Events. An Affirmation of the Eurasians*, edited by Petr Savitskii et al., 30–40. Idyllwood, CA: Charles Schlacks, Jr., 1996.

———. *Collected Works*. Vol. 1, *Bible, Church, Tradition: An Eastern Orthodox View*. Belmont, MA: Nordland, 1972.

———. *Collected Works*. Vol. 6, *Ways of Russian Theology. Part II*. Translated by Robert L. Nichols. Vaduz: Büchervertriebsanstalt, 1987.

———. "Patristics and Modern Theology." In *Procès-verbaux du premier Congrès de Théologie Orthodoxe a Athènes, 29 Novembre–6 Décembre 1936*, edited by Amilkas S. Alivizatos, 238–42. Athens: Pyrsos, 1939.

———. "Revelation, Philosophy, and Theology." In *Collected Works*. Vol. 3, *Creation and Redemption*, 21–40. Belmont, MA: Nordland, 1976.

Franke, William. "Franz Rosenzweig and the Emergence of a Post-Secular Philosophy of the Unsayable." *International Journal for Philosophy of Religion* 58 (2005) 161–80.

Habermas, Jürgen. "Religion in the Public Sphere." *European Journal of Philosophy* 14/1 (2006) 1–25.

Kirill, Patriarkh Moskovskiy i vseya Rusi. "Tserkovnaya zhizn' dolzhna byt' sluzheniyem." *Izvestiya*, May 12, 2009.

Kyrlezhev, Aleksandr. "Postsekulyarnaya epokha." *Kontinent* 120 (2004). Online: http://magazines.russ.ru/continent/2004/120/kyr16.html.

Martínez, Javier, Archbishop of Granada. *Beyond Secular Reason. Más allá de la razón secular*. Granada: Editorial Nuevo Inicio, 2008.

Mrovchinski-Van Allen, Artur. "Russkiye mysliteli i Evropa segodnya." In *XX Ezhegodnaya Bogoslovskaya konferentsiya Pravoslavnogo Svyato-Tikhonovskogo Gumanitarnogo Universiteta: Materialy*, edited by Vladimir N. Vorob'yev, 87–91. Moscow: Izdatel'stvo Pravoslavnogo Svyato-Tikhonovskogo Gumanitarnogo Universiteta, 2010.

Taylor, Charles. *A Secular Age*. Cambridge, MA: Harvard University Press, 2007.

Vaganova, Nataliya. *Sofiologiya protoiyereiya Sergiya Bulgakova*. Moscow: Izdatel'stvo Pravoslavnogo Svyato-Tikhonovskogo Gumanitarnogo Universiteta, 2010.

Vasilenko, Leonid I. *Vvedeniye v russkuyu religioznuyu filosofiyu*. Moscow: Izdatel'stvo Pravoslavnogo Svyato-Tikhonovskogo Gumanitarnogo Universiteta, 2009.

Voegelin, Eric. *History of Political Ideas*. Vol. 4, *Renaissance and Reformation*. Columbia: University of Missouri Press, 1998.

Zander, Lev. *Bog i mir. Mirosozertsaniye ottsa Sergiya Bulgakova*. Vol. 1. Paris: YMCA, 1948.

Zhuravskiy, Aleksandr. "Religioznaya traditsiya v usloviyakh krizisa sekulyarizma." *Kontinent* 120 (2004). Online: http://magazines.russ.ru/continent/2004/120/zh17.html.

2

"Secularization" and "Post-Secular" in Russian Religious Thought

Main Features

Konstantin Antonov

The term "secularization" in its philosophical meaning appeared relatively late in Russian thought. In the entry "Secularization" from the Russian *Brockhaus Encyclopedia*, Nikolai Kareev described "the liberation of thinking and social activity from church patrimony" as an additional, recently appeared meaning of that historical term.[1] The notion of secularization was used sporadically in religious philosophy at the beginning of the twentieth century as a synonym for the growth of culture worldliness, its separation from religion.[2] Nevertheless, the philosophical conceptions which may be called theories of secularization (in the sense of their attempt to explain that very process), are found in Russia at an early stage of the development of religious thought. Their appearance may be considered to be the result of the reception of conservative romantic thought and the German classics, mostly Hegel and the late Shelling.

It should be noted that Russian thinkers were very prejudiced. The problem of secularization was not an abstract sociological question for them, but rather a matter of practical action, tightly connected with the problems of life and death. Atheists, such as Vissarion Belinsky, Alexander Herzen and Nikolai Bakunin, accomplished secularization by the very fact of their thinking having an explicitly propagandistic character. They saw

---

1. Kareev, "Sekulyarizaciya," 332.
2. See, for instance, Bulgakov, *Dva grada*, 105.

a significant aspect of a "liberating movement" in it, which had universal perspectives. Meanwhile, their opponents tried to give some explanation of the secularization process, insert it into a framework of a religious world picture, and overcome it in the end. They also realized that by the very fact and the manner of addressing this matter they facilitated a counter-secularization process, which also had a global historical and even an eschatological perspective. Those counter-secular thinkers will be in the focus of our investigation.

The ideas mentioned above were formed at the intersection of philosophy of history, philosophy of religion and political thought but it is the philosophy of religion which played a fundamental role here. An understanding of the course of the history and contemporary political processes is determined by an understanding of religion and its place in history and culture.

Soloviev and the Metanarrative of the Post-Secular

The idea of the overcoming of the split between faith and reason that characterizes the Enlightenment, the project of the union of philosophy and religion, as the main tool of this overcoming, and finally the philosophical use of the criticism of religion for the sake of the strengthening of the positions of Christianity in European culture, are clearly reflected in Peter Chaadaev's *Philosophical Letters* and in his private correspondence.[3]

In the works of Ivan Kireevsky, we find for the first time in Russian literature an extensive description of the development of European culture as a process of secularization. In the sequence of papers: "In Response to A. S. Khomiakov," "On the Nature of European Culture and on Its Relationship to Russian Culture," and "On the Necessity and Possibility of New Principles of Philosophy," he described the process of the gradual transformation of the Christian authority of European culture and its further decay.[4] The main active force of this process is rationality, borrowed from the ancient world. The important thing is that Kireevsky marked the coming of a new age each time he addresses this issue. He depicted the frustration of reason, the beginning of religious searches, their relative failure, and finally the possibility of solution of the crises due to the growth of Orthodox culture in Russia.

---

3. See Chaadaev, "The Philosophical Letters," and also letters to Schelling, Turgenev, princess Meshcherskaya.

4. See Kireevsky, "On the Nature of European Culture," "On the Necessity and Possibility of New Principles."

His description, excluding the last point, is comparable with some modern descriptions of a post-secular situation.

The most detailed interpretation of these developments was given, however, by Vladimir Soloviev. This may be found in such works as *Lectures on Divine Humanity* (1877–1881), *History and Future of Theocracy* (1885–1887), *Russia and the Universal Church* and some others. The metanarrative created by him enclosed in a unified way an extensive description of both secularizing and desecularizing processes.

Let us consider this metanarrative more closely. In spite of some differences in details, other authors generally follow his model. We can easily see in Soloviev's writings that the starting point of this model is a specific understanding of the nature of religion based on personal experience and a recognition of the contrast between the very nature of religion and its actual place in the modern world.

In *Lectures on Divine Humanity* Soloviev says: "Speaking generally and abstractly, religion is the connection of humanity and the world with the absolute principle and focus of all that exists."[5] The religion thus understood must stay at the centre of human life.

> It must determine all interests and the whole content of human life and consciousness. All that is essential in what we do, what we know, and what we create must be determined by and referred to such principle.[6]

But actually religion does not have this universal and central significance. "Instead of being all in all"—writes Soloviev—"it is hidden in a very small and remote corner of our inner world. It is just one of a multitude of different interests that divide our attention."[7] Therefore, Soloviev recognizes wholly secular character of modern Western civilization, which tries "to organize humanity outside of the absolute religious sphere, to establish itself and make itself comfortable in the realm of temporal, finite interests."[8] The most striking expressions of this intention he supposes to be are socialism in social life and positivism in knowledge.[9]

An exposition of the general course of history serves to explain this state of affairs. Soloviev makes it more than once with some variations, but the general model remains, I believe, invariable. In a short but important

5. Solovyov, *Lectures on Divine Humanity*, 1.
6. Ibid.
7. Ibid.
8. Ibid., 2.
9. Ibid.

text for Soloviev "On the Law of Historical Development" (which he considered to be a general historical introduction to his early unfinished treatise *The Philosophical Principles of Integral Knowledge*) history as a whole mostly longs for secularization. It must be noted, however, that in the works of the same period (chiefly in *Lectures*) history is presented by Soloviev as a process of the development of religious consciousness, as a "revelation of divine principle" determined by "a real interaction between God and humanity."[10] As a result, the described "progressive separation of various spheres and elements of human existence"[11] (in the very same words Nikolai Berdyaev later defined the secularization), their liberation from the authority of religion loses the negative character traditionally assigned to it and becomes ambiguous.

The paradox consists already in the fact that in Greece and Rome this process was only outlined, while it was Christianity which gave it a real impact. Being the "beginning of real freedom" it "deals a final blow to this external, involuntary unity."[12] It is the original Christianity which constantly provides the principle of division between the sacred and the profane in all fields. First of all, it divides the church as a holy community from the profane world, particularly from the state, which loses in the eyes of the first Christians all spiritual significance.[13]

The situation changed from the moment of the conversion of Constantine the Great, when the church connected its fate with the fate of the state which had become Christian only in name. Soloviev calls such connection an "outward compromise," but in various works he expresses different attitudes to it. Nevertheless, the general model remains more or less the same: an artificial character of a medieval synthesis becomes a starting point and justification of modern secularization processes. Most sharply Soloviev expresses this position in his famous thesis "The Collapse of the Mediaeval World-Conception."

While in the earlier works Soloviev talked about factual compromise, determined by the fact that reviving force of Christianity "could not spread instantly over the whole organism of humankind,"[14] here he talks about fundamental compromise with paganism as the basis of the medieval understanding of Christianity.[15] Soloviev highlights three essential features of this

---

10. Ibid., 33–34.
11. Solovyov, *The Philosophical Principles*, 35.
12. Ibid.
13. Ibid.
14. Ibid., 37.
15. Solovyov, "The Collapse of the Mediaeval World-Conception," 64–65.

compromise: dogmatism, individualism, and spiritualism. He understands dogmatism as a transformation of vivid truths of faith into abstract dogmas whose meaning is not clear for most worshippers and the recognition of which is considered as a necessary condition of salvation. By individualism he means the reduction of soteriology to the idea of personal salvation. The consequences of individualism is a disappearance of the idea of the Christian transformation of society as a necessary task of church on the one side, and the spiritualization of Christianity on the other, which abandons the idea of incarnation in practice, the denial of the significance of material nature. Taken together, these aspects of a medieval synthesis helped, as Soloviev supposed, to set up the mechanism of repressions both in the West and in the East of the Christian world.

All these aspects of a medieval synthesis are the results of a reinterpretation of Christianity from the point of view of pagan foundations of life and thought. In this respect Soloviev develops, generalizes and specifies the Slavophile ideas about ancient rationalism as a source of the weakening and decline of Western Church. At the same time his views are close to Adolf von Harnack's idea of the Hellenization of Christianity. The domination of these aspects undermines a medieval worldview and caused "necessarily, but also justly," a "disintegrating movement of thought and life."[16] This movement, however, in its turn "leads to a triumph of the true Christianity—living, social and universal—not denying, but transforming human and natural life."[17]

Soloviev's thesis evoked an extensive discussion in Russian society. On the one hand, it attracted a common attention to religious problems, and on the other Soloviev's ideas became the *loci classicus* in discussions of the beginning of twentieth century and the following period. Their development and revision became a starting point both for so-called "new religious consciousness" (Dmitry Merezhkovskiy, Vasily Rozanov, etc.), as well as for more conservative and church-centered trends ("*puteystvo*," Mikhail Novoselov's circle, etc.). The popularity of Soloviev's ideas explains the efficiency and durability of the metanarrative he suggested. But let us return to the summary of the course of events.

Presenting a medieval mentality as a compromise (accidental or principal) between Christianity and paganism, Soloviev gets an opportunity to give a religious justification to modern times and the secularization associated with it. He inserts this history into the general scheme of the history of

---

16. Solov'yev, "Polozheniya k chteniyu," 357.
17. Ibid.

humankind, where a disappointment in the previous stage always precedes a transition to the new level of religious consciousness.[18]

But the modern secularization process not only has a negative but also a positive meaning: it not only destroys unsatisfactory medieval synthesis, but also discloses the potential for human freedom, which is very important in the general course of history. "The unbelieving promoters of modern progress" do the essentially Christian work of a humanistic transformation of human life and prepare forms for a new stage of Christian history: vivid, social, universal.[19]

Nevertheless, the immediate results of this process are negative: "The second force—writes Soloviev—which directed the development of western civilization, when acts freely, irrepressibly leads to a general decomposition into smaller parts, and to the loss of any universal content and absolute principles of existence."[20]

"Atomism" in life, science and art, the fragmentation and superficiality of existence, and ultimately the denial of life are the last words of Western civilization. Producing the forms of a secular culture, according to Soloviev, leads to the perishing of its content. Therefore, we reach the limit of the process of secularization, and its ultimate meaning is discovered in its "self-denial."[21] Here a sort of criticism of the criticism of religion begins. This is a starting point for the "third force" activity and the process of desecularization begins. Soloviev analyzes this process it in the majority of his works, and takes is as a new "revelation of a higher divine world."[22]

This stage of history Soloviev defines as acceptance of the idea of "virtuous life" in the framework of new universal god-man culture, as a unity of free theurgy, free theosophy and free theocracy. Soloviev's commentators, beginning with Evgeniy Trubetskoi, characterize this project as a utopia and trace its connections back to first Slavophile ideas concerning "the necessity of the fulfillment of the Christian ideal in all spheres of human life."[23] Indeed, Soloviev gave a classic expression of the metanarrative first outlined by the Slavophiles. Subsequently he worked out previously sketched ideas: the reflection on secularization, based on the disadvantages of the previous religious age, the worldliness of medieval Christianity, as a justification of

18. See Antonov, "Koncept religioznogo obrashcheniya v filosofii Vl. Solov'eva," 177–78.

19. Solovyov, "The Collapse of the Mediaeval World-Conception," 70–71.

20. Solovyov, *The Philosophical Principles*, 171. A conception of "forces" or "potencies" taking place in history, Soloviev takes from Schelling.

21. Solovyov, *Lectures on Divine Humanity*, 6.

22. Solovyov, *The Philosophical Principles*, 51.

23. Trubetskoi, *Mirosozertsanie Vl. S. Solovyova*, 1:417.

the emergence of secular modernity, new secularism ("rationalism" in the works of Slavophiles), as a continuation of a medieval reception of paganism, and so on.

In the meantime we need to recognize that a certain element of utopianism is essential for any metanarrative, and to a considerable degree it determines its effectiveness, i.e., the ability to satisfy human need to perceive life as a whole. Soloviev explicitly pursued this aim and successfully realized it in many respects. The main point of his objections against medieval Christianity boils down to its inability to provide an acceptable meaning to the life of a modern man.

The first Christians were prepared for martyrdom or the "impending end of the world." Afterwards the First and the Second Comings of Christ "lost their vital significance, became an object of abstract faith," and "human life . . . retained all its material senseless and inertia."[24] An idea of personal salvation was powerless to change this situation and that is why the violence in the religious sphere became necessary. The revision of Christianity "as a morally-historical, universally human task"[25] should allow, according to Soloviev, the true foundations of Christian life to emerge, solving the fundamental problems, and formulate clear perspectives for modern humankind.

This metanarrative played an enormous role in the history of the Russian and European thought of the twentieth century. It provided the understanding of the aim of history and the concept of Christian activity in the world capable of competing with different secular theories of progress.[26] As a result, it undoubtedly became a kind of self-realizing prophecy which drove the process of religious renovation at the beginning of the twentieth century.

Opponents and Followers

Within the described metanarrative a number of theories appeared which developed some of its aspects, but in general corresponded to Soloviev's model.

I shall consider them in the following aspects: (1) the relation to the Middle Ages and "historical church," (2) the relation to secularizing

---

24. Solovyov, "The Collapse of the Mediaeval World-Conception," 66.

25. Ibid.

26. The criticism of secular theories of progress and utopias from Soloviev's position became an important part of Russian religious renovation, see for instance Bulgakov, "Osnovnye problemy teorii progressa," Novgorodtsev, *Ob obshchestvvennom ideale*.

processes of modern times, (3) the understanding of modernity, and, finally, (4) the perspectives of religion in the world.

Konstantin Leontiev

Firstly, let us look at the most important alternative to Soloviev's project, the theory of Konstantin Leontiev. He formulated his own "laws of development,"[27] which determined his evaluations of history and contemporary events. The distinctive feature of Leontiev's theory is the positive evaluation of the Middle Ages as the time of "blossoming complexity." The medieval world was not a monolith. On the contrary, this was a complex organized whole, determined by conflicts between the sacred and the profane in all its spheres. Leontiev considers Christianity first of all as a spiritualistic religion of personal salvation, which was formed in that epoch and dominated the church. He disregarded any of the attempts of Tolstoy, Dostoevsky or Soloviev to join Christianity with the idea of progress, called it "pink Christianity."[28] The process, which most of the authors of his time evaluated as "progress," was for him simply a "secondary simplification" and degradation of culture, society, and religion. Secularization from his point of view consists not in autonomization of particular fields of culture (on the contrary, he talks about their mixture) but in general the decline of religious consciousness, a weakening of the mystical element in life, and the domination of ethics in religion. Unlike Soloviev, Leontiev did not see positive moments in this processes, and did not expect a religious revival in the nearest future. For him the current stage of culture was not the final form of decay. Analyzing the possibilities of increasing of religious influence in culture, Leontiev stressed its ambivalence: struggling against the banality of contemporary life increased not only Christianity, but also occult-demonic mysticism.

From this point of view, Leontiev may hardly be called a theorist of a "post-secular world." Nevertheless the following thinkers (Berdyaev first of all) took his ideas and his fate as a kind of prophecy about that, what we now call "the post-secular."

In spite of the obviously polemical character of Leontiev's attitude toward Soloviev, his understanding of the church supported Soloviev's view. The features highlighted "The Collapse of the Mediaeval World-Conception"—dogmatism, individualism, and spiritualism—became truly

---

27. Leontyev, "Vizantism i slavyanstvo," 69, 75.
28. See Leontyev, *Nashi novye khristiane*, 14

commonplace. They were used under different names both in the criticism, aimed at "historical Christianity," and in the self-criticism of church thinkers.

Dmitry Merezhkovsky

The most radical interpretation of Soloviev's metanarrative was proposed Dmitry Merezhkovsky in the beginning of the twentieth century. He practically rejected the "churchness" of the church on the basis of Soloviev's arguments, which he extended to all forms of "historical Christianity." Christianity, by introducing the opposition of the spirit and the flesh, actually destroyed the monolith of the ancient religious life, but was not a higher, but lower form of religious consciousness. Spiritualism (asceticism), dogmatism, and individualism—according to Merezhkovsky (and in this he is close to Leontiev)—are not the result of a compromise between Christianity and paganism, but its essential features. Thus Christianity inevitably provoked the emergence of modernity as a "vindication of the rights of the flesh." Besides, "not holy flesh of non-Christian world is closer to the union of Holy Spirit with Holy Flesh then a fleshless holiness of Christianity."[29]

But Merezhkovsky not only formulated a religious license to secularization, even in the aggressive revolutionary style, but also showed its dead ends. It consists first of all of the antinomy of personality and society, the struggle between socialism and anarchism and the problem of philistinism: "denying God, man inevitably falls into absolute philistinism."[30] Merezhkovsky turned this idea upside down: the one who fights against philistinism seeks God by this very fact. The spiritual searches of Belinsky, Herzen, and Bakunin were based on this quest for God, even though they were afraid to recognize this.[31] From this point of view, the atheism of Russian revolution looks rather like an accident. It has in fact a religious foundation and the revolution would have won if it had recognized its religious nature. In the paper "Revolution and Religion" Merezhkovsky traces the symptoms of a new religious revival both among simple people ("searches for Kitezh"), and intellectuals. "Russian decadents—he claims—are the first self-generated mystics in Russian educated society beyond any church tradition."[32] The highest point of these searches was religious meetings, which he considered as the first stage of a religious revolution which should precede a politi-

29. Merezhkovskiy, "Mech," 168.
30. Merezhkovskiy, "Gryadushchiy kham," 6.
31. Ibid., 9–10.
32. Merezhkovskiy, "Revolyuciya i religiya," 204.

cal one. Taken together, they were supposed to build a church, the realm of the Third Testament, the true religion of the Spirit—the final God-man synthesis.

Nikolai Berdyaev

Nikolai Berdyaev had much more reasonable, realistic and analytical views, though within the same tradition. He tried to show the relevance of Soloviev's metanarrative in completely new social and cultural circumstances: in the period between the First and the Second World Wars. The result of this effort is a set of texts, dedicated to the problems of philosophy of history and the contemporary situation: *The Meaning of History* (1922), *The New Middle Ages* (published in English as *The End of our Time*) (1924), and *The Fate of Man in the Modern World* (1934).

His description of the Middle Ages, based on the ideas of Soloviev, Leontiev, and partly Merezhkovsky, also takes into account the criticism of Christianity by such thinkers as Nietzsche and Rozanov, and as a result is much more differentiated. Berdyaev often turns the evaluations made by his predecessors upside down: "abstract dogmatism" he turns into "contemplative metaphysics and mysticism,"[33] ascetic individualism into "forging and strengthening of a human personality," and spiritualism into "liberation of human spirit from the subsoil of the nature."[34] The much more detailed picture reached in this way allows him to play freely with the shades of meanings by distinguishing their positive or negative aspects depending on context. He nevertheless preserves the main negative characteristics of a medieval synthesis: its obligatory character, which justified the process of differentiation and autonomization, which he called "the secularization of human culture."[35] From this point of view "the secularization of state and society has positive religious meaning, it prepares free god-man life."[36]

Berdyaev proposes a similarly complex interpretation of the dialectics of Renaissance humanism, which he identifies with the modern times as well as with the secular period. In general, however, his conclusions are quite close to those of his predecessors. He wrote: "Self-assertion of a man leads to his self-destruction. An exposure of free game of human powers, which are not connected to the ultimate goal, leads to an extinction of

---

33. Berdyaev, *The Meaning of History*, 109.
34. Ibid., 116, 126.
35. Ibid., 128–30.
36. Berdyaev, *The Meaning of the Creative Act*, 272, 299.

creative powers,"[37] and to the notorious "atomization" and the domination of "the average."

But that is not all. Berdyaev also highlighted the transition from atomization to collectivism, including an active involvement of masses in the history, the appearance of machines, and the decomposition of the human image. He called that period the "New Middle Ages." On the one hand, it extends the main trends of the secular period, but on the other, it marks the beginning of a post-secular period. Among the most significant features of this period Berdyaev indicated a return of religion to the sphere of social activity: "Religion cannot be each mans private concern, as is enunciated nowadays . . . Real Religion is in the highest degree generalized and collective, and holds the first place in society."[38] Soviet aggressive atheism, from his point of view, proved his claim.

> I do not mean that the religion of the one God, the faith of Jesus Christ, is going to triumph absolutely and in order of quantity, but that all aspects of life will be engaged in a religious struggle, grouped under opposes religious principles.[39]

An outline of a positive ideal drawn by Berdyaev would be the "free theocracy" of Soloviev: the religious overcoming of atomism in church.[40] "Forms of knowledge and of society must spring from within, flowing from the freedom of a religious spirit."[41] Religion "as free spiritual energy, must renew the face of the earth."[42] Here, again, secularization turns out to be a step toward a renewal of religious consciousness since it got rid of the repressive elements of the Middle Ages.

But in his *The Fate of Man in Modern World*, Berdyaev proposed a much more pessimistic vision. The New Middle Ages appeared here in the form of the continuing decay of humanism and its culture. Its source was, as Berdyaev suggested, "the crisis of Christianity and religious consciousness in general."[43] The symptoms of religious conversion indicated in his previous works are absent here, and the search for new spirituality is presented here rather as a desired way out from the dead end of collective insanity then as a real process. This change of accents is only partially explained by a change in

---

37. Berdyaev, *The Meaning of History*, 142.
38. Berdyaev, *The End of Our Time*, 81.
39. Ibid., 82.
40. Ibid., 109.
41. Ibid., 104.
42. Ibid., 109, translation modified.
43. Berdyaev, *The Fate of Man in Modern World*, 109.

the historical situation, i.e., the coming to power of Hitler in Germany and beginning of The Great Purge in the Soviet Union. It seems that Berdyaev realized that we were facing global change: the end of the cycle of religious revival of the beginning of twentieth century and transition to the secular cycle in the second half of the century. The ideal of the religious renovation of the world was again located in the sphere of utopianism.

Therefore, we can see that Soloviev's metanarrative became a highly successful conceptualization of the spiritual processes of the end of the nineteenth and the first quarter of twentieth century. His key idea of giving a positive religious meaning to secularization has counterparts in such western authors as Henri de Lubac, Paul Tillich and Paul Ricoeur. It was also similar with some of the contemporary theories of the post-secular world. Paradoxically, this fact undermines one of their most important claims that the post-secular stage of the world had no precedents.

Conclusions

All of the observations provided above allow us to point to some of the general features of theories of secularization, characterizing Russian thought up to the middle of the twentieth century. I will conclude by briefly listing them:

First of all, the thesis of John Milbank that "once there was no secular"[44] seems to be false from the considered point of view. The period of an initial religious integrity of consciousness was located in the earliest historical or even pre-historical times, and was considered only as a starting point for further decomposition.

Christianity itself is supposed to be an important factor of secularization. For the first time it introduced the strict distinction between the religious and the secular aspects of human life. From this point of view, medieval theocracy looks like an artificial and violent synthesis, already open for the processes of secularization with such phenomena as "abstract dogmatism," "individualism," and "spiritualism."

Correspondingly, the resistance against this synthesis in modern times was considered something positive. Secularization acquired a positive religious meaning, which creates a conceptual foundation for communication between the religious and the secular segments of culture. The religious criticism of secularism, therefore, even in most radical forms, has always preserved a constructive and dialogical character.

---

44. Milbank, *Theology and Social Theory*, 1.

Therefore, there are two aspects of Russian religious thought on the post-secular: Firstly, by setting the dialog between the religious and the secular, Russian religious thought actually started the post-secular period, preceding contemporary discussions. Secondly, it outlined a post-secular stage of society, paying attention first of all to the fundamental self-reconsideration and self-transformation of the church on which the changes in secular society depend.

Bibliography

Antonov, Konstantin. "Koncept religioznogo obrashcheniya v filosofii Vl. Solov'yeva." *Vestnik Pravoslavnogo Svyato-Tikhonovskogo Gumanitarnogo Universiteta* 2 (2004) 159–89.

Berdyaev, Nicolas. *The End of Our Time*. Translated by Donald Attwater. London: Sheed & Ward, 1933.

———. *The Fate of Man in Modern World*. Translated by Donald A. Lowrie. Ann Arbor: University of Michigan Press, 1961.

———. *The Meaning of the Creative Act*. Translated by Donald A. Lowrie. New York: Collier, 1955.

———. *The Meaning of History*. New Brunswick, New Jersey: Transaction, 2009.

Bulgakov, Sergey. *Dva grada. Issledovaniya o prirode obschestvennih idealov*. Saint Petersburg: RHGA, 1997.

———. "Osnovnye problemy teorii progressa." In *Ot marksisma k idealismu*, 113–60. Saint Petersburg: Obschestvennaya pol'za, 1903.

Chaadaev, Peter, "The Philosophical Letters to a Lady." In *Philosophical Works of Peter Chaadaev*, 18–101. Translated by Raymond T. McNally, Richard Tempest. Dordrecht: Kluwer, 1991.

Kareev, Nikolay. "Sekulyarizaciya." In *Entsiklopedicheskiy slovar' Brokgausa i Efrona*. Vol. 29, 330–32. Saint Petersburg: Brokgafuz i Efron, 1900.

Kireevsky, Ivan. "On the Nature of European Culture and on Its Relationship to Russian Culture." Translated by Valentine Snow. In *On Spiritual Unity. A Slavophile Reader. Alexei Khomiakov. Ivan Kireevsky*, edited by Boris Jakim and Robert Bird, 187–234. Hudson, NY: Lindisfarne, 1998.

———. "On the Necessity and Possibility of New Principles of Philosophy." Translated by Peter K. Christoff. In *On Spiritual Unity. A Slavophile Reader. Alexei Khomiakov. Ivan Kireevsky*, edited by Boris Jakim and Robert Bird, 233–73. Hudson, NY: Lindisfarne, 1998.

Leont'yev, Konstantin. *Nashi novye khristiane: F. M. Dostoyevskiy i gr. Lev Tolstoy*. Moscow: Tipografiya E.I. Pogodinoy, 1882.

———. "Vizantism i slavyanstvo." In *Izbrannoe*, 19–118. Moscow: Rarog, Moskovskiy rabochiy, 1993.

Merezhkovskiy, Dmitriy. "Gryadushchiy kham." In *Gryadushchiy kham*, 4–26. Moscow: Respublika, 2004.

———. "Mech." In *Gryadushchiy kham*, 154–73. Moscow: Respublika, 2004.

———. "Revolyuciya i religiya." In *Gryadushchiy kham*, 174–212. Moscow: Respublika, 2004.

Milbank, John. *Theology and Social Theory: Beyond Secular Reason.* Oxford: Blackwell, 1991.

Novgorodtsev, Pavel. *Ob obshchestvennom ideale.* Moscow: Pressa, 1991.

Solovyov, Vladimir. "The Collapse of the Mediaeval World-Conception." In *A Solovyov Reader*, edited by Semen Frank, 60–71. Translated by Natalie Duddington. London: SCM, 1950.

———. *Lectures on Divine Humanity.* Translated by Boris Jakim. Hudson, NY: Lindisfarne, 1995.

———. *The Philosophical Principles of Integrate Knowledge.* Grand Rapids, MI: Eerdmans, 2008.

Solov'yev, Vladimir S. "Polozheniya k chteniyu Vladimira Solov'yeva *O prichinakh upadka srednevekovogo mirosozertsaniya*." In *Sochineniya v dvukh tomakh.* Vol. 2, *Chteniya o bogochelovechestve. Filosofskaya publitsistika*, 356–57. Moscow: Izdatel'stvo Pravda, 1989.

Trubetskoi, Evgeniy. *Mirosozertsanie VI. S. Solovyova.* Vol. 1. Moscow: Medium, 1995.

3

Post-Secularity vs. All-Unity

Grigory Gutner

In many studies of the phenomenon of post-secularity the triadic scheme is adopted. According to it the "pre-secular," "secular" and "post-secular" epochs are distinguished. However, Russian religious philosophy can hardly be associated with any of them. It is a rather strange and unique school of thought: it forms an alternative to the secularity, however it is neither a restoration of the pre-secular ideas, nor a precursor of the post-secularity. In this paper I shall try to discuss, on one hand, the meaning of the alternative to secular ideas which Russian religious philosophy tries to develop. On the other, I shall try to demonstrate some essential similarities between this philosophy and secular thought and their principal differences from post-secular ideas.

Some Notes on the Idea of Secularity

First of all, I should say something about pre-secular and secular epochs. The pre-secularity forms the integral Universe, which includes both natural and super-natural realities. The integrity of the Universe is determined by the fact that it is created and permanently supported by God. The unity of the Universe is perfectly expressed in the image of the Cosmic Liturgy. Each created thing is a participant of the Liturgy because it participates in mystical action of God. This has an important implication for each aspect of human activity. Cognition, social and private life, political activity are the ways of the participation in God's action. So science, ethics, policy are derivate from theology.

Secularization is an emancipation of these (and some other) spheres of life. Throughout the seventeenth and eighteenth centuries they became autonomous and in some way self-sufficient and the pioneer of this autonomous development was science. The Aristotelian paradigm which previously dominated presupposed a teleological explanation of things. The understanding of anything implied knowing the aim (*telos*) of its existence. Science depends on theology, because its aims ultimately reside in the Divine Mind. However, the new scientific paradigm refused teleological explanation. The understanding of phenomena in this paradigm means knowing not aims but causes. Causal explanation implied understanding nature from itself, without appeal to its transcendent Creator. After the Scientific Revolution of the seventeenth century, scientific research has been quite independent of Christian faith. The latter is the private matter of a scientist. Science, on the contrary, becomes universal and it is the same for Christians, Muslims, Jews, atheists etc.

Another important sphere of secularization is policy and political philosophy. The first significant step in this direction made Thomas Hobbes with his theory of state. He presupposed that the state appeared as a result of social contract. So political power does not have divine but rather human origins. We have no need for the theological justification of power since it is independent of any religion. The situation is similar to science since the State cannot be Christian, Islamic, Judaic, atheistic etc. This is the private matter of every citizen (including politicians and state officials). The state, however, is common for all of them.

Morality is in the same situation and this is especially strange because morality is usually an important part of religion. Most religions include moral commandments but Pierre Bayle, already in the seventeenth century, tried to demonstrate that morality is founded on the principle of reason and needs no justification by means of Holy Scripture or religious tradition. Immanuel Kant developed this idea in his moral philosophy, demonstrating the fact that the moral cannot be deduced from religion. The autonomy of the moral will in Kant's ethic is correlated with the universality of moral law. It must be the same for both religious and non-religious people.

Not only science, policy and morality become independent on religion. The same can be said about other spheres of human life: art, economy, professional activity etc. Most of them (although not all) became autonomous. They have their justification only in themselves. Religion remains a private matter, some specific sphere of life which exists as an equal to (even, maybe, less significant) others.

As a result, the integrity of the world disappeared. The life of a medieval man was united by his faith, because all aspects of this life had an essential religious component. The life of man of the secular epoch is divided between several autonomous spheres. The Enlightenment made an attempt to find a new wholeness. The foundation of the wholeness must be reason. All aspects of human life must be based on clear and distinctive principles, evident for each reasonable being. However, nobody could ultimately formulate such principles and philosophers could not agree about their nature and origin, to say nothing of definite content.

The search for wholeness took an essential place in minds of Europeans during the nineteenth century and even the first half of the twentieth century. The main hope lay with science. Projects developed in the frame of Positivism considered the human being as some part of nature. As physics, chemistry and biology give us objective knowledge of nature, so psychology and sociology can obtain objective knowledge of human life. Ultimately, some unified scientific image of the world was expected to appear. All human problems must be solved by means of scientific approaches.

The failure of these hopes became evident after World War I. Husserl described the fact as the crisis of European science. New attempts to find some wholeness resulted in monstrous consequences: totalitarian regimes in Germany and Soviet Union. Totalitarian movements tried to create absolute wholeness (totality) on the base of ideology. The latter was the strange hybrid of scientific theory and religious doctrine. Nevertheless it appeared quite effective for uniting the masses. The experience of totalitarianism is the evidence of the failure of all secular attempts to create some wholeness. We must stop on the way to it, because the price of the wholeness is the destruction of the human being.

Russian Religious Philosophy

Russian religious philosophy develops some alternatives to European secular thought. The latter, as we can see, failed to create any wholeness on the base of reason or science. Many Russian religious thinkers insist that reason itself is not able to produce any organic integrity by its very nature. Any rational activity has a dominant intention to distinguish and divide. Rational efforts to integrate something are always an attempt to construct some device from separate details.

As a result, secular reason produces not a wholeness but permanent separations. It separated moral, science, police and religion and divided science into separate disciplines. It divided spirit and body and faced with an insoluble problem of interaction between physical and spiritual realities. It dissociated the spirit from itself and the latter is especially evident in the phenomenon of alienation (*Entfremdung*), described by Hegel and Marx.

All these (and some other) accusations were declared by various Russian philosophers from Slavophiles to Nikolai Berdyaev.

So the main aim of religious thought is the search for some new integrity. This integrity, however, cannot be the same as medieval pre-secular integrity. It must provide the conditions for the freedom of human personality, the free development of knowledge and true progress of society. All these branches must be, however, united by some free spirituality of renewed Christianity. There cannot be non-religious morality, non-religious science, non-religious state etc. However, "being religious" is not considered as a limitation for free development.

The first project of such an integrity was developed by Alexei Khomiakov in the concept of "Sobornost." However, the most evident expression of this idea is the doctrine of the "All-Unity" of Vladimir Soloviev. Although other Russian religious thinkers do not follow Soloviev in his pursuit of universal totality, all of them share his care for integrity and his criticism of rational philosophy. Seeking wholeness in various spheres of the human existence is the main point of Russian religious philosophy. This wholeness is based on religious principles and implies the supremacy of the religion over all other forms of human life.

I suppose that all those who are identified as "Russian religious philosophers" are the descendants of Soloviev, in spite of all the disagreements between them. They sought different ways for the theoretical justification and practical implementation of the same project. The main problem for both justification and implementation is, as I have noted before, the fact that the project cannot imply the restoration of pre-secular situation. The new wholeness cannot be the wholeness of medieval Christianity. In fact, Russian religious philosophers borrow rather a lot from secular thought. They never deny liberal ideas of free personality and human dignity. They cannot reject also the free development of science and art, autonomous moral choice, humanistic oriented policy. Ultimately, they must admit that reason has a right for free and autonomous thought, which is not suppressed by any external factors. However, on the other hand, this free autonomous reason must agree with the supremacy of religious faith. Science and philosophy must occupy a hierarchically lower place than renewed theology or *theosophy* (if we use Soloviev's term). A person can be free and autonomous but subject to a religious community. Reason as well can be free and autonomous if submitted to religious faith or mystical intuition. That is an unavoidable internal contradiction of Russian religious philosophy.

Fortunately, Russian philosophers had at their disposal the perfect instrument for dealing with contradictions. This instrument was Hegelian dialectics. They used Hegel's concept of freedom as an internally adopted necessity. According to the concept, a person is not free when he or she acts under external constraint. The latter means that the external demand (for example the demand of law, or moral, or tradition) differs from an internal intention of the person, and he/she is forced to act against his/her own will. So the freedom is a correspondence of external demand and internal intention. Due to this correspondence personal submission to the whole is the realization of an internal intention. Berdyaev described the orthodox understanding of freedom in practically the same terms. A religious person is free in the church because "the religious collective is found within the religious person."[1]

The relationship between faith and reason is understood in a similar manner and a good example can be found in the work of Semen Frank in his article *Philosophy and Religion*.[2] First of all, Frank describes them as quite different types of human activity. They both try to find a way to the *absolute*, to the first foundation of life and being. In other words, they are both directed to God but their approaches are quite different. Religion seeks a direct personal communion with God. Philosophy tries to learn God and to describe Him by means of logical categories. Ultimately the very subject seems to be different: alive, personal God for religion and an abstract absolute for philosophy.

However, Frank insists that we can overcome the contradiction. Philosophy can find the object of its research only in mystical intuition. The beginning of proper philosophical thought is some kind of revelation. According to Frank, philosophy is not rational in its genuine depth. The system of rationally ordered categories has the only proper task: it must express transcendent being which dwells far beyond the limits of any rational construction. This attempt can be successful, if the thought keeps its connection with its irrational initial point. The thought in each of its act is directed by "seeing of super-logical, intuitive base."[3] In other words, philosophy "must be based on the alive religious experience."[4]

This implies that philosophy is free in its research and nevertheless subordinated to religion. It is free because religion does not limit philosophy

---

1. Berdyaev, "Truth of Orthodoxy."
2. Frank, "Filosofiya i religiya," 324–32.
3. Ibid., 327.
4. Ibid., 330.

with some external frame. Religion is initially inside philosophy. Philosophy develops its own internal intention if, and only if, it is religious.

A similar consideration can be applied not only to philosophy but, with some variations, to any activity of thought, ultimately to any human activity. Rather interesting attempts at such an application have been made by various Russian philosophers. For example, they sought for religion beginning in science (Vladimir Soloviev, Pavel Florensky), art (Pavel Florensky), economy (Sergey Bulgakov), policy and social life (Nikolai Berdyaev, Sergey Bulgakov). All these attempts, I suppose, can be considered as various approaches to the realization of Soloviev's initial project of All-Unity.

I must admit that this project is quite ambiguous as it implies two opposite possibilities. Let us return to the Frank's article to demonstrate it. On one hand, the fact that thought has some transcendent source and is based on "super-logical intuition" implies the real freedom of thought. The latter cannot be transformed in rigid logical schemes. It cannot cease its development and decide that everything is already known, that there is nothing in reality except logically consistent ideal constructions. It must make new and new efforts to seek better expression of reality and clarify the initial intuition. And it cannot admit any result of these efforts quite complete. The complete understanding of its object would imply that thought is reduced to an unchangeable conceptual system. In fact it is the death of thought and so the connection with infinite transcendent reality makes the thought alive. Without such a connection it cannot be a thought in a proper meaning of the word but becomes an ideology which is in fact hostile to thought.

On the other hand, however, the approach of Russian philosophy has quite the opposite and rather dangerous implication. This implication is, strange as it may seem, ideological. As we just have seen, Frank insists, that philosophy tries to learn God and must be based on "alive religious experience." This means that if some thinker does not satisfy these two conditions, he/she is not a true philosopher. Using this criterion we can admit a great plenty of thinkers—from Kant to Derrida, including Husserl and Heidegger and to say nothing of the Anglo-Saxon analytical tradition as being false philosophers. In the same manner we can discern true art from false art, a true political system from a false political system etc.

Some Russian philosophers quite willingly made this demarcation. An important example is an attitude of such thinkers as Ern and Florensky to Kant. Florensky also develops quite a sharp critique of European art of Renaissance and the following period. Berdyaev rejects the Western political and economic system (democracy and capitalism). They considered all these phenomena as the results of some deep distortion, the fatal mistake of human spirit, which tried to gain absolute autonomy and act without God.

In other words, all these authors believe, that these phenomena of European thought and culture are not based on the "alive religious experience."

Many Russian intellectuals nowadays continue this tradition and their critique often has a rather aggressive and vulgar form. References to Russian religious philosophy are rather popular and unfortunately not always irrelevant.

So freedom (even in the Hegelian meaning) is hardly possible in the frame of the All-Unity project. Only a religious person can judge whether there is "alive religious experience" at the heart of a philosophical theory (work of art, social or political system etc.) or not. So the religion must not only be inside these phenomena of human spirit but must form some external frame for them and even acquires a right for some kind of censorship.

From Religious Philosophy to Post-Secularity

Let us now consider the first implication of Frank's analysis of philosophy. Thought, as we could see, deals with the transcendent, which is presented by means of intuition. This intuition is initially rather vague. Thought tries to get some clear presentation of its object but absolute clearness is, however, impossible. The thought cannot capture its object completely so intuition is always necessary for the connection of thought and reality. What kind of intuition is it? What is the reality the thought deal with? We can give some approximate answers only from the position of developed thought. It is not known *a priori*. Thought can answer these questions only after long and difficult search for its own beginning. This search of the beginning is the matter of philosophy. So I do not agree with Frank when he insists that God is the only object of philosophy. Thought can find different answers. The search for the beginning led Husserl to the concept of *Lebenswelt* (Lifeworld) and Heidegger to the concept of *Sein* (Being). No answer, however, is complete. It can always be corrected, changed, rejected. We cannot even say that there is the only beginning of thought. Different branches of thought can be based on different intuitions. There is such branch which actually starts from the *religious* intuition and it is theology. However, theology cannot cover all the variety of human thought.

The variety of human thought originated from a variety of initial intuitions. If we follow the Husserlian idea, we must confess that *Lebenswelt* is not homogenous. We cannot *a priori* expect that it will be reduced to some universal foundation. So we must confess that the activity of the human spirit cannot be organized in the frame of universal wholeness. Neither science nor religion could play the role of an absolute unifying factor. We can hardly expect that any other such factor will ever appear. This does not mean, however, that any unity is impossible. We can find other ways to unity nowadays and one of them is known as post-secularity.

The post-secular interpretation of religion is quite opposite the position of Russian religious philosophy yet it is also opposed to secular rationality. This paradoxical situation becomes clear if we notice some essential similarity between the Russian religious project and rational secular project. Both projects try to be total and they oppose each other, because they seek different totalities. Secular rationality seeks for the totality of scientific reason while religious philosophy tries to include reason. Distinct from both, post-secularity refuses any kind of totality. The post-secular project does not presuppose to construct any integrity but the main concept of this project is complementarity. The totality of scientific reason expels religion to the private life while post-secularity means its return to the public sphere. However, this return is neither the restoration of its supremacy, nor a new integrity on religious principles. It implies the partnership of different discourses which are complementary to each other.

Various intuitions initiate different thinking or discursive practices of our life. We develop moral discourse, scientific discourse, political discourse etc. Religious discourse is one important discourse among others. All discourses come in touch with each other and need to interact. They permanently disclose common objects for interaction. Each discourse has its own objects and its specific concepts to describe them. For example, the interaction between God and human being is the object of Christian discourse. This discourse develops its specific concepts to express this interaction. These concepts, for example, are obedience, love, sin, grace, redemption and salvation. However, Christian discourse also deals with objects which it shares with other discourses. For example such objects as nature or world are the common ones for Christian and scientific discourses. They use different concepts for the objects.

Three strategies are possible in this situation. The first one is based on the presupposition that the concepts of the other discourse are false and the discourse as a whole produces illusions. That is the dominant strategy of the secular epoch. According to it the Christian (and any religious in general) views on Nature are mere prejudices and must be eliminated because only science properly deals with the subject. The other strategy is more tolerant. Its main presupposition is that the other discourse can develop its own concepts, however these concepts are dependent on the concepts of some dominant discourse. That was the strategy of Russian religion philosophy. According to it, the philosophical and scientific concepts must ultimately be derived from religious ones.

The third strategy must be characterized as a post-secular one. It presupposes an equality between discourses. Different discourses develop different concepts on the same object. It is impossible to reduce one conceptual system or discourse to any other. They are autonomous and complement to each other. This complementarity presupposes the following conditions:

1. Each discourse has some limits. It acts within some conceptual area and uses its own language and its own procedures to constitute and clarify its concepts. That is why each discourse must admit other discourses which act in their own limits.

2. Different discourses meet each other on their borders. They have some common objects, which they describe by means of different concepts. Dealing with the same objects results in an interaction between discourses. So the complementarity stimulates changing and clarification of initial concepts and the search for consensus.

3. Every consensus is not forever and about everything. The consensuses are ever local and incomplete. We must permanently make new and newer efforts to achieve another agreement in the interaction of discourses.

So post-secularity implies that religious discourse acts in the public sphere in the interaction with other discourses. The principle of complementarity is valid not only for religion and science. It can be applied to religion and morality, religion and policy and in general to the interaction of any discourses. It is important that complementarity is not the universal principle, which could make some fixed frame for interaction of all discourses. The complementarity of religion and science is something other than the complementarity of science and policy. They are both quite different from the complementarity of morality and economy. The form of the interaction must be relevant to the objects and concepts the discourses deal with.

So we shall never have global unity which is based on the eternal principles. However, we are not doomed to disintegration and hopeless relativism. Post-secularity implies an alive and changing unity which is based on permanent interaction. In other words, the unity is not given from the beginning and forever. It is not a rigid construction which could be built on some unchangeable foundation either. Unity needs permanent renewal by means of our communicative actions and is in permanent danger of disintegration if we cease our efforts. However, we must remember about the other danger—ceasing thought and its transformation into an ideology. We must resist two temptations: total disintegration and total unification. So we need to permanently seek a narrow passage between two monsters.

Bibliography

Berdyaev, Nikolai. "The Truth of Orthodoxy." Translated by A. Smirensky. Online: http://www.chebucto.ns.ca/Philosophy/Sui-Generis/Berdyaev/essays/orthodox.htm.

Frank, Semyon L. "Filosofiya i religiya." In *Na perelome. Filosofiya i mirovozzreniye. Filosofskiye diskussii 20-kh godov*, edited by Petr V. Alekseev, 324–32. Moscow: Izdatel'stvo politicheskoy literatury, 1990.

4

Post-Secularism

A Preliminary Outline of the Issue with a Certain Ancient Russian Context[1]

Janusz Dobieszewski

Perhaps every reflection in the domain of religious studies or the philosophy of religion should quite distinctly, but not necessarily persistently, express a conviction about the possibility of some autonomy and separateness between religiousness and confessionalism, between religion and the church, between an internal experience and an external institution. The conviction that religion takes an adequate shape only together with the aspect of cult, social and institutional, should be treated very seriously, but we should also pay attention to the risk of trivialization and instrumentalization and allow the philosophical right to free thinking on these issues.

Furthermore, there exists a strong conviction which determines both past events and the status of contemporary awareness, that religion is connected with conservative and traditionalist beliefs, that it opposes (or at least is suspicious of) social and scientific progress, that is close to the political right wing and far from, or even hostile toward, left-wing, liberal ideas. Moreover, it is thought that these attitudes are mutual. This type of negative dependency between religion and the left (with the idea of social progress) were formed and dominated mostly in the modern period, in the era of modernism, which tried to reduce religion to an obscure superstition, an atavism of human nature, an expression of immaturity. Religion, in its

---

1. This chapter was written as a part of a research project "Epistemology of Religious Experience in the Twentieth-Century Russian and Jewish Philosophy," funded by National Science Center, Poland, No. DEC-2014/13/B/HS1/00761.

turn, accused the left of the ungodly shallowing and instrumentalization of man, reversing the hierarchy of needs and values defining man, and rejecting roots and memory which must lead to a deep crisis, disintegration, degeneration and even the diabolization of humanity.

We should notice, however, that the crisis of modernity and recent proclamation of pro-modernity, together with new re-interpretations of historical and cultural events, have also influenced this negative dependency between the left wing and religion, which is no longer obvious. Overcoming the modern practices in this area was a long process and it still continues, but there is a certain point which is quite commonly considered to be a turning one.

Before we identify and discuss this point, we should notice another more general matter connected with the topic of the relation between religion and the left-right issue. The left is permeated—so to say—with the spirit of activism, action, social freedom, transformation of the world, negation of the existing rules and standards, going beyond what is obvious and natural in the existing order of the world. This has usually been accompanied by a spirit of freedom and human solidarity, dealing with social evils, suffering, injustice, which easily assumed a form of messianism and utopianism believing in the possibility of the satisfying of all human desires. Such an approach to the world seems to be close to philosophical idealism or transcendentalism, i.e., approaches which are quite close to a religious vision of the world. As we know, left-wing programs, on the other hand, were more willing to refer to the materialist philosophy, to the naturalist vision of the actual order and nature of society. This led left-wing thinking to numerous contradictions and antinomies (the need for a free and subjective act was motivated by an objective guarantee of what this act should bring and this contradiction gave sleepless nights to many representatives of the left) and to the philosophical primitiveness of left-wing projects. Such works as *Anty-Dühring* by Friedrich Engels or *Materialism and Empirio-Criticism* by Vladimir Lenin were defended with surprising energy as if the fate of the world was to depend on their rightness. These were weak, philosophically banal works in the sense that they moved back thinking to the position of pre-Kantian philosophy. For an activist ideology with a strong subjective moment, that was a demobilizing absurdity. Actually, all attempts at any ideal-related reforms formulated in the left camp, at reforms which were not limited to hard, objective laws of the world or social and historical development, were based on an introduction of various types idealistic philosophies into its ideology. Kantianism, Fichteanism, Hegelianism, existentialism, personalism, and also even Christian philosophy simply captured the left ethos much more appropriately.

A Preliminary Outline

Now, let us return to the indicated turning point in contemporary philosophy. This is about Jürgen Habermas's paper "Faith and Knowledge," which is a record of a lecture delivered in Frankfurt, October 14, 2001.[2] Habermas formulated in this text a notion of post-secularism which expresses the contemporary re-birth of religious problems in a context which seemed to be hostile or at least strictly indifferent towards religion, namely in the context of a contemporary liberal state and the left.

The notion of the post-secular shows a certain helplessness of modernity in removing, reducing or overcoming religion and also a certain failure in understanding man as a fully rational, transparent, autonomous and subjective being. It has been noticed that religion emerges from various sources, that it has extraordinary liveliness, and that irrational faith inspires thinking and speaking with cognitively valuable content. Moreover, it turns out that notions obviously connected with secularization have theological or religious flipsides. Contradictions, antinomies, crises and catastrophes of modernity, its failures and lost illusions, make the modern world fall back into the arms of myth, fate, providence, and mercy. As Gianni Vattimo puts it with certain exaggeration and exaltation: "religion is coming back in a great style." What is more, and it seems that this was actually what Habermas tried to emphasize, religion can be an ally of modern—or rather postmodern—society in defending it from the greatest threats of the modern era, for which the religion was sometimes blamed, but which were probably created by the modernity itself.

This last aspect plays the greatest role in Habermas's paper. Modernity was forced to critical self-reflection by what it excited itself: (1) fundamentalism, which uses the language of religion, but is a purely modern phenomenon (the whole matter was clearly seen in the New York attacks); (2) genetic engineering together with other achievements and, at the same time, threats connected with contemporary science; (3) religious irrationalism, popular and childish, which easily manipulates people and becomes an expression of social and individual neurosis.

These phenomena show that secularization has in some way been stopped. Fortunately, apart from religion and science, which were in conflict for a long time, there still exists a certain neutral area which also had numerous flaws, but which could be a middle ground limiting the radicalism of the science-religion opposition. According to Habermas, common sense can guard a certain level of social and worldview health.

---

2. Habermas, "Faith and Knowledge."

The contemporary situation also makes religion face a lot of important challenges, particularly the awareness of co-existence with other religions with similar aspirations, the necessity to adjust to the authority of sciences, and finally the recognition of a constitution state based on lay morality.

Religions, especially major monotheistic ones, were basically able to handle these challenges. What is more, for large religions, handling them is a kind of reconciliation with modern liberal society. It is advantageous due to the hazards of fundamentalism, irrationalism and to far-reaching claims of the scientific image of the world.

Thus, we have a kind of solidarity between religion and modernity (or postmodernity) with an additionally enhanced role of common sense, which always remains slightly alienated towards fundamentalism and irrationalism and, at the same time, retains a distance towards science and religion. Common sense is a third paradigm which always shows at least a hypothetical way out of radicalism, dogmatism, and one-sidedness.

According to Habermas this whole situation, defined by the need for compromise, makes the modern mind aware that its universalism and egalitarianism has its roots in the mental revolution which converges with the development of the world's major religions. It was the religions which limited various types of particularism, mythologism and substantialism within the understanding of man, and, on the other hand, opposed, as religions, to bringing this universalism and egalitarianism to enlightened rationalism, to scientism, contractualism and utilitarianism. But also, and what is particularly important here, this distance to rationalism is repeated by religious irrationalism, individual-mystic religiousness and also fundamentalist claims. The major religions "disenchanted magic, overcame myth, sublimed sacrifice, and disclosed the secret";[3] they seem to enter the path of the open, self-controlling, and self-critical reason.

Looking at it from the other side, religion allows modern reason to state a permanent question and desire, which nevertheless seems naive and childish in the era of secularism. A question of putting an end to the suffering inflicted on somebody, a problem (raised by Lev Shestov) of reversing the past events and suffering. Here the famous Max Horkheimer thesis about critical theory gains sense: "This theory knows that there is no God but faith in him is present anyway." What is more, Habermas adds, it is God's transcendence and the idea of creation (as opposed to emanationism and pantheism) that frees humans from absolute divine determination (laws of nature, strict rules of existence) and—what is obvious—from natural determination and opens field of human freedom and self-determination.

3. Ibid., 113.

The name of Horkheimer referred to above reminds us that Habermas is the direct heir of the Frankfurt School, an excellent and influential philosophical formation with a distinctly left-wing character. Thus, in the context of post-secularism, religious interests gain a new meaning, especially indicated by Horkheimer, Adorno and Benjamin, which could be called pre-post-secularism. That meaning has been announced and expressed in the famous *Dialectic of Enlightenment*, which described the fate of European reason with criticism and distance.[4]

In a late text with a promising title *The Longing for the Totally Other*,[5] Horkheimer identifies the need for a transcendent Absolute as an object of the most remote human longing, as a hope that the phenomenal world characterized by injustice will not have the last word. This hope, at the same time, rejects to a certain point "daft optimism" as regards transformations of social life, stating that it will be possible to achieve the state of absolute happiness in a phenomenal and historical reality. The religion that meets these most remote human hopes, which is deprived of illusions about the current existence is Judaism not Christianity in Horkheimer's opinion.

Another attempt to connect religion and left ideas are the theoretical concepts of thinkers such as Alain Badiou and Slavoj Žižek. The Frankfurt School referred to religion to enrich the image of the world and classifies exaggerated thoughts connected with social transformations, while Badiou and Žižek see in Christianity a significant partner for the creation of a new social order. Christianity is not merely a reflection, but also mobilizes and motivates social action as well. Christianity can also deepen the image of historical development and the vision of social conflicts with religious and metaphysical grounds, and deepen the image of history as an area where the drama of salvation is resolved. The participation in social actions turns out to have a messianic and eschatological character here.

The existing order of things, as it is claimed here, covers the truth; in other words, it obscures the higher religious and at the same time an alternative social order. However, there occur "events" in the existence, kinds of cracks, epiphanies, interferences of other things, overcoming the entire existing order and the perception of the world. In the "event" humans can go beyond themselves, transcend their egoism and interests, change their ontological status and everything around as well. Humans find themselves in a perspective of universalizing power that gives sense to the whole of existence, eliminates all exclusion, including the exclusion from life (promise of resurrection). The return of theological perspective allows for re-birth

---

4. Horkheimer, Adorno, *Dialectic of Enlightenment*.
5. Horkheimer, *Die Sehnsucht nach dem ganz Anderen*.

and re-formation of all social ideals which became shallow and banal in the modern era. Christianity, as Žižek puts it, has a "subversive core" which can never be noticed by fundamentalists and conservatives, Christianity, therefore, cannot be left to them since it is too valuable. Religion becomes a paradigm of revolution here. Both of them requires constant continuation. They are closely related and give sense to one another. In other words, justice (social truth) turns out to be a counterpart here or the other side of resurrection (religious truth).

Ancient Russian Context

The post-secular terminology leads toyet another place, to the work *History of Russian Philosophy* by Vasily Zenkovsky.[6] According to him, the essence of Russian philosophy is its genetic dependence on the religious tradition. Zenkovsky, just like by Berdyaev, takes contradictions and antinomies as specific characteristics of the entire Russian thought. They are considered as secondary features which result, probably inevitably, from going away from the bond of religion. This process is defined as the secularization of philosophical culture. According to Zenkovsky, religiousness is a state of fullness, harmony, and consolation in which a philosophical crack, a gap, a dichotomy appears.

Thus, Russian philosophy is at its base—just like any other philosophy—a manifestation of thought being freed from the authority of faith; but despite the fact of secularization, Russian philosophy assumed a specific form, separated from West European thought, a form which maintains a more or less camouflaged bond with its religious source. As shown by Zenkovsky, while Western philosophy, especially modern one, distinctly focuses on epistemological problems and perspectives, Russian thought is characterized by ontologism; it focuses on existential problems, which, in turn, results in anthropocentrism and theocentrism, panmoralistic and historiosophical character of Russian philosophy, and its striving for going beyond borders between theory and practice. That last feature was called "theurgic anxiety." A further result of such a shape of Russian philosophy is the idea of wholeness, synthesis and integrity. The religious motives are very distinct here. This idea was inspired by the development of a de-secularization trend, parallel to the secular tendency in the Russian thought. The formation of opposites of religious (de-secularization) philosophy and secular philosophy were called by Zenkovsky "the second polarization of the Russian thought" (after the initial independence of philosophy and religion).

6. Zenkovsky, *History of Russian Philosophy*.

Zenkovsky described in the largest parts of his work a process of formation, maturation, and separation of these two trends. The secularization trend was followed by various forms of aestheticism in Russian culture, by occidentalism, materialism, positivism, radicalism and social revolutionism and, finally, socialism and liberalism. Very often philosophical concepts born within these trends were characterized by a holistic and integral perspective, a moral rigorism and the passion for transforming the world. That is why they might be labeled as "secularized religiousness" or "religious immanentism"; Zenkovsky does so for Bakunin for example. This trend, according to Berdyaev for instance, was developed through its subsequent crises (Nikolai Chernyshevsky, Dmitry Pisarev, Pyotr Lavrov), revealed dead ends (Alexander Hercen), to go down to fanaticism and caricature of the Russian philosophy and a strong religious aspect is still present in it.

The de-secularization tendency in the Russian philosophy, on the other hand, was reflected in Peter Chaadayev's religious and historical concepts, in Slavophiles' and Soloviev's theories, the Russian Renaissance of the turn of the nineteenth and twentieth centuries, the twentieth century sophiology and all-unity theory. In all these trends a holistic approach to reality and history was only possible in the context of religion, in the context of an idea , which is not only moral, but also metaphysical.

Zenkovsky clearly sympathizes with this trend, but also shows limitations in its development. Chaadayev for instance was too individualistic, in Slavophiles there is not enough "theurgic anxiety," philosophers of Russian Renaissance were too opposed towards historical Christianity, which in the case Rozanov leaded to provocative criticism of the church. A significant danger, which can be seen particularly in Berdyaev, was also a failure to guarantee the divine transcendence, which resulted in a risk of solipsism. All these limitations for Zenkovsky shows the need of the further scrupulous intellectual work, however, the general philosophical perspective was right. Exactly this kind of religious philosophy, which undertakes dispute with secularism, guarantees a chance of overcoming all these errors.

On the other hand, when issues related to these limitations gain autonomy, if, for example, "theurgic anxiety" is "set free" (and, in this way, moral postulates are deprived of metaphysical grounds), then it must lead to impatience, hasty solutions and, finally, to fanaticism. Fanaticism, which might be of a political or a religious variety, sees brave new world coming just "round the corner." Post-secularism, instead, both in the current shape, and in a form which could be found in the most eminent representatives of Russian religious philosophy at the end of the nineteenth and then twentieth century, seems to be characterized by mature loathing to of utopianism and a mobilizing, life-giving distance of the theoretical thought to any "already now."

Bibliography

Habermas, Jürgen. "Faith and Knowledge." In *The Future of Human Nature*, 101–15. Translated by Hella Beister, and Max Pensky. Cambridge: Polity, 2003.

Horkheimer, Max. *Die Sehnsucht nach dem ganz Anderen: Ein Interview mit Kommentar von Helmut Gumnior*. Hamburg: Furche, 1970.

———, and Theodor W. Adorno. *Dialectic of Enlightenment: Philosophical Fragments*. Translated by Edmund Jephcott. Stanford: Stanford University Press, 2002.

Zenkovsky, Vasily. *History of Russian Philosophy*. 2 vols. Translated by George L. Kline. New York: Columbia University Press, 1967.

PART II

Systematic Studies

5

Eleusa

Secularism, Post-Secularism, and Russian Sophiology

Aaron Riches

In *Pascendi dominici gregis*, Pope Pius X warned that the most pernicious "designs" of the ruin of the church come "not from without but from within," as an illness "present almost in the very veins and heart of the church."[1] Msgr. Javier Martínez has often argued precisely this about secularism: laicist laws imposed upon the church by the secular state, may be unjust and may cripple her legal freedom, but they are not such a grave threat to the living history of Christianity as is the permeation of the church herself with what John Milbank calls "secular reason."[2] Concern with the the colonization within of the church's self-identity is one key by which we can unlock programmatic battle of the current pontificate of Pope Francis, his war against "spiritual worldliness."

In his last intervention before the conclave that elected him pope, Cardinal Bergoglio offered that the 266th successor of Peter would need to be a man who could effectively fight "that evil which is so grave, that of spiritual worldliness (according to [Henri] de Lubac, the worst evil into which the church can fall)."[3] The expression "spiritual worldliness" comes from de Lubac's *Méditation sur l'Église*, where the Jesuit theologian delineates "spiritual worldliness" as "the most subversive temptation, the one that is ever and

---

1. Pius X, *Pascendi dominici gregis*, 3.
2. See Milbank, *Theology and Social Theory*.
3. Magister, "The Last Words of Bergoglio."

insidiously reborn when all the rest are overcome."[4] In the words of Abbot Anscar Vonier, which de Lubac quotes, this "most subversive temptation" is "the practical relinquishing of other-worldliness, so that moral and even spiritual standards should be based, not on the glory of the Lord, but on what is the profit of man; an entirely anthropocentric outlook."[5] De Lubac goes on to say that this "worldliness of the spirit" will corrupt the church at her very heart, the very origin of her experience, which concerns her foundational encounter with what is other-worldly: the Word made flesh. To be sure it is a dualistic construal of the "worldly" and "otherworldly" that makes the temptation possible; and in this way it is internally related to de Lubac's diagnosis of the extrinsic relation of nature and the supernatural construed in modern theology as a result of the Neo-Scholastic doctrine of *natura pura*, which according to him made possible "secular humanism," that "worldliness of the spirit" that animates the "entirely anthropocentric outlook" of modernity.

This paper outlines the move from the dualist foundation of secularism to the monistic nihilism of the post-secular as a basis to explore the Russian sophiology of Sergey Bulgakov, suggesting that therein we find a key resource for a post-secular theology. The paper has five parts: (i) "*Natura pura* and the invention of secular humanity," which outlines de Lubac's account of the theological foundations of modern secularism; (ii) "Nihilism and the move towards the post-secular," which explores the post-secular as a theological turn to nihilism; (iii) "Radical orthodoxy and *ressourcement* of sophiology," which treats John Milbank's turn to the sophiological tradition as key resource for Christian post-secularism; (iv) "Sophia and divine-humanity," which offers an account of the non-dualism of Sophia in contrast to the doctrine of *natura pura*; and in conclusion (v) "Christology and Sophia," which outlines the Christological heart of Sophia as the key to personal overcoming of spiritual worldliness and modernist logic of secularism.

Natura pura and the Invention of Secular Humanity

While the Neo-Scholastic doctrine of *natura pura* has precedence in the sixteenth-century Thomist commentator Cardinal Cajetan, the solidification of the doctrine came a century later in the work of the Granadino Jesuit, Francisco Suárez. In its classical form it involves a twofold claim:

---

4. Lubac, *Splendour of the Church*, 287.
5. Ibid., 288.

1. even here and now, in the concrete order, there is impressed upon each human person a natural order to the proximate, proportionate, natural end from which the species of man is derived, an end that is in principle naturally knowable and distinct from the final and supernatural end; and

2. that the human person could *without injustice* have been created with this natural ordering alone, outside of sanctifying grace, *in puris naturalibus*, and without the further ordering of man to supernatural beatific vision (for the call to grace is an unmerited gift).[6]

The "proximate, proportionate, natural end from which the species of man is derived," entails that the human being, in his essential nature, flourishes *humanly* within the parameters of proportionality set by his "nature," that is, in a purely natural or "worldly" way. If we want to talk about the human *qua* human, there is no need to invoke the otherworldly or the "supernatural." As the Victor Cathrein put it in the early twentieth century, the human creature is created with a natural *finis ultimus*, an end that corresponds to the limits of mere "nature."[7] Unlike deifying vision of God that is the supernatural *finis ultimus* received in Christ, the merely natural *finis ultimus* "perfectly satisfies," the longings of the "natural appetite," such the natural *finis ultimus* is "*perfect* insofar as it is proportionate with respect to human nature."[8]

For adherents of *natura pura*, the doctrine is salutary in at least two basic ways. The first is theological and otherworldly; the second is pragmatic and worldly. The theological and otherworldly advantage of the doctrine concerns the ease with which it effectively is said to safeguard the gratuity of grace and the supernatural order, while affirming the ontological density and goodness of creation or nature. It does this by the way it understands the *duplex ordo* of nature and the supernatural in terms of the above *duplex finis ultimus*. Presenting the Christian vocation as a supra-human reality, directed beyond the human to an otherworldly *finis ultimus*, the supernatural end is construed as a complete *novum*, a gift gratuitous precisely because it is wholly disproportionate. But the gratuity of the supernatural end, on this scheme, is secured precisely to the extent that it is *extrinsic*, and is not the mysterious correlate of the Augustinian *inquietum cor*. Setting aside the unity of the Christian vocation and the desire of the human heart that entails from the Augustinian vision, the Suarezian doctrine of *natura pura* was

---

6. Long, *Natura Pura*, 8; emphasis is Long's.
7. Cathrein, "De naturali hominis beatitudine."
8. Ibid., 403.

expedient "to protect the supernatural from all contamination,"[9] and so safeguard the radical gratuity of grace by configuring it as a super-addition to the basic infrastructure of human being. Thus Suárez took it to himself

> to cut off (*praescindere*) whatever surpasses nature; that not only could have been made by intellect, but that may actually have been made by God: *what to our eyes is already almost as certain* as it is certain that all these supernatural goods are purely gratuitous.[10]

The dual purity of "nature" and "grace" must be established with no intermediating reference to each other: the gratuity of grace, the good news of the Gospel and the utter surprise of heavenly bliss, is predicated on nature's capacity to fully flourish without the supernatural. The "species of man," then, his essence and his worldly being, is derived not from Christ or from any otherworldly reality, but wholly and exclusively from the "proximate, proportionate, natural end" of his putatively "pure" human nature.

The act of bracketing everything that "surpasses nature," if it is fundamental to establish the nature of nature and the gratuity of grace, leads to a second more pragmatic and worldly advantage: it establishes a salutary terrain of alleged mere human on which Christians and non-Christians find common ground. In the first place the doctrine allowed that the human being was not necessarily, in the first place, a theological fact. Nature now possessed an integrity and density by which the *dignitas* of the human person could be rooted the soil of human being itself, and need not be directly linked to the creation of the human being in the image of God. This allowed for a new kind of pluralism: if an atheist, a Buddhist and Christian are bound to disagree fundamentally on the otherworldly questions of "religion," on the merely natural question of their common human "nature" there is no reason in principle why they cannot come to agreement. The laws of nature and the rights of human beings could now be established apart from any referent to Christianity. According to de Lubac, this new situation had the negative effect of making grace and the supernatural seem more and more an "artificial and arbitrary superstructure."[11] And so the sharp distinction Suárez drew between nature and the supernatural helped to make possible secular humanism, a zone of mere human life and society in which a plurality of view about God can be lightly set aside in order to agree on the universal category of mere humanity. And thus: "isolated from

---

9. Lubac, "Nature and Grace," 32.

10. Suárez, *De ultimo fine hominis*, dis. 15, sec. 2.

11. Lubac, "Nature and Grace," 32. See Rowland, *Culture and the Thomist Tradition*, 100–104, especially, 102–103.

the life of the mind, and from social life, the field [of human life] was left clear for the invasion of secularism."[12] We need only look at the purported influence of Suárez on the Jeffersonian *Declaration of Independence*[13] as an example of how on the level of politics, the separation of nature and grace and the natural from the supernatural began to be enshrined.

As de Lubac rightly saw, the conclusion of this Suarezianism over the long haul was to supplant the Christian identity of a people, who understood themselves and their human experience as constituted by the concrete history of the church, exchanging this new identity with a new sense of human progress realized in "a total secularization that would banish God not only from social life but from culture and even from the relationships of private life."[14] Drawing on de Lubac's analysis, the end result of this process, as Tracey Rowland puts it, was the following:

> [T]he infrastructural properties of religious faith . . . [are] dissolved and all that remains is a privatised superstructural religious sentiment which may sometimes find expression in privatised religious practices and tribal denominational loyalties . . . [A] culture might look Christian and its adherents appear to have a life of the soul but this may be largely fragmentary, formalistic and vacuous.[15]

And thus, as Msgr. Martínez argues, the effect of the Suarezian bifurcations of human nature from the supernatural, of human experience from the life of grace is that,

> "Christian" has come to designate not so much a concrete human experience and endowment that cannot be understood apart from its "particular" categories, but rather now a particular self-enclosed world, [defined in relation to] . . . a humanity *without Christ*, which now becomes the "universal."[16]

Being Christian, on this view, becomes less and less a way of being that permeates the whole of human experience or answers the deepest question of what it means to be human, and now becomes more and more a punctiliar activity that begins and ends with an a good deed, a pious devotion, a Sunday obligation fulfilled.

---

12. Lubac, "Nature and Grace," 33.
13. See Fortin, "The Catholic Church and the Enlightenment."
14. Lubac, "Nature and Grace," 33.
15. Rowland, *Culture and the Thomist Tradition*, 102.
16. Martínez, "Prefacio," 1.

Nihilism and the Move towards the Post-Secular

If the secular is the tidy separation of the worldly from the otherworldly, nature from the supernatural, reason from faith, the human from God, then what is the post-secular? The post-secular can be summed up in four epiphanies that destabilize the logic of *separatio* that animates the Suarezian parsing and the foundation of secular humanism:

1. Faith is the element of all human cognition.
2. Once there was no "secular."
3. He who does not pray to the Lord, prays to the Devil.
4. If the God of monotheism has been dead a long time . . . the man of humanism has not survived the twentieth century.

I will take these epiphanies in turn.

The first epiphany is that of Friedrich Jacobi: "Every avenue of demonstration [that is, every attempt of reason to establish for itself its own basis] ends up in fatalism [that is, nihilism]. We can only demonstrate similarities. [Therefore:] Every proof presupposes something already proven, the principle of which is Revelation. [And so:] Faith is the element of all human cognition and activity."[17] Jacobi is of course famous for popularizing the term "nihilism," which he understood as internal to the Enlightenment project, and particularly its exaltation of reason above religious belief. What Jacobi clearly grasped was the inability of mere reason to master its own powers or provide sufficient ground for its own "rationality." The paradox of reason is that rests upon an original trust, an aboriginal faith, which meant that ever purely rational attempt at a metaphysical system could only end in atheism and nihilism. Faith is therefore inescapable, No mode of human reason is aloof or neutral with regards theological commitment and the original decision to trust. As Jacobi put it in a letter to Mendelssohn "My dear Mendelssohn, we were all born in faith, and we must remain in faith, just as we were all born in society and must remain in it."[18] Why is this? Because all rational demonstration has to break off at some point, since the first principle of demonstration is, finally, indemonstrable. The upshot of this radical non-neutrality of reason with regards faith finally entails Jacobi to declare: "man has this choice and this alone: nothing or God."

"Once, there was no 'secular.' And the secular was not latent, waiting to fill more space with the steam of the 'purely human' . . . Instead there

---

17. Jacobi, "Concernong the Doctrine of Spinoza," 234.
18. As quoted in Beiser, *The Fate of Reason*, 89.

was the single community of Christendom."[19] This second epiphany, the opening words of the first chapter of Milbank's *Theology and Social Theory*, remember a time *before* the idea of secular "space," a zone of neutrality indifferent to the question of God, and therefore essentially separable from the supernatural and the otherworldly. Rather what there was, Milbank reminds us, a "single community of Christendom," a difference in unity of the "dual aspects of *sacerdotium*, and *regnum*." The *saeculum*, then, was not a *zone* but a *time*, a history before the consummation of the world "where coercive justice, private property and impaired natural reason must make shift to cope with the unredeemed."

Milbank's memory in itself deconstructs the secular and "secular reason" because it entails that the secular is itself contingent, and so not a perennial a-temporal and universal foundation, but rather a particular historical idea, of a comparatively recent genesis. What is more, discovering that the secular is not the a-temporal, universal foundation it purports to be, unmasks that, far from being aloof of of the religious, it is itself a theology, a negative theology with no *telos* to the good or the true, but a theology governed by an absolute will-to-power, since every attempt to separate the term "good" from "God" invariably leads to the priority of "right" over the "good" and so to the abandonment of every objective *telos* of human life. All of this anticipates our third post-secular epiphany: "Celui qui ne prie pas le Seigneur, prie le diable."

This third epiphany is taken from the ninetieth-century French writer and poet, Léon Bloy. Quoted by Pope Francis in his inaugural homily in the Sistine Chapel, the sentence specifies that the pontifical program against "spiritual wordiness" is aimed precisely against the secular dualism that would suppose that there is an active, a moment, or a space where there religious question can be set aside. The character of the human being is the religious sense, such that ever moment, every fact, every event involves a concrete decision of radical non-neutrality: either Jesus Christ or the Devil, either true piety or nihilism. There is no secular ground. Friedrich Nietzsche of course understood this well. In the *Gay Science*, when he famously proclaimed the "death of God," he proclaimed it with fear and trembling: "How were we able to drink up the sea? Who gave us the sponge to wipe away the entire horizon? What did we do when we unchained the earth from its sun?"[20] The whole infrastructure of being human, as Nietzsche saw, resists the Suarezian dualism that would lightly bracket the question of God to answer the question of what it is to be human. This leads to our last and dra-

---

19. Milbank, *Theology and Social Theory*, 9.
20. Nietzsche, *Gay Science*, 181.

matic epiphany: if "the God of monotheism has been dead for a long time ... [then] the man of humanism has not survived the twentieth century."[21]

This fourth epiphany, which deeply recalls Jacobi, awakens us to the ultimate anti-humanist character of the post-secularist condition; it comes from the contemporary French Marxist, Alain Badiou.[22] Recapitulating the anti-humanist legacy of Michel Foucault and Louis Althusser against Jean Paul Sartre's radical humanism, Badiou contends that Nietzsche's "desperate intervention" was never about "god," but instead aimed to "undo" the "un-decidable predicate" that tied God to the human being, the impossible correlate that makes the human unthinkable apart from God.[23] And so Nietzsche, far from merely pronouncing the death of God, was forced to proclaim at the same time the death of the human, or as Badiou puts it, he forced a decision at the point of the un-decidable: "God must die and Man must be overcome."[24] The death of God is the death of the human unless humanity can achieve the *Übermensch*, his own self-deification. The old anarchist slogan "Neither God nor master!" must be transformed into a new post-secular mantra: "Neither God nor Man!"[25]

Radical Orthodoxy and *Ressourcement* of Sophiology

De Lubac fully perceived the nihilist entailment of the secular worldview. In his book the *Drama of Atheist Humanism*, he wrote: "It is not true, as is sometimes said, that man cannot organize the world without God. What is true is that, without God, he can only organize it against man."[26] In the face of secular humanism, and knowing well that the groundwork for it was laid in previous innovations in modern theology, de Lubac set out to recover the theology of the Fathers. Therein he found no great gulf between nature and the supernatural since for the Fathers humanity is constitutively orientated in its fundamental being to receiving the gift of supernatural grace. In other words, the real and necessary *distinctio* between grace and nature, rather than involving a *separatio* as the Suarezian construal presumes, is rather built on a *correlatio* of nature in relation to grace, such that, by grace, nature possesses an integral density. Following the Fathers, Thomas Aquinas's axiom that the gift of grace presupposes nature signifies that nature,

21. Badiou, *The Century*, 166.
22. See Riches, "Christology and Anti-Humanism."
23. Badiou, *The Century*, 167.
24. Ibid., 168.
25. Ibid., 166, n. 53.
26. Lubac, *The Drama of Atheist Humanism*, 14.

in her difference, is not replete but is an unfathomable openness to what is more intimate to nature than nature is to itself. The surprise of the gift of grace reveals a heretofore-unknowable meaning in nature beyond every expectation.

In some sense the best of late twentieth century Catholic thought is dedicated to expounding the irreducible dissimilarity of nature in relation to grace in terms of the more fundamental communion of nature in grace, in which the principle of correlation is based on a union of *maior dissimilitudo* and not a parallelism of *separatio*. This program was carried out chiefly through theologians associated with *"ressourcement,"* including figures such as de Lubac, Jean Daniélou, Hans Urs von Balthasar, as well as Joseph Ratzinger. In a more philosophical mode the program was brought forward by figures such as Maurice Blondel, Karol Wojtyła, Erich Przywara and Ferdinand Ulrich. The common task of these theologians and philosophers can be well understood as a concerted effort at healing the deepest problematics of Latin Christian thought in the modern age, beginning with the theological invention of the self-secularizing idea of *natura pura*.

Of course it would be reductive and imprecise to say that the whole the modern crisis of the church is simply based on the idea of *natura pura*. The factors are complex and not merely notional. In addition to the dualistic construal of the relation of nature and grace, there is the anterior metaphysical shift to a univocal conception of being, made possible above all by John Duns Scotus.[27] Along with a loss of the sense of the mystical sense of Scripture, the reification and standardization of the liturgy and the loss of the internal relation of spatiality and the science of theology. What is in all cases clear is that the Suarezian dualism, if it did not directly precipitate the secularization of the Christian mind, nevertheless gave it one of its first major possibilities of expression. In this regard, the tradition of Eastern theology through the modern period has, on the question of the relation of grace and nature, stood as a provocative reminder of the traditional non-dualist view. As Vladimir Lossky put it in his *Mystical Theology of the Eastern Church*:

> The Eastern tradition knows nothing of "pure nature" to which grace is added as a supernatural gift. For it, there is no natural or "normal" state, since grace is implied in the act of creation itself . . . "Pure nature," for Eastern theology, would thus be a philosophical fiction . . . [since for Eastern theology, the] world . . . [is]

---

27. De Lubac at times takes a positive view of Scotus, and certainly there is much in subtle doctor to comment, but with regards *natura pura*, clearly de Lubac was of the opinion that this doctrine was a "piece of Scotism," specifically the univocal conception of God, wrongly absorbed by Thomism "because it was extremely convenient in the refutation of Baianism." Lubac, *Mémoire sur l'occasion de mes écrits*, 188.

created in order that it might be deified . . . [that it might have its] center in the Word, the hypostatic Wisdom of the Father.[28]

If Lossky's description is somewhat idealized, it is nevertheless fair to say that the logic of *separatio* never took root in the East the way it did in the West. The *sensus fidei* of Orthodoxy remained basically integrated: the human being was created for deification; while the God's highest glory consisted in his humanization.

Situated more or less outside the problematic inventions of modern Western theology, Orthodoxy did not need to "return to sources" in order to rediscover a non-extrinsic theology of grace. According to John Milbank, allowed Eastern theology to be uniquely situated to respond to secularism and make the special post-secular contribution it did. The salient contribution, according to Milbank, lies in Russian sophiology, which he calls "most significant theology of the two preceding centuries."[29] Milbank's most important commentary on Russian sophiology focuses especially on Sergey Bulgakov.[30]

According to Milbank, the genius of the Russian sophiological tradition lies in its encounter with this post-secular aspect of German idealism, and specifically in a two-fold apprehension of it. In the first place, Russian sophiology was keenly aware that the nihilist problematic underpinned *tout court* the various projects of German idealism, and in this sense could see that German idealism represented itself a "theological turn" of sorts. In the second place, the Russians fully grasped that, in making this turn, German idealism had restored the integral unity of faith and reason—and so grace and nature, spirit and history—through a positing of reason *over* faith, and so in a heretical and Gnostic variant that needed to be both critiqued and recapitulated from an orthodox and theological point of view. In this way, on Milbank's reading, the sophiological tradition from Soloviev to Bulgakov should be understood as simultaneously extending the German idealist attempt to think rationally after Jacobi, while overdetermining its heretical residuals. And herein lies what is truly radical of the sophiological tradition.

In the first place the sophiological tradition is radical in the sense of the Latin "radix," it represents a return to sources, patristic and biblical, underdeveloped or forgotten in tradition, by which the tradition can be marshaled from its source to enter into a profound dialogue with (and critique of) modernity. Armed with the old "newness" of the wisdom literature and patristic commentary on it, the sophiologists were able to confront the new

---

28. Lossky, *The Mystical Theology of the Eastern Church*, 101.
29. Milbank, "Sophiology and Theurgy," 45.
30. Ibid.

questions thrown up by modernity with a fresh boldness, both in tandem with the German idealist critique of modernity, but also as recapitulating the German idealist "solution." According to Milbank, the inexorable anthropological insight raised by modernity and grasped by German idealism coalesces around the heretofore-unimaginable realization that—far from possessing a static nature—the human being is constitutively and basically dynamic and creative in character. The human creature is, by nature, the possessor of what de Lubac called an "unstable ontological constitution" (*constitution ontologique instable*).[31] And if the human being is constitutively dynamic; his being is radically rooted in the temporal unfolding of his experience, which is bound in the historical experience of a wider community. A series of questions arise from this. Milbank lists the following:[32]

1. Why, philosophically and theologically, is there life in time?
2. Why are there successive human generations?
3. Is human collective existence primary over individual existence?
4. What exactly is it that binds together the human collectivity that composes human nature?
5. If human creativity possesses a seemingly unlimited and potentially catastrophic power to transform non-human nature, then what exactly is our role within nature and what is the meaning of nature for us?

According to Milbank, in the face of this new understanding, the genius of the Russian sophiologists was their ability, first, to discriminate between was in the ineluctable in modernity and what is ideological and problematic, and second, to forge a Christian response that attempted to meet the challenges of modernity head on through a contemplative fusion of biblical sophianic literature, the writings of the Fathers and the popular Russian devotion to the feminine figure of Sophia. The result is a paradoxical recapitulation of the insights of modernity, now understood within a theological vision, of which Milbank highlights three:[33]

1. To take better account of the dynamism of nature, appeal is made to a nontemporal heart of nature which is created Sophia as the world-soul.
2. In order to take better account of human historicity and collectivity, appeal is made to some sort of ahistorical [or perhaps better, eternal] Adam-Kadmon figure.

---

31. Lubac, *Le Mystère du surnaturel*, 149.
32. Milbank, "Sophiology and Theurgy," 48.
33. Ibid., 49.

3. In order to come to terms with evolutionary struggle [and seeming flux of life towards death], the primacy of life and the unreality of death is invoked.

Dogmatic aporias that result from the seemingly ineluctable insights of modernity, which would appear to contradict outright the traditional doctrinal formulations of the church, are now freshly reinterpreted through a sophianic lens. Critically, the dogmatic impetus here is rooted, first of all, in Trinitarian theology: between the persons of the Trinity, defined as substantive relations, there can be no third term. This concerns the classical doctrine of the mutual penetration, *circumincedere* of the Trinitarian persons on account of the undivided divine essence.[34] The doctrine is based on the words of Jesus himself: "I am *in* the Father and the Father is *in* me" (John 14:10); "I and the Father are one" (John 10:30). This principle of divine filiation applies, moreover and equally, to the indwelling of the Holy Spirit, who also is wholly *in* the Father and Son, who in turn are equally *in* the Spirit, since the Spirit abides, knows and searches "even the depths of God" himself (1 Cor 2:10). Trinitarian mediation, then, involves not middle terms but a paradoxical abiding of each term in the other.

The Trinitarian principle of mediation applies, as Milbank points out, equally to at least four other relations, each different from other but alike insofar as they are realized by the mediatory possibilities of Trinitarian circumincession. The first relation is that between God and creation: we have mediation with no *tertium quid* because between created and uncreated being there is precisely "nothing." At once there is a perfect intimacy of being coupled with a maximal difference of being: created being is so related to uncreated being so as to exist wholly constituted in relation to the latter, while the latter impossibly has no need of created being in order to be *the Creator*. As Milbank puts it: "if God were related to the creation and not just the Creation constitutively related to God, there would be a greater than God and God would not be God."[35] And so: God is more intimate to creation than creation is to itself.

The second relation in which the principle of Trinitarian mediation is at work is that of the hypostatic union: it is axiomatic of orthodox Christology that Christ is both fully human and fully, while no *tertium quid* results from this unity. In Jesus there is nothing "between" divinity and humanity, rather he simply *is* the eternal Son who is wholly *in* the Father and in

---

34. See the Council of Florence: "Because of this unity the Father is entirely in the Son and entirely in the Holy Spirit; the Son is entirely in the Father and entirely in the Holy Spirit; the Holy Spirit is entirely in the Father and entirely in the Son," (DS 704).

35. Milbank, "Sophiology and Theurgy," 49.

whom the Father wholly is. This Christological truth is formulated in the Chalcedonian *Definitio* and forms also the basis of the patristic doctrine of *communicatio idiomatum*, but it receives its most powerful and provocative articulation in the axiom of Dionysius the pseudo-Areopagite who specifies that Jesus does not do divine things divinely and human things humanly, but rather does human things divinely and divine things humanly.[36] There is a perfect interpenetration, a perfect circumincession of divinity and humanity in the "one" Jesus.

The third relation of third-term-less mediation applies to the Holy Spirit in relation to the infallible church and the inerrant Scriptures. The former is of course composed of exceedingly fallible human beings and institutionally lead by fallible priestly ministers and bishops, while the latter, the Scriptures, are texts that are entirely human (in composition and interpretation). Nevertheless both the church and the Scriptures, by the indwelling of the Spirit, are simultaneously otherwise: the church is the spotless bride of Christ and the Scriptures are inbreathed to be Holy Writ.

Perhaps most daringly and mysteriously, but really the total sum of relations (1), (2) and (3), is the fourth relation, which is that of the human being to God. The human being is "the only creature on earth that God has willed for its own sake," as *Gaudium et spes* put it (no. 22), and as such his relation of God so intimate so as to make of his being a question in relation to the divine answer. Only God saves the human being. All this entails from the fact that, again as *Gaudium et spes* taught and as John Paul II loved to repeat, Christ "reveals man to himself and brings to light his most high calling" (no. 24). And so between the God who is able in Christ to become man and the human being whose destiny is revealed in that theandric fact, there is again no *tertium quid*. The patristic axiom according to which God became man that man might become God could as easily be rephrased: God became man that man might become human.

According to Milbank sophiology is best understood as the most remarkable twentieth-century attempt to think through this unique mediation of difference with no "middle," where mediation appears at once as seemingly impossible (because not enabled by a "thing" that one can point to), while at the same time arising form the very source of being, the Trinitarian fact that is God himself. Sophia designates the *metaxu* that does not lie "between" the two terms of difference, nor on one side or the other, but rather abides simultaneously *within* both poles at once. This means, as Milbank puts it, that Sophia "does not subsist before the two poles," but rather she "co-arises with them such that they can only exist according to a

---

36. Denys the Areopagite, *Epistula* 4 (PG 3:1072b-c).

mediated communication which remains purely occult, a matter of utterly inscrutable affinity."[37]

Sophia and Divine-Humanity

As much as we can retrospectively "define" Sophia as the *metaxu*, the mysterious "co-arising" that gives expression to the intimacy of theological mediation, for Bulgakov Sophia was less a figure that could be "defined" and was more a figure that had to be intuited and seen. Andrew Louth offers that Bulgakov's evocative and poetic description of Hagia Sophia is, for this reason, his most precise statement of the nature of Sophia.[38] Bulgakov writes:

> Human tongue cannot express the lightness, the clarity, the simplicity, the wonderful harmony which completely dispels all sense of heaviness—the heaviness of the cupola and the walls. A sea of light pours from above and dominates all this space, enclosed and yet free. The grace of the columns and the beauty of their marble lace, the royal dignity—not luxury, but regality—of the golden walls and the marvellous [sic] ornamentation: it captivates and melts the heart, subdues and convinces. It creates a sense of inner transparency; the weightiness and limitations of the small and suffering self disappear . . . the soul is healed . . . It becomes the world: I am in the world and the world is in me . . . This is indeed Sophia, the real unity of the world in the Logos, the co-inherence of all with all, the world of divine ideas . . . Truly, the church of Hagia Sophia is the artistic, tangible proof and manifestation of Hagia Sophia—of the Sophianic nature of the world . . . How true was our ancestors' feeling in this temple, how right they were in saying that they did not know whether they were in heaven or on earth! Indeed they were neither in heaven nor on earth, they were in Hagia Sophia—between the two: this is the *metaxu* . . . O Lord, how holy, how marvellous [sic], how precious is this manifestation![39]

The clarity of the description lies in its mood. Bulgakov is neither trying to "define" Sophia, much less to "defend" her. Rather he is *intuiting* the sophianic, evoking her, which would seem to be the most precise and

---

37. Milbank, "Sophiology and Theurgy," 50.
38. Louth, "Father Sergii Bulgakov on the Mother of God," 151.
39. Bulgakov, "Authobiographical Notes," 13–14. Cf. Louth, "Father Sergii Bulgakov on the Mother of God," 150–51; italics are mine, and I have modified the spelling of "*metaxuv*" to "*metaxu*."

correspondent was to approach her. Sophia is best understood, then, not as a doctrine but as a liminal reality that can only be approached or seen in the most aesthetic of ways. Sophia is apprehended, not with the rigor of the scientific lens, but with the eyes of the heart that sense her and feels she is at the deepest mystery of reality. What is key is the metaxological mode of her being; she is "the co-inherence of all with all."

Keeping this invocation of Sophia in mind, we can now turn to a more technical explication of Sophia. Bulgakov begins with the *Quicumque vult*, the so-called "Athanasian Creed." The key passage concerns the Trinitarian third-term-less mediation we touched on above: *ut unum Deum in Trinitate, et Trinitatem in unitate veneremur*.[40] What one God in Trinity and Trinity in unity signifies is the paradoxical status of perfect unity and difference as mutually internal to one another, that is not exclusive. If God is truly "one," he is perfect unity, the simple oneness to which every unity gestures; while if God is truly "many" (triune), then it follows that he contains within himself perfect difference, and so the interval of every distinction. God, then, embraces within himself—within his simple oneness—the perfect intimacy of otherness and total dissimilitude, in which the maximality of difference must be equally as great as the simplicity of divine "oneness." According to Bulgakov this paradoxical coincidence of unity and difference was unevenly probed in the development of Trinitarian thought. While the trihypostatic reality of God was clearly grasped and contemplated in the three persons of the Trinity (Father, Son and Spirit), the face of the theological consubstantiality of their difference in unity remained, he thought, obscure in the mainline tradition. The face of consubstantiality Bulgakov sought to discover, he caught a glimpse of it in the biblical figure of Sophia.

Drawing on the wisdom literature of Old Testament, especially Prov 8:22–31, Bulgakov suggests that Sophia herself is the *ousia* of God, the principle of "oneness" which is the unity of the trihypostatic life of the God. She is the "personal" face of the principle of unity (*ousia*) correspondent to the concretely different "persons" of Father, Son and Spirit (*hypostasis*). From this, Bulgakov goes on to argue that the *ousia*-Sophia of God is the principle of God's "self revelation," such that the unity of God's life, which is a genuine other in relation to God's trihypostatic reality, is paradoxically the condition of the possibility of God's extra divine self positing (first in creation, then in the Incarnation).[41] In other words, in God it is not only that difference is mediated by unity, but also unity in relation to difference is itself an alterity that both *is* the unity of divine difference and *is* the openness of the divine

---

40. Boulgakov, *La Sagesse de Dieu*, 19–26.
41. Ibid., 37.

life to what is not divine. Here, indeed, Bulgakov stretches the bounds of traditional orthodox Trinitarian theology narrowly conceive. Whether he does so to the breaking point is contestable. Whether the extent to which "sophiology" represents a linguistic innovation more distracting than useful is again another issue. What, however, is indubitable is the fact that the whole of Bulgakov's sophiology, on the strictly theological level, is at pains to articulate something rather convertible with a basic insight of classical Augustinian theology: the principle of "otherness" in God is the principle of his self-communication in love.

God is Love (1 John 4:16). For Bulgakov, as for Augustine, this is the most basic thing we can say about God.[42] "Love" specifies God's Trinitarian being; it is the basis of his inner life and of his going out from himself in creation and in the Incarnation. As soon as we affirm that God is Love we affirm the mystery of unity and difference in God, since the God who "*is* Love," must *actively love* "love."[43] "God is love, and it is proper for love to love and to expand in love."[44] Because God is Love, God is paradoxically *both* "inside" and "outside" himself. Sophia is precisely the term or name of this "inside-out" loving of divine Love, both eternally *in* God (as God's *ousia*) and *outside* God in the primeval divine idea that is the economy of creation and Incarnation, what we call the "world soul."[45] The Sophia of God's own life, then, the economy of love that interpenetrates the divine persons and constitutes both their unity and difference, is also the ground of the being of the world. Sophia is both created and uncreated, inside and outside, not as "two discrete things," but rather as the differentiation of *co-incidentia oppositorum*. Sophia is the identity in distinction and differentiation in union of the created and uncreated realms of interpenetrating love that is the Love of God himself.[46]

For Bulgakov all of this means that Sophia is neither "divine nature" nor a mythological "person." This is crucial to emphasize. The persons of God are three. The divine nature does not exist apart from the three divine persons, as a fourth "thing." Rather, as Rowan Williams clarifies, Bulgakov's Sophia is an "aspect of the divine nature *in action*."[47] This reality of Sophia as "action" (*energia*) is the crux of the essential clarification Bulgakov made

---

42. Ibid., 25.
43. Bulgakov, "The Unfailing Light," 134.
44. Bulgakov, *Lamb of God*, 120.
45. Williams, *Sergii Bulgakov*, 128.
46. Boulgakov, *La Sagesse de Dieu*, 50.
47. Williams, *Sergii Bulgakov*, 165.

in his crucial 1925 essay, "Hypostasis and Hypostaticity."[48] Moved to defend himself from the accusation of heresy, Bulgakov was forced to clarify that, in contradistinction to an infamous and unfortunate formulation of Pavel Florensky, Sophia is in no way a "fourth hypostasis." Sophia, Bulgakov clarified, is rather "hypostaticity" or "hypostasising energy," a personalization the reaches the depth of all being in the act of love. The hypostasising energy of divine love, the uncreated life of God, is that out of which creation is drawn; while it is not a person or hypostasis, it is somehow "personalizing," it is the capacity of all being to be enfolded in love. Here an interpretation of Milbank is helpful:

> Sophia [for Bulgakov] is the Creation in God; Sophia is also God in the Creation. [*But:*] There is not one Sophia, hovering onto-theologically between God and the Creation; there are two Sophias on two sides of the chasm, yet somehow their deep-beyond-deep affinity renders them after all but one. But not "one" in the sense of an hypostasis; one rather in the sense of a shared essence or character or power-to-personify.[49]

A "deep-beyond-deep affinity," Sophia is the "co-inherence" of reality in the act of love, which is not only a personal act but also an act that personalizes. And herein lies the distinction for Bulgakov between Sophia and humanity on the one hand, and the Christological accomplishment of humanity on the other. As Williams explains:

> God as personal (hypostatic) love, love in action, loves also the *fact* that self emptying love is *what* God is. And that "what," which is not simply conceptually identical with any or all of the Trinitarian hypostases, that eternal object of divine love, is Sophia. As object of eternal love, it is the prototype of the created world, or, speaking boldly, the prototype of *humanity*—because humanity is the perfection of the world's being as object of divine love; what is loved is always love itself, but love cannot exist without loving *agents*, and so when God loves the world he cannot but love in it the capacity of the world to be "hypostatic," a world of agents and subjects. Thus what God loves is the directedness of the world towards the human; God loves the heavenly image or idea of humanity, the "Heavenly Adam." And that reality is fully actualised when Christ, the divine person, brings created humanity to perfection because he introduces

---

48. Bulgakov, "Hypostasis and Hypostaticity."
49. Milbank, "Sophiology and Theurgy," 65.

into humanity the action of the perfect other-directed hypostatic life that belongs to the Holy Trinity.[50]

Drawing together these strands of interpretation of Bulgakov by Williams and Milbank we begin to see how the hominization of creation is the perfection of created being, since the human person is the hypostatic realization of the sophianic reality of creation as such. The human creature is creation capable of love; creation, that is, capable of receiving and giving the "I" of love that is at the source of all reality, created and uncreated. In this way, the human being is the still point at which created being and triune being cohere.

Christology and Sophia

With this in mind, I want now to turn to the Christological heart of Bulgakov's theology. I want to do so, ultimately, in order to offer Bulgakov's Christology as the basic touchstone of the irreducible "co-" entailed by his sophiological *metaxu*, and so the secret source of his post-secular theological vision.

For the Fathers, from Ignatius of Antioch to Maximus the Confessor, from Irenaeus of Lyon to Cyril of Alexandria, the Incarnation of the Son of God is not only *the* unrepeatable metaphysical exception of human history, it is also ultimate and definitive illumination of the enigma of human being.[51] From its origin, then, Christology entails a double focus: it concerns the transcendent revelation of Wholly-Other in the face of the only begotten Son of the Father made flesh, while at the same time it concerns the most intimate unveiling of the interior mystery of universal human experience.

For Bulgakov, the interface between Christology and anthropology is based in the three principle modalities of "image" posited by John of Damascus: (1) the Son as the *Imago Dei perfecta*; (2) the "divine ideas" (*paradigmata*) of creation in the mind of God; and (3) the human being, the created *imago Dei*.[52] The *Imago Dei perfecta* is the Son, which means that he is is the *ens realissimum* of the human creature, the creature God created according to the divine image, *ad imaginem Dei*. This means that the human being—created according to the image of the Son, and "as the created image" of the eternal "divine ideas" of God—is himself the "hinge"

---

50. Williams, *Sergii Bulgakov*, 166.

51. See Ratzinger, "Concerning the notion of person in theology," 450.

52. John of Damascus, *De imaginibus*, Oratio III, 18–20 (PG 94:1337C–1341A), cf. Boulgakov, *La Sagesse de Dieu*, 51, n. 38.

of the relation of creation to the Creator. For Bulgakov three things entail from this: (1) the "divinity" of the human being created in the image of God; (2) the "microcosmic" reality of the human as the imaging unity of the "divine ideas"; and (3) the "humanity" of God according to the apostle Paul's notion of humanity as the offspring of God (see Acts 17:29).[53] There is thus, for Bulgakov, a internal relation between "divinity" and "humanity," the uncreated and the created, nature and grace, the natural and the supernatural, all of which converge on the human being, on the one hand, and the divine person of the Son, on the other. The trajectories of human experience (of the desire that sets the human being on the path to his divine destiny) and of divine love (that sets God ultimately outside himself in the path of descent of the Son of God) overlap in the life of divine-humanity, which is sophiological. Central to the life of divine-humanity is the hypostatic nature of the human being, the mode by which he is a "created person," a created being capable of giving personal voice to the sophiological depth of the cosmic reality.

The personal being of the human creature is rooted in the fact that he is created in the image of God, which is his "divine origin," the locus of his reception of the "spirit" or "breath" of God (see Gen 2:7).[54] The human being is thus an "incarnate spirit."[55] This is both what makes him a creature capable of being a "partaker of the divine nature" (2 Pet 1:4), and what makes him a "person." Personhood is thus, for Bulgakov, convertible with "spirit" such that the human "person" is supernatural, the embodiment of a divine principle of "spirit" breathed into creation out of God's own life. In *The Lamb of God* (1933),[56] the first volume of his trilogy on divine-humanity, Bulgakov clarifies how the pneumatic and personal core of anthropology interlocks with Christology through a creative rereading of Apollinaris of Laodicea (d. 390), the "first to pose the problem of divine-humanity."[57]

Condemned at Constantinople I (381), according to Bulgakov, Apollinaris's opponents wholly misunderstood his Christological proposal. While Apollinaris was taken to have suggested that Christ's human "mind" (*nous*) was replaced with the Logos such that the natural faculty of the human "rational soul" would have to be found lacking in Jesus, according to Bulgakov this was not Apollinaris's doctrine properly understood. According to Bulgakov Apollinaris in no way meant to suggest that in Jesus the faculty of

---

53. Boulgakov, *La Sagesse de Dieu*, 51.
54. Ibid., 57.
55. Ibid., 38.
56. Bulgakov, *Lamb of God*.
57. Ibid., 3.

human soul was absent. But to the contrary: Jesus is a fully human being, with all the faculties of human nature, but he is, as Chalcedon would clarify latter, *not a human person*, rather Jesus is the divine person of the Logos. For Bulgakov, that this is Apollinaris's doctrine is clarified when we understand the Pauline tripartite anthropology Apollinaris presumed. On this scheme, the human is not a mere composite of "soul" and "body," rather his is "spirit" (*pneuma-nous*), "soul" (*psuche*) and "body" (*soma*). While "soul" and "body" are faculties of human nature, "spirit" (*pneuma-nous*) is not a faculty of nature but rather the principle of personal being, the hypostatic term.[58] When Apollinaris is reread in this light, he is understood to have said, not that Jesus lacks some infrastructure of human nature, but rather that the Logos in Jesus took the place of human personhood: that Jesus was not a human hypostasis, but the divine hypostasis of the Son. According to this rereading Apollinaris is made to fully anticipate Chalcedonian orthodoxy, which of course holds that the hypostasis/person of Jesus simply *is* the divine Son, such that Jesus is not a "human person" but rather is a "divine person." Moreover, according to Bulgakov, by this method "Apollinaris . . . understood the christological problem also as an anthropological one and indissolubly linked these two problems."[59]

Leaving aside the question of whether Bulgakov's rereading of Apollinaris is historically justifiable, the key dogmatic point he wants to make concerns the recovery of the Pauline trichotomy as internal to the sophiological vision of divine-humanity. The Pauline trichotomy is, in a sense, the hinge on which Christology and anthropology turn. On Bulgakov's scheme it allows that "the postulate of the Incarnation" involves a "primordial identity" between the Logos, the divine hypostasis of the Second Person, and human personhood ("spirit").[60] Moreover, his personal "primordial identity" establishes a correlate identity between human being in general and the filiation of the Son: humanity aims at the divine life, which is to say that human personhood internally tends to its personal perfection in the life of God. The "man from heaven" is the personal *link* that binds creation to God and God to creation, while the flesh of human being is the soil of inner-penetration (*circumincedere*) of the cosmos in God and God in the cosmos. In this way, Bulgakov specifies the Christological nature of how human nature is wholly correlative, a relation to the supernatural that is unthinkable apart from it. Moreover, he specifies what is at stake in the claim that the human is the "microcosm," the "world soul," the created face of Sophia. Bulgakov writes:

58. See ibid., 8–9.
59. Ibid., 12.
60. Ibid., 186.

> The human hypostatic spirit, which lives in man and which fundamentally distinguishes him from the animal world, has a divine, uncreated origin from "God's breath" [see Gen 2:7]. This spirit is a spark of Divinity that is endowed by God with a creaturely hypostatic face in the image of the Logos and, through Him, in the image of the entire Holy Trinity . . . Through his spirit, man communes with the Divine essence and is capable of being "deified." Being united with and living by the divine nature, man is not only man but also potentially—by predestination, by his formal structure—a god-man. At the same time, in his nature, as the soul of the world, as "flesh" (i.e., through his animate body), man unites in himself the entire world, which in this sense is his humanity. Man consists of an uncreated, divine spirit, hypostatized by a creaturely I, and of a created soul and body.[61]

In this passage we see how the Damascene's three modes of "image" converge on the human being. First, the human is the summary of the "divine ideas," he "unites in himself the entire world, which in this sense is his humanity." Second, he is uniquely a created image of God, the "image of the entire Holy Trinity" who is endowed with "hypostatic spirit," a "spark" of the divine life itself. Finally, the human is, "by his formal structure" predestined to be "a god-man" because his "hypostatic face" is the created "image of the Logos."

Created according to the image of the *Imago Dei perfecta*, the Logos is thus the proto-Image according to which the human is created and hypostatically perfected.[62] "The Logos is the eternal man, the prototype of humanity; he is the Lamb slain from the foundation of the world [see Rev 13:8], who is predestined to become the earthly man."[63] This personal destiny of Logos to become human corresponds to the destiny of human personhood to perfect creation through becoming a participant of the divine nature. This means that there is both a "divinity" of human being and a "humanity" of God. All of this comes together when we recognize how the Logos is the proto-Image of humanity, and thus "the eternal Man," the "Man from Heaven," the Man who "comes down" from above.[64] Thus:

> Man is created in the image of God but this means that he is created in the image of Christ; for man, Christ is the revelation and

---

61. Ibid.
62. Ibid., 113.
63. Boulgakov, *La Sagesse de Dieu*, 52.
64. Bulgakov, *Lamb of God*, 113.

accomplishment of this image. The image of the coming Christ is imprinted in the first man not only in his body, which is an image of the sophianic world [i.e., the "divine ideas"], and not only in his spirit, which in a certain sense is sent from heaven. It is also imprinted in the structure of man in the union of two natures (spiritual and psycho-corporeal) in one hypostasis.[65]

The destiny of the human being to deification is constitutive: "He desires to become a son of God and to enter into the glory of creation, for he is predestined to this."[66] Anthropology in this light must be unfolded in concretely Christological terms: "Man bears within himself the coming Christ; and prior to Christ's coming, man does not have the power to become himself (i.e., the true man)."[67] To heal the world and deify human flesh, Christ cannot merely "assume" humanity, he must bring it "down from above."

Divine-Humanity and the Man who "Came Down" from Above

The Bulgakovian ideas we have explored thus far establish two inter-related anthropological premises: (1) the human being bears within himself the coming of Christ, the True Man who is the "Heavenly Man" who "came down" from above; and (2) the human person is the hypostatic realization of the wisdom of God, Sophia, the created act of receiving the personal Love of the uncreated God and responding in turn with a love that likewise is fully personal, but now wholly created. On the one hand this thesis is strictly Christocentric, while on the other hand it is (as we shall see) a Mariological opening of Christology through which the *metaxu* of Sophia is incarnated in the double gaze of love loving love. This expansion is rooted in the primordial pneumatological fact that while the Logos is the "hypostasis" proper to the theanthropic truth of humanity, it is the Holy Spirit who is the "principle" of divine-humanity.[68]

For Bulgakov, the dyadic relation of the Son and Spirit is crucial to economy of the Incarnation. In the first place this means recognizing that the Father is revealed—not by the Logos alone—but by the interrelation of the Logos with the Spirit.[69] The dyadic descent of the Logos and the Spirit

65. Ibid., 139.
66. Ibid., 187.
67. Ibid.
68. Boulgakov, *La Sagesse de Dieu*, 52.
69. See Bulgakov, *Comforter*, 177–218.

in the Incarnation is attested to in the Creed: *Et incarnatus est de Spiritu Sancto ex Maria Virgine.*[70] Bulgakov finds the crucial patristic resource to the dyadic interrelation of the Logos and the Spirit in the Trinitarian theology of John of Damascus, outlined in his *De fide orthodoxa*.

According the Damascene, the Spirit is the "breath" of the Father's utterance: "for the Word there must be breath (*pneuma*), for our word too is not without breath."[71] Accordingly, the Spirit is the power of the Logos's annunciation, apart from which the Logos does not sound. A one sided theology that forgets the Spirit, then, ends by silencing the Logos. The uncreated sophiological life of the Trinity is rooted here, in the way the Son is un-abstractable from the Spirit. The Damascene fuses his Trinitarian understanding of the Spirit-Logos dyad with the narrative characterization of their interrelation in the Gospel, where the Spirit is characterized repeatedly as "resting" on the Son (in the overshadowed womb of Mary, at the baptism in the Jordan, on Mount Tabor, in the resurrected body in the tomb). This "rest" of the Spirit constitutes, for the Damascene, the Spirit's procession: the Spirit proceeds from the Father to "rest" upon/in the Logos in order that the Logos might sound.[72] The Son's revelation of the Father always implies this fundamental interrelation with the Spirit. This interrelation is precisely the intimation of uncreated Sophia, the life of Love that loves love. And this means, for Bulgakov, that just as the Father is revealed by the dyadic reciprocity of the Logos and the Spirit, so the sophianic reality of humanity/creation must be revealed in a correspondent dyadic rationality: the *divine* hypostasis of Logos, the God-Man, the Heavenly Man, must sound in relation to a genuine *human* hypostasis, in whom the Spirit, the principle of divine-humanity, has descended and become transparent.

The co-constitutive nature of divine-humanity in the dyadic relation of the Logos and Spirit is, moreover, reflected in the creation of the human being, "male" and "female." The reciprocal correlation that animates the human experience from the beginning, thus, analogically intimates the dyadic revelation of the Father in the Son and the Spirit.[73] Just as the reciprocity of the Son and the Spirit reveal the Father, so the reciprocity of the "masculine" and the "feminine" together achieve the *similitudo Dei* of humanity created according to the image of God.[74] This points to the mystical logic of the

---

70. Bulgakov, *Lamb of God*, 177.

71. John of Damascus, *De fide orthodoxa*, 1.7 (PG 94:804C), quoted in Bulgakov, *The Comforter*, 49.

72. John of Damascus, *De fide orthodoxa*, 1.7 (PG 94:805B), quoted in Bulgakov, *The Comforter*, 84.

73. Boulgakov, *La Sagesse de Dieu*, 52.

74. Ibid.

unity of Christ and the church, which is the concrete instantiation of divine-humanity. Accordingly it entails that divine-humanity is only achievable within a relation of mutual union between God and the human, where the divine hypostasis of the God-Man is put in dyadic relation to a created-feminine hypostatic representative of the church, that is to say a human hypostasis that perfectly bears the Spirit, the principle of divine-humanity. Precisely this interrelation of divine-humanity is personified in the love of Jesus and Mary, which correspond in their mutuality to the Logos and the Spirit.

The meaning of the dyadic relation of Jesus and Mary for Bulgakov is based, first of all, on a reread of the Annunciation that is mindful of the co-descent of the Spirit with Logos. Mary becomes the Theotokos when she receives the overshadowing Spirit who incarnates her Son. Thus the pattern of divine-humanity unfolds as a two-fold event:

> [T]he Second Person is incarnate and becomes the hypostatic God-Man, while the Third Person is not himself incarnate but rather impregnates human nature, to abide in it and deify it. The dyadic descent of these Hypostases from heaven aims to achieve divine-humanity, the unity of the divine life with human life, to establish the communion of created humanity with the uncreated humanity of heaven.[75]

Crucially, the Holy Spirit—the "principle" of divine-humanity—is not hypostatically incarnated, but rather "impregnates" and "abides" in the flesh and heart of a created hypostatic spirit. In this way, the Spirit enables a created spirit to personally correspond to the uncreated hypostasis of the Logos, the Heavenly Man. The Logos "alone," then, does not hypostatically accomplish the human vocation: there is a genuine sophianic/created "response" to God uttered by a created person. This is crucial for Bulgakov since (1) the Logos himself—even while he is the Heavenly Man—is nonetheless a "divine" person/hypostasis, and (2) he is dependent on a creature to prepare a body for him, he is humanly dependent on the "Yes" of a human "spirit." Mary's hypostatic response—enabled by the Holy Spirit—is thus internal to the becoming human of the divine hypostasis of the Son, and so to the full manifestation of divine-humanity.[76]

In Bulgakov's theology the correlation between Mary and the Spirit is thereby intimately linked to the hypostatic union. Mary is "the human manifestation of the Holy Spirit."[77] Just as the divine Son is the God-Man,

---

75. Ibid., 69.
76. Ibid., 76.
77. Boulgakov, "Hypostasis and Hypostaticity," 34.

the human Mother is the "Spirit-bearer."[78] Mary is the "epiphany" of the Holy Spirit.[79] In being the "epiphany" of the Spirit, Mary is fulfilled as a created person in such a way that she truly fulfills the "hypostaticity" of sophianic creation as such. Thus, "in her person, [Mary] represents the whole of humanity."[80] "Mary is creation."[81]

The dyadic reciprocity of Logos and Spirit is thereby "incarnated" in the mother-child reciprocity of Jesus and Mary. The God-Man and the Spirit-bearer together realize the internality of the Logos (the principle of humanity) with human nature (the capacity for deification, the "hypostaticity" capable of personal response). The Son alone is not the image of divine-humanity, but rather it is the Son *with* the Mother. This is the icon of Sophia, she is act of love that loves love flowing between the Son and the Mother, she is revealed in the divine-humanity of these two faces gazing upon each other: the face of the divine person of Son become flesh, and the face the human person of the Mother become Theotokos.

Conclusion

With the icon of the Mother and the Son before us, we can return both to the Pian war against the self-secularizing modernism in the church and the Franciscan war against spiritual wordiness.

The only answer to the bifurcations of modernity, of nature and grace, of God and human life, is an icon of the circuminession of divine-human love. This is one meaning of Sophia: she is for us a post-secular epiphany of the unity in difference of divinity and humanity. Here the iconic co-relation of divine-humanity makes the theoretical dualism of *natura pura* irrelevant. In the face of this icon, concrete human experience is reveled in the mutual sophianic responsiveness of Mary and Jesus. While it now becomes impossible to think of the human experience apart from Christ, equally it becomes impossible to think of the revelation of God without the "Yes" of the Virgin Theotokos. The future of humanity becomes ever more clearly post-secular: either the death of man in the will-to-power of the *Übermensch*, or the God-Man in the *fiat mihi* of the Virgin of Nazareth.

---

78. Bulgakov, *Comforter*, 187; *Lamb of God*, 140.
79. Schmemann, *Virgin Mary*, 75.
80. Bulgakov, *Orthodox Church*, 177.
81. Bulgakov, "Hypostasis and Hypostaticity," 34.

Bibliography

Badiou, Alain. *The Century*. Translated by Alberto Toscano. New York: Polity, 2007.
Beiser, Frederick C. *The Fate of Reason: German Philosophy from Kant to Fichte*. Cambridge, MA: Harvard University Press, 1993.
Boulgakov, Serge. *La Sagesse de Dieu: Résumé de sophiologie*. Translated by Constantin Andronikof. Lausanne, Suisse: L'Age d'homme, 1983.
Bulgakov, Sergey. "Authobiographical Notes." In *A Bulgakov Anthology*, edited by James Pain and Nicolas Zernov, 3–27. London: SPCK, 1976.
———. *The Comforter*. Translated by Boris Jakim. Grand Rapids, MI: Eerdmans, 2004.
———. "Hypostasis and Hypostaticity: Scholia to the Unfading Light." Translated by A. F. Dobbie Bateman, Anastassy Brandon Gallaher and Irina Kukota. *St. Vladimir's Theological Quarterly* 49 (2005) 5–46.
———. *The Lamb of God*. Translated by Boris Jakim. Grand Rapids, MI: Eerdmans, 2008.
———. *The Orthodox Church*. Translated by Lydia Kesich. Crestwood, NY: St. Vladimir's Seminary Press, 1988.
———. "The Unfailing Light." Translated by Rowan Williams. In *Sergii Bulgakov: Towards a Russian Political Theology*, 113–62. Edinburgh: T&T Clark, 1999.
Cathrein, Victor. "De naturali hominis beatitudine." *Gregorianum* 11 (1930) 398–409.
Council of Florence.
Fortin, Ernest L. "The Catholic Church and the Enlightenment: Changing Configurations." In *Collected* Essays. Vol. 4, *Ever Ancient, Ever New: Ruminations on the City, the Soul, and the Church*, edited by Michael P. Foley, 137–46. New York: Rowman & Littlefield, 2007.
Jacobi, Friedrich Heinrich. "Concerning the Doctrine of Spinoza (1785)." In *The Main Philosophical Writings and the Novel Allwill*, edited and translated by George Di Giocanni, 173–252. Montreal: McGill-Queen's University Press, 1994.
Long, Steven A. *Natura Pura: On the Recovery of Nature*. New York: Fordham University Press, 2010.
Lossky, Vladimir. *The Mystical Theology of the Eastern Church*. Crestwood, NY: Saint Vladimir's Seminary Press, 1976.
Louth, Andrew. "Father Sergii Bulgakov on the Mother of God." *St. Vladimir's Theological Quarterly* 49 (2005) 145–64.
Lubac, Henri de. *The Drama of Atheist Humanism*. Translated by Edith M. Riely, Anne Englund Nash, and Marc Sebanc. San Francisco: Ignatius, 1998.
———. *Mémoire sur l'occasion de mes écrits*. Namur: Culture et vérité, 1989.
———. *Le Mystère du surnaturel*. Paris: Aubier, 1965.
———. "Nature and Grace." In *The Word in History: The St. Xavier Symposium*, edited by T. Patrick Burke. London: Collins, 1968.
———. *Splendour of the Church*. Translated by Michael Mason. New York: Sheed and Ward, 1956.
Magister, Sandro. "The Last Words of Bergoglio Before the Conclave." Online: http://chiesa.espresso.repubblica.it/articolo/1350484?eng=y.
Martínez, Francisco Javier, Arzobispo de Granada. "Prefacio a la Edición de 2008." In Luigi Giussani, *El Sentido Religioso, Curso Básico de Cristianismo*. Vol. 1. Translated by José Miguel Oriol, 1–6. Madrid: Ediciones Encuentro, 2008.

Milbank, John. "Sophiology and Theurgy: the New Theological Horizon." In *Encounter Between Eastern Orthodoxy and Radical Orthodoxy: Transfiguring The World Through The Word*, edited by Adrian Pabst and Christoph Schneider, 45–85. Aldershot: Ashgate, 2008.

———. *Theology and Social Theory: Beyond Secular Reason*, Second Edition. Oxford: Blackwell, 2006.

Nietzsche, Friedrich. *The Gay Science*. Translated by Walter Kaufmann. New York: Vintage, 1974.

Pius X, *Pascendi dominici gregis*, September 8, 1907.

Ratzinger, Joseph, Cardinal. "Concerning the notion of person in theology." Translated by Michael Waldstein. *Communio* 17 (1990) 439–54.

Riches, Aaron. "Christology and Anti-Humanism." *Modern Theology* 29 (2013) 311–37.

Rowland, Tracey. *Culture and the Thomist Tradition: After Vatican II*. London: Routledge, 2003.

Schmemann, Alexander. *The Virgin Mary*. Translated by John A. Jillions. Crestwood, NY: St. Vladimir's Seminary Press, 1995.

Speyr, Adrienne von. *Handmaid of the Lord*. Translated by E. A. Nelson. San Francisco: Ignatius, 1985.

Williams, Rowan, editor. *Sergii Bulgakov: Towards a Russian Political Theology*. Edinburgh: T&T Clark, 1999.

6

Russian Sophiology and the Problem of the Subject in Modern Philosophy

Natalia Vaganova

In his early writing, notably entitled *The Crisis of Western Philosophy*, Vladimir Soloviev wrote about a certain need to create a new philosophy that would have the form of a universal synthesis of science, philosophy and religion. I would claim that the main problem of sophiology was the question of searching and asserting what the subject of this universal synthesis (or *vseyedinstvo*) was to be. Soloviev suggested it should be "not an abstract substance, not an *empty unity*, but the concrete, all-one, *all-embracing spirit*. And this spirit does not have a negative relation to the other, to particular being, but, on the contrary, itself posits this being."[1]

Such an existent subject, or a particularly-universal being—which is all-human subject of thought and deed and, at the same time, the bearer of each particular subjectivity—was for Soloviev and his successors Sophia, as a specific being, connecting God, nature and human being. Sophiology defines this indefinitely-real being with its four predicates: divinity, feminity, universality and individuality; it is stated to be perceived through the unity of mystical, rational and practical realms of life.

Identifying this search for such a subject with contemporary conceptions of an autonomous subject as the fundamental idea of modernity and discourse would certainly be a strained interpretation and a very inaccurate modernization. Still, two remarks are worth keeping in mind for our analysis of the Russian sophilogists' particular doctrines. First, Jürgen Habermas's observation, that Modernity changes religious life, state and society, as well as science, morality and art, into correspondent embodiments

1. Solovyov, *The Crisis of Western Philosophy*, 148.

of the subjectivity principle. Second, the significant statement of Romano Guardini, that the notion of spirit correlates individual subjectivity with subjectivity of the universe, that is, the world spirit, so the realm of human action and creativity appears between the nature and the subject spirit, and this realm becomes an autonomous actor in the important for modern philosophy notion of "the culture."

As Habermas points out in *The Philosophical Discourse of Modernity*, according to Hegel, the specific trait of Modernity is the subjectivity principle. It means that at the heart of modernity lies an autonomous reflecting spirit, forming structure of the world and simultaneously criticizing it (in this case it means also self-criticism).

Analyzing the Modern Age, Guardini marks three main spheres where the emancipation of a personal subject from religion took place: these are nature, personality and culture. It is these three spheres where cognition discovers the being. Having subjectivity as their common substance, these three phenomena form the indivisible whole, which is "the ultimate impermeable basis of everything" and a source of spontaneity and creativity. Significant change in understanding these elements of the universe means for Guardini leaving the framework of the Modern Age. He describes these new phenomena as "unnatural" nature, "inhumane" human and "uncultured" culture. One can imagine "irreligious" religion as well. Guardini supposes that in the realm of faith people have to overcome the liberal project of creating an emancipated subject, connected with the notion of "personality." This process leads to such a mode of individual existence that is closer to the notion of "person," and probably of "hypostasis" in its dogmatic meaning, freed from modern absolutization of the rights and freedom of the individual.

Guardini's idea appeared in the middle of the twentieth century. By that time the sophiological project in the Russian philosophy already had a long history and was completed in the doctrine of Fr. Sergey Bulgakov. Sophiology addressed the indecomposable basis of the being, comprehended in experience. Such an address should oppose the autonomization of the subject, the decay and degradation of the life with some synthesis, searching for a unity of the natural, the humane and the divine.

Now I will examine three sophiological theories, pointed out in regard to the question of constructing a subject of sophiological synthesis. We will observe how this problem was dealt with by Vladimir Soloviev, Fr. Pavel Florensky, and Fr. Sergey Bulgakov.

Vladimir Soloviev

The first attempt was undertaken by Soloviev in his early treatise *La Sophie* written in French that was published more than one hundred years after its creation. This composition is a surprising result of Soloviev's trip to London, where he studied Gnosticism in the British Museum, and of his visionary experiences he had in London and near Cairo on his way to the Thebaid desert.

The treatise was not finished by Soloviev and remained inaccessible for his contemporaries and successors, and it still remains relatively unstudied by historians of philosophy, so the interpretation and analysis of this peculiar text seems to be not a very easy task.

Nevertheless, in this early writing Soloviev already formed the basis for his metaphysics of the "whole-unity" (*vseyedinstvo*), developing many themes and intuitions of his future doctrine. But he did it in a peculiar form of authorial myth I will retell later. In the ideas and concepts of *La Sophie* one can observe influence of gnostic, theogonic, cosmologic, and historic-philosophical motives, dating back to the works of Plato, the Gnostics, the Corpus Hermeticum, Philo of Alexandria, Jacob Boehme, Franz von Baader, Johann Gottlieb Fichte, Friedrich Wilhelm Joseph von Schelling, Arthur Schopenhauer, Friedrich Nietzsche, etc.

La Sophie is composed of four unfinished fragments. The first part, entitled "Principles of Universal Doctrine," can be interpreted as metaphysical preamble to the cosmological myth, developed in the other three parts. In the second part: "On three phases [of nature] of absolute principle and on three hypostases," three characters of the myth appear: Satan, Demiurge and Sophia. This part also contains fragments of mediumistic writing (as we know, Soloviev had ability of automatic writing). In these fragments we hear the voice of a "transcendent" character, whose name Soloviev writes with Russian and Greek letters: Соφια. There are some fragments of that style in the treatise which I will not analyze, but I should say that they do not appear spontaneously, but in connection with the whole composition of the text.

In two dialogues, one in Cairo and one in Sorrento, the Philosopher talks with Sophie. She teaches him about "the absolute principle as the unity." Then the author of the treatise extensively discusses connection between "cosmic and historic processes," these two leading to foundation of the new universal religion of the "whole-unity"; Sophie is silent here.

In the "Principles of Universal Doctrine" Soloviev tells about a "metaphysic need," making human reaching out for the existent good and the existent truth. They are both identical to each other and are not identical to nature—they cannot be discovered in the phenomenal order of the nature.

If so, the human has to overcome nature as the objective "outer reality," and as his subjective foundation of identity as well. As a result of this overcoming, the human should become the highest being, existing beyond the "ordinary" physical nature in the realm of metaphysical nature. According to Soloviev, all systems of religion and philosophy are devoted to this aim. Thus the main problem of the treatise is the question of ontological status of human-being as metaphysical being.

The next step in Soloviev's discussion seems somewhat unexpected: as the first metaphysical capability of human-being he denotes laughter. There is no other natural species that can laugh. By laughing the human fulfills—unconsciously or intentionally—his freedom, since he mocks the "vain reality" and his own phenomenal "vain state" as unauthentic, by these means affirming the nature to be of a superior order and to have its roots in the transcendent reality.

Understanding laughter as a divine principle leads us to the concept of irony elaborated by the Jena romantics. For Friedrich von Schlegel, irony and the wittiness of genius is a way to the highest synthesis of creativity, where science, art, poetry and philosophy are combined together.

The Romantic principle of irony was developed in Schelling's idea of "divine irony" (in his "Philosophy of Revelation"). Schelling suggests a necessary intermediate link, *something between* eternal existence of God and his creation. God detects this intermediate *something* in Himself and begins some divine game *cheering* Him up. It is a mediator between God and the creation, the *capability* for creation. Being the first object of divine cognition, it is the very divine Wisdom, Sophia. God wills to turn it into the different from Himself, to turn the invisible of his divinity into the visible and universal whole-in-difference of the world, without altering Himself, but *feigning* to be the other—and this is the divine art of irony.

Accordingly, having defined the human-being as laughing-being, Soloviev identifies him with Schelling's Creator of the world. This middle reality, connecting God and human through irony as spontaneous freedom of self-expression, is Sophia. Logically, one can suggest, that human god-likeness should has its final proof in his capability to somehow replicate God's activity—which is to transcend his own substance in a free creative game, first by perceiving it as an object of cognition, and second by putting the variety of the inner reality into the outside.

The second phenomenon where human metaphysical nature expresses itself is art and poetry. It is so because precisely in these realms human creates a specific, supernatural reality. In the sophiological perspective it is the creation of some particular syntheses ("unions"), different from both the ordinary, non-universal, individuals of the phenomenal-natural world, and from the abstract and non-individual universals of cognition.

Such a being, or *such beings* are above our reality, but they correspond with it and even guide it. They also correspond with the Absolute being (i.e. with God), who never reveals Himself directly, but only manifests through these mediators. Not anyone can contact them, but only some representatives of human-beings, who have inspiration, intuition, imagination etc. as specific means of communication. This communication is certainly not of a rational cognitive nature, but is a mystic communion. And here, on the margins of the manuscript, certain evidence of such communication appear—some notes dictated to Soloviev by Sophia (her name he writes mixing Greek and Russian letters, as "*Coφια*").

After that Soloviev tells the history of the Universe in the genre of an authorial myth. Having departed from the Absolute, the Soul of the world, la Sophie tries to fulfill herself also in an absolute manner—but this is her fault, since her nature is passive ("feminine"). She consequently turned away from her divine root and fell under the influence of active "cosmourges." The Gnostic genesis of this myth is obvious.

The later development of the world is determined by the struggle between Satan, Demiurge and Sophia. The substance of the cosmos is under Satan's power, ideal forms are determined by Demiurge. The Soul, Sophia, who is responsible for "particular unities," is not able to approve their stable existence, consequences of that are death and decay of the world, the ostensibility of time and space, and other troubles. But Sophie succeeded in establishing a "conscious center" of the world, which is human-being. The human has the inner unity of everything, and history is now influenced by him. The process of the liberation of Sophie begins, and it ends in a final synthesis, identifying the individual with the universal. That is what the human is necessary for.

At the time Demiurge and Satan continue their intrigues, mainly in the sphere of religion. Trying to overcome them, human creates universal systems of religion and culture. And religious process is flourishing when Sophia becomes the object of these systems. Being already aware of her faults, she stands on the path of improvement and is ready to act through her earthly agent, which is a particular human's soul. Thus, the myth goes about birth of the God-man. But is it the final end of the world progress? According to the logic of Soloviev's project of universal synthesis, it is certainly not.

Sophia told the Philosopher:

> The true universal religion is a tree with countless fruit-laden branches that spreads its tabernacle over the entire earth and over the worlds to come. This is not the product of abstractions and generalizations. It is the real and spontaneous synthesis of all religions that takes nothing positive away from them, and instead gives them something more than they had had.[2]

The outline of this religion is presented here only in draft form, and we can only guess how Soloviev suggested his own participation in the forming of the new religious and philosophical synthesis. In the well-known letter to his bride Ekaterina Romanova, written three years earlier, he sees himself just as a theoretician and theologian, however he was ready to go to the world in order to transfigure it. Let us suppose that in this treatise, "inspired" by Sophia, unfinished and consequently unpublished, Soloviev in his most bold intentions saw himself as not only a theoretician, but also a prophet and establisher, even a priest-theurgist of the future religion of the Whole-unity. On this way he himself had to join the "mythical" process being the chosen one of Sophia.

The ideas elaborated in the unfinished treatise were developed in Soloviev's later writings. For example, in the nineties of the nineteenth century he wrote *The Meaning of Love*, where a "gender" interpretation of divine love appears again, for this time also approving significance of this love for cosmic and historic teleology. The universal religion is the end of the world's process, which *in toto* is a process of realization of the perfect Feminine and of its embodiment in the vast variety of forms and degrees; and this religion will become "a real, not merely subjective but also objective, reunion of the individual human being with God."[3]

Later Soloviev chose to remain a theoretical thinker and not to become a priest-theurgist of the new religion, nevertheless, the idea of "embodied Sophia" was popular among his contemporaries. During his life already, and we should say, to his great surprise in the ordinary reality appeared some applicants for this role. So, Anna Schmidt proclaimed herself to be Sophia, and Lubov Mendeleeva-Blok became an object of the sophiological intuitions of Alexander Blok and Andrei Bely.

Fr. Pavel Florensky

It was in this context in which Pavel Florensky became interested in the sophiological problems. By the end of his first year of studies in Moscow

2. Solovyov, *Divine Sophia*, 122.
3. Solovyov, *The Meaning of Love*, 92.

Ecclesiastical Academy this interest developed to purposeful preparation for a theoretical research. In his letter to Andrei Bely, Florensky reported that he was collecting iconographic material for *Sophia*, that finally became his thesis and book *The Pillar and Ground of the Truth*. In this letter he also mentioned his recent article *On the Types of Growing*, in which he undertook mathematical and psychological preparations for treating the question of "individuals who are under *the special patronage* of S.," i.e. of Sophia. It turns out, that besides the two named ladies there is another "particularly graceful" person.

Florensky admits that in the ordinary life there appear some individuals "of another nature." These "angels in flesh" are known to ascetic authors, and their existence can be proven scientifically thanks to recent discoveries in mathematics. This point Florensky tries to demonstrate in his paper *On the Types of Growing*, resting on the theory of mathematical function introduced by his university professor Nikolai Bugaev (the father of Andrei Bely).

There is no doubt that all these speculations have a personal-biographical motivation. The underlying reason of this "scientific-ascetic" theorization on the "empirical data" was necessity of intellectual reflection on Florensky's devotion to Sergey Troitsky, an acquaintance he made in the Ecclesiastical Academy. It is well known, that this friend tragically passed away is anonymously presented in *The Pillar and Ground of the Truth*.

In the book Sophia reveals herself in ascending insight as the church, through the inner experience ("the living religious experience"). The highest point of the ascension is, according to the apostle, the hidden inner incorruptible Beauty. Florensky defines this experience positively, not as abstract religiosity, but as "ecclesiality." He proclaims it should be treated not in "juridical and archeological" concepts, "but biological and aesthetic ones."[4] Ecclesiality is the new life in the Spirit, and the Beauty is the criterion of it. It is achieved through ascetics as the highest art, which is identic to the profane art.

Sophia in the doctrine of *The Pillar* is certainly neither a metaphysical substance in any understanding of the latter, nor is it any particular being of subjective character, in spite of its definition as the "fourth hypostasis." It only can be interpreted as a symbol of some perceptible, but not rationally expressed content of inner religious experience, which can be discovered in each ontological layer of the created hierarchy, while these layers lead to more and more ineffable mystical focus. This focus is called the Truth in the book. But essentially there is no logical cognition, only a scientifically

---

4. Florensky, *The Pillar and Ground of the Truth*, 8.

masked mystagogy, a kind of mystical heuristics, symbolic ascends to the Truth, proceeding from a station to a station, and then the question of the real existence of described phenomena has no meaning.

Being aware of the risk of subjectivizaton to the results of research, Florensky raised the question whether his method would lead to the substitution of reality with psychological illusion, if the author's biography were to be proclaimed to be dialectics. He finds a solution in an understanding of philosophy as a kind of ascetics and as an object of religious activity, the result of which would be the building of the philosopher's own personal spirit.

Fr. Sergey Bulgakov

Now we will consider the sophiology of Fr. Sergey Bulgakov. I believe that the central problem of this sophiological doctrine is connected with Kant's teaching on the transcendental subject.

The difficult relation of Russian religious philosophy to Kant is well known. Semen Frank even suggested that the struggle against Kantianism was a constant problem of Russian philosophy. At the same time in their constant attempts to complete Kant with Plato, Russian philosophers could hardly dispense with Kant himself, for his thought offered some interesting possibilities. In his second *Critique* Kant speaks about the necessity for reason to hypostasize the transcendental idea of the ethical good, and it is hardly just a disclosure of the process of creating metaphysical phantoms.

In the *Critique of Pure Reason* Kant says that the existence of God cannot be a problem of gnoseology, but still the question is gnoseologically significant, since gnoseology demonstrates to the reason frames of its ambitions "in order to give some space for faith." The existence of God is an ethical problem (consequently it is dealt in the *Critique of Practical Reason*, while in the first *Critique* there is only some negative discussion); and it is not an aesthetic problem, neither in the sense of transcendental aesthetics as a sphere of sensual perception (the *Critique of Pure Reason*), nor in the sense of aesthetics as a possibility for artistic judgment (the third *Critique*, where the divine is understood as teleology of aesthetics, but there is no discussion of what is there behind the gates of supersensual).

Kantian rational "apophatic" could not be suitable for sophiology, essentially a kataphatic doctrine. In transcendental schematism sophiologists saw the threat of the desubstantialization of the world which appeared to Bulgakov to be "a way to the Berkeleianism."

Kantian principles did not correspond to the religious experience of sophiological thinkers. We have already discussed the first intuitions of

Soloviev and Florensky. In Bulgakov's case, the first sophiological experiences that were adopted as certain approval of reality of *the other*—the divine being—were of an aesthetic nature.

This is why Bulgakov regarded Kant as the most *a-sophian* philosopher of all times. He saw him as a logical end of European rationalism since Descartes, denying the existent being of the nature.

How fair is this accusation? Kant is certainly far from sophian poetry, but there is at least one "sophilogical" text by him. In the treatise *Idea for a Universal History with a Cosmopolitan Purpose* (1784) he speculates on the wisdom of the nature that is observed in intentional realization of some "secret plan" for human-beings. History here is a fulfillment of this plan leading to the foundation of the perfect state organization, when the nature would be able to become perfect humanity. This problematics was adopted by Russian thinkers through the works of Herder and Schelling and can be found in Soloviev's theurgistic project, where natural and historical processes are included into the common supernatural ascent towards the highest good (having universal theocracy as a rather feasible ideal). The same problematics can be seen in Bulgakov's doctrine, when he proclaims that historical reality of the world should be enlightened and transfigured through Sophia's creativity—in economics, knowledge and art.

Paradoxically, Bulgakov insists on the a-sophianity of Kant, however using Kantian concepts in definitions of Sophia. In his *Philosophy of Economy* Sophia is described as a "transcendental subject of economy," likewise it is the "transcendental subject of cognition" and the transcendental subject of culture. The same situation is in the *Unfading Light*, already opening with a Kantian question: "How is religion possible?" The question, he goes on, is only how to deal with religion in the realm of transcendental—and that it is possible in the same manner as for science, ethics and aesthetics.

The only condition is: *there should be no presupposition*—be it metaphysical, speculative, dogmatic or empirical. If so, the question of religion arises only in a clear consciousness, in a phenomenological field of spontaneous, undetermined religious experience. Bulgakov denotes that religion in this respect becomes such a general fact of human life that it cannot be denied. One cannot deny *an experience, a living religious experience*, and he presents it in a particularly personal shape. In the *Unfading Light* this undetermined and consequently perceived as irresistible experience is described as entering *the particular personal* of *the other*. The *Presence* of the divine imperatively demanded reciprocal entrance into its realm.

The essential feature of religious experience is that it *produces* a direct contact with other worlds, the experience of ultimate divine reality, the experience of God that is not abstract, but is *in concreto* for a *certain* person.

One has first to *experience* God before he *recognizes* Him. In this regard religious experience should be connected with Sophia—but how?

Certainly, such an appeal to Sophia in relation to religious experience raised a question for Sophiology: whether Sophia is *something* or *somebody*. Is Sophia a certain metaphysical being? I believe this is just an imaginary problem. It occurs each time one tries—intentionally or not—to imagine Sophia as a particular being—and then it is necessarily criticized as some fabrication *ad hoc*. But each metaphysical being of all classical metaphysical systems are fabricated ad hoc—as a case that is necessary for all other cases.

Having understood it, Bulgakov tried to step aside from such an interpretation of Sophia and proposed a concept of *hypostaticity* instead of *hypostasis*. In this regard we are facing what can be called the Kantian problem of sophiology, that is, the problem of metaphysics of subject after Kant. It is clear that Sophia cannot be understood as a metaphysical personal being—neither "after Kant," nor "before Kant." But, being aware of an impossibility of impersonal interpretation of Sophia, Bulgakov defined it as "not hypostasis, but hypostaticity," as not *self*-dependent, but adopted (or given) existence before its actualization in the reality.

Having examined particular sophiological doctrines (on the one hand those were synthetic systems, while on the other hand they appealed to synthesis as an activity) we can interpret sophiology as a branch of competing projects. In this concern, Kantian definitions of creative abilities and the limits of a subject were ultimately significant for sophiology. The subject cannot hypostatize objective realms—for example the nature (the life as a system of organisms), and the divine reality as well. He is just able to create "illusionary" syntheses of these two "actual" realities, and these syntheses turn out to be very unstable and need permanent care and renovation. But the two actual realities appear to be bound together nowhere else but in these creative constructions of a subject. Art is the most evident example of such synthesis, but actually it is the case with the whole of human culture. In this realm, not "existence," but "meaning" is significant. This escape from all attempts at the ontologization of "reality" that we can define as symbolic remains the only "world," where humans can dwell, and consequently it is created only for this purpose.

Bibliography

Florensky, Pavel. *The Pillar and Ground of the Truth: An Essay in Orthodox Theodicy in Twelve Letters*. Translated by Boris Jakim. Princeton: Princeton University Press, 2004.

Solovyov, Vladimir. *The Crisis of Western Philosophy: Against the Positivists*. Translated by Boris Jakim. Hudson, NY: Lindisfarne, 1996.

———. *Divine Sophia: The Wisdom Writngs of Vladimir Solovyov*. Translated by Boris Jakim, Judith Deutsch Kornblatt, and Laury Magnys. Ithaca, NY: Cornell University Press, 2009.

———. *The Meaning of Love*. Translated by Jane Marshall, revised by Thomas R. Beyer, Jr. Hudson, NY: Lindisfarne, 1985.

7

Post-Secular Metaphysics

Georges Florovsky's Project of Theological Philosophy[1]

Paweł Rojek

Once there was no real distinction between philosophy and theology. The difference was a matter of emphasis. Although philosophy started from the study of nature, and theology began from listening to revelation, they were moving to the same final end, which was the highest and the most universal wisdom. The study of creation readily led to the discovery of its ultimate source, and the inquiry of divinity casts light on the whole universe. Modern times brought about a separation between them and as a result we arrived at the project of pure natural philosophy on the one hand, and the idea of pure revealed theology on the other. Interestingly enough, in both cases theology lost: in the former account it becomes redundant, in the latter meaningless. There are, however, at least two different ways in which one can restore the link between theology and philosophy. First, philosophy may enter to the field of theology to provide her with some concepts and principles and attempts to justify her claims; second, theology may intervene in philosophy by suggesting some problems, categories and claims to be applied for the natural world. That first project might be roughly called a philosophical theology, the second one might be termed theological philosophy.

It seems that the Western philosophical imagination was dominated by the first way of proceeding. The task of philosophy was usually seen as an

---

1. This publication is a result of research generously supported by a grant from the National Science Center, Poland, No. 2014/15/B/HS1/01620.

independent inquiry not drawing on any revealed truth, ultimately culminating in natural theology, that is a philosophical justification of some basic theological claims. There is, however, also a second way of doing philosophy, which starts with revelation and then approaches the natural world. The possibility and the need for such philosophical enterprise was recently indicated by Alasdair MacIntyre:

> Philosophical enquiry begins by considering what it would be to understand the order of things rightly and so moves in its enquiries toward affirming the existence of God. But philosophical enquiry finds a second beginning in considering how we need to understand the order of things in the light of God's self-revelation. So philosophy and theology each need and complement the other.[2]

In the first case, philosophy attempts to rational reconstruct religious beliefs, providing the concepts and principles for theology. In the second one, conversely, the revelation suggests categories and principles by which the natural world might be described and explained. The former is the path of philosophical theology, the latter is a way of theological philosophy. Both moves constitute the integral program of Christian philosophy.

In this chapter I would like to argue that the Russian religious philosophy of the turn of the nineteenth and twentieth century was in large part an outstanding attempt to formulate and realize the project of theological philosophy in this sense. Russian religious philosophers, at least from the time of the Slavophiles, not only opposed the secular modernity, linking philosophy and theology again, but did it in the most provocative way. They intentionally drew some basic concepts and axioms from Christian theology and adopted them in various fields of philosophy, attaining many interesting and important results. I think that this particular intellectual strategy is the most original and valuable characteristic of Russian religious thought, which makes it probably the first conscious project of post-secular philosophy.

In the first part of this chapter I would present briefly the possible relations between philosophy and theology.[3] The classification proposed here is an attempt at the systematization of a typology suggested by John Paul II's in *Fides et Ratio*, an encyclical letter addressed to the relation between philosophy and theology. Theological philosophy is an old, but not always rightly understood idea. Classical examples of enriching philosophical enquiry by

---

2. MacIntyre, *God, Philosophy, Universities*, 166.

3. This part draws on a part of my paper in Polish "Rosyjska filozofia teologiczna," 23–33.

faith might be found in the Church Fathers, in Aquinas, in his theory of being for instance, or in Palamas, in his distinction between essence and energies. Nevertheless this classical path was abandoned in modernity and for a long time few philosophers, even among declared Christians, saw a need to enter it again. In the second part I am going to discuss an idea of theological philosophy presented by one of the most recognized Russian Orthodox theologians, Georges Florovsky (1893–1979). I believe that Florovsky, especially in his famous paper "Revelation, Philosophy and Theology," published in 1931, nicely summarized and generalized the Russian post-secular approach to the relation between philosophy and theology. He was the man who finally realized, like Monsieur Jourdain, that he was speaking prose all his life. Quite surprisingly, Florovsky for some unclear reasons denied that it was the proper tradition of Russian religious thought. So, in the third part, I will suggest that many Russian ideas in metaphysics, epistemology, anthropology and social philosophy perfectly fit the pattern discovered by Florovsky. Particularly, I will focus on the early program of Russian philosophy sketched by Ivan Kireevsky (1806–1856) and then turn back to Florovsky's critique of Russian religious philosophy, which seems to be based on the confusion of two different charges. I believe that almost all of Russian religious philosophy might be interpreted as a realization of post-secular program of philosophical enquiry directly inspired by theological revelation. And I suppose that it was the very reason John Paul II highlighted the Russian thinkers Vladimir Soloviev and Pavel Florensky as "significant examples of a process of philosophical enquiry which was enriched by engaging the data of faith."[4]

Relations between Philosophy and Theology

Philosophy and theology share the same general structure. Both disciplines, as all other kinds of knowledge, elaborate their own concepts, formulate general principles and arrive to some particular thesis. The fundamental difference between them lies in the direct object of inquiry. Philosophy starts with the natural reality, theology with the divine revelation.

Now, generally, various kinds of knowledge might influence each other on different levels. In many cases some concepts, principles or even the particular claims of one discipline might be borrowed and reused by another. There are plenty of examples: sociology, for instance, vigorously developed after the adoption of some concepts and metaphors from nineteenth century biology; semantic antirealism in philosophy appeared as a result of the

4. John Paul II, *Fides et Ratio*, 74.

implementation of some ideas from mathematical intuitionism; structural anthropology in social science was built on the basis of some linguistic concepts. In many cases an appropriate transfer of concepts or principles from one kind of knowledge to another leads to great results.

The same interrelations might occur between philosophy and theology. Theology might owe her concepts and principles to philosophy, and philosophy might also have borrowed some axioms and ideas from theology. In the long history of the exchange between philosophy and theology, the former case seems to be more popular, though many theologian regard it as a potentially dangerous situation. It seems, however, that some important philosophical ideas also sprang from theology, such as the doctrine of existence which was presumably possible solely as a philosophical expression of the religious dogma of the creation *ex nihilo*.

The general ways of possible influences between any two disciplines make possible a simple classification of different types of philosophy and theology. In fact a kind of such classification was suggested in *Fides et Ratio*, where John Paul II distinguished between three kinds of knowledge: a "philosophy completely independent of the Revelation," a "theology . . . which itself calls upon philosophy," and a "Christian philosophy."[5]

Firstly, an "independent philosophy" claims to not rely on theology in any respect. Philosophy of this kind was presumably developed before Christ and is still practiced by those few who still do not know Christianity and the many who intentionally attempt to deny or ignore it. Such "independent philosophy" might be in principle considerably open for the truth coming from revelation, if only it was not consciously built on the negation of revelation.

Secondly, a "theology which calls upon philosophy," according to *Fides et Ratio*, uses philosophical concepts in analyzing divine revelation. Perhaps every kind of theology is implicitly philosophical in this way. Theology, as a rational activity, always rest on some kind of general philosophical framework, moreover revelation itself is a part of the given reality, so it also might be inquired after by philosophy. In many cases, however, theologians consciously and intentionally used philosophy to analyzing the revelation. In this respect philosophy was a true *ancilla theologiae*.

Finally, a "Christian philosophy" is "a Christian way of philosophizing, a philosophical speculation conceived in dynamic union with faith," and this kind of philosophical thinking, as underlines John Paul II, "would not have happened without the direct or indirect contribution of Christian

---

5. Ibid., 75–79.

faith."[6] Christian philosophy deals with the questions suggested by revelation, such as the reason of all being, the personal character of God, the meaning of life, or the problem of evil. It is not, however, simply a rational analysis of faith, as in the case of "theology which calls upon philosophy," but rather an extension of the scope of natural philosophy. New philosophy owes its problems and the inspirations for their solution to theology. Obviously, as John Paul II reminded us, there is no single officially admitted particular "Christian philosophy" but there might in fact be many different realizations of the same program. *Fides et Ratio* quite surprisingly praises Christian phenomenology along with the Thomist tradition. It seems therefore that different philosophical schools might take their inspirations from revelation. Theological concepts, intuitions and claims might be embodied in various philosophical systems in many different ways.

The interrelation between philosophy and theology in the two cases of "theology which calls upon philosophy" and "Christian philosophy" remains, however, somehow unclear. John Paul II focused on sharing questions between these two disciplines. No doubt, there were great theological problems, such as free will or creation *ex nihilo*, which was subsequently taken by philosophy. In this way revelation, as noticed John Paul II, "extended" philosophical research "to new aspects of truth" and it might be really said that "a good part of modern and contemporary philosophy would not exist without this stimulus of the word of God."[7] Undoubtedly, also some specific philosophical issues, such as aesthetics or the philosophy of labor, have subsequently received theological explanation. Nevertheless it seems that the exchange between philosophy and theology was even deeper than simply extending the scope of inquiry. Both disciplines also borrowed some concepts, principles and claims from each other. The concept of substance, for instance, was apparently taken by dogmatic theology from ancient philosophy, whereas the concept of the person presumably migrated from the doctrine of Christ and the Trinity to philosophical anthropology. The same might be found on the level of principles and claims. The logical principle of contradiction, for instance, was generally accepted in theology, and the idea of original sin, on the other hand, received many interpretations in the social philosophy. It seems even that the exchanges of concepts and principles were even more illuminating and fruitful than mere extending of the scope of the both disciplines.

The typology sketched in *Fides et Ratio* might easily be developed into a clear classification of kinds of philosophies and theologies. Philosophy

6. Ibid., 76.
7. Ibid.

and theology differs in their immediate objects: philosophy speaks first of all about natural reality, whereas theology starts with revelation. Both disciplines developed their own concepts and formulated their own claims concerning their own immediate domains. Exactly that concepts and claims might be subsequently transferred from one discipline to another. Therefore, there are four possible ideal types of philosophy and theology (see Fig. 1).

	Object of Philosophy	Object of Theology
Language of Philosophy	Philosophical Philosophy	Philosophical Theology
Language of Theology	Theological Philosophy	Theological Theology

Fig. 1. Four ideal types of philosophy and theology

Philosophical philosophy is simply pure philosophy, corresponding to an "independent philosophy" from *Fides et Ratio*. It speaks about its own domain in its own language. An ideal of a pure theology, significantly missing in John Paul II typology, is theological theology, speaking in own way on its own subject. The meeting of philosophy and theology might result either in philosophical theology or in theological philosophy. The former corresponds to a "theology which calls upon philosophy," described in *Fides et Ratio*, whereas the latter fits to a "Christian philosophy," if it is understood not only as extending the scope of philosophy, but also as borrowing concepts and principles from theology. Now I would like to analyze these four types of general inquiry a little bit more.

Philosophical Philosophy

Philosophical philosophy is, paraphrasing Kant, "a philosophy within the limits of reason alone." There are plenty of philosophical theories which do not adopt any principles, concepts, or even problems from revelation, the large part of contemporary analytical philosophy fitting this category. There is nothing wrong with this from a Christian perspective since such theories have a rightful autonomy, nevertheless they should also respect the autonomy of faith, that is to not exclude the possibility of their complementation by revelation.

Nevertheless any serious attempt to realize the ideal of philosophy, that is a universal wisdom, nevertheless leads to the problem of revealed religion. To ignore this would mean to arbitrarily restrict the scope of philosophy. To focus on it means to switch either to philosophical theology or theological philosophy.

Philosophical Theology

Philosophical theology is the first way of meeting of philosophy and theology. It is an intellectual reflection on revelation with the help of philosophical concepts and principles. Categories developed for analyzing the natural world are used here for the interpretation of the divine truths. Philosophical theology in this sense consists exactly in the conscious and intentional use of philosophical tools to develop reflection on faith.

The first attempts to use natural pagan philosophy for theological purposes were made by the very first Christian thinkers, the Apologetics and the Church Fathers. It was often said that by doing so they followed the Jews, who stole pagan gold and silver vestments before escaping Egypt and using them for the cult of the true God, or young David, who wrest the sword from the hands of Goliath and killed him with his own weapon. Both metaphors recalled Pope Leo XIII in his encyclical on Christian philosophy.[8] Philosophy serves here theology, providing language used for a precise expression of the truths of faith. In general, traditional Christian dogmatics, formulated in philosophical language, with categories of substance, nature, *hypostasis* and so on, seems to be a result of the process of adoption philosophical concepts to theological purposes.

There are of course great doubts concerning the influence of philosophical language on the truths of faith. Philosophy has not been revealed and no particular philosophical system fits the content of revelation perfectly. The use of philosophy is therefore always burdened by the risk of distortion of the depositions of faith. Not all theologians and philosophers agreed with Aquinas, who famously claimed in *Super Boetium De trinitate* (q. 2, a. 3, ad 5) that "those who use the works of the philosophers in sacred doctrine, by bringing them into the service of faith, do not mix water with wine, but rather change water into wine."[9] Some of them indicated that many times in history we can see instead of the "Christianization" of pagan philosophy we have rather been witness to the "paganization" of Christian faith. Mixing wine and water we simply we lost wine and were left with water. For that reason many theologians in recent centuries formulated a

---

8. Leo XIII, *Aeterni Patris*, 4, 7.
9. Aquinas, *Faith, Reason, and Theology*, 19–20.

postulate to abandon the whole project of philosophical theology and to retreat to pure theology, that is theological theology.

However, the defenders of philosophical theology, such as John Paul II, indicate that the Apologetics and the Church Fathers "were not naïve thinkers."[10] They did not simply express the truths of faith in the existing philosophical categories, but rather transformed the philosophical systems, modifying, correcting and developing them to fit the message of faith. The adjustment of Platonism for Christianity is clearly seen in Origen, Pseudo-Dionisius Areopagite or Saint Augustine, the similar adaptation of Aristotelianism might be found in Saint Thomas Aquinas or in Blessed John Duns Scotus. If it is so, however, it looks like these masters realized in fact not the project of pure philosophical theology, but rather theological philosophy. It seems therefore that the dialectics of philosophy and theology leads either to theological theology or to theological philosophy.

Theological Theology

The criticism of the philosophical theology led many authors to heroic attempts at the formulation of an independent theology. Such a theology would be in strict opposition to the pure philosophy mentioned in *Fides et Ratio*. Such a theological theology seeks to understand the content of revelation exclusively in reference to the categories and concepts already contained within it. This leads to the postulate of the purification of theology from any kind of philosophical additions and deformations, which had corrupted revelation during the centuries of the cultivation of philosophical theology.

This tendency is obviously most explicit in protestant theology. Martin Luther famously called the faith to "slaughter" and "kill the reason," as an offering for a sacrifice,[11] still his followers maintain that the metaphysics is the fundamental evil in Christian theology. Paul Tillich for instance claimed that "to argue that God exists is to deny him,"[12] and Karl Barth viewed the doctrine of *analogia entis* as "the invention of Antichrist."[13] Similar formulations, though usually less colorful, might be found among some analytical philosophers of religion, especially those inspired by the late Ludwig Wittgenstein. According to Devi Z. Phillips, the very first Christians went wrong by using philosophical concepts of being, cause or substance to

---

10. John Paul II, *Fides et Ratio*, 41.
11. Luther, *A Commentary on Saint Paul's Epistle*, 195.
12. Tillich, *Systematic Theology*, 1:205.
13. Barth, *Church Dogmatics*, 1/1:xiii.

for understanding and expressing their faith. This original mistake gravely distorted the true meaning of Christianity and is about to bring about its collapse.[14]

The postulate of pure theology faces however a straightforward difficulty since in some sense theology is always a part of philosophy. Philosophy aims to understand all reality, theology starts with a part of it, namely revelation. One cannot therefore build theology without any philosophical presuppositions. The demand of "de-philosophization" of theology always amounts to replacing one philosophical paradigm by another. It was clearly seen in the famed Polish debate on Thomism in the seventies. Fr. Józef Tischner declared the "decline of thomistic Christianity" and called for the abandonment of all remains of outdated medieval outlook.[15] The rejection of the allegedly unnecessary burden of philosophy did not however leaded to the liberation of theology from philosophy in general, but rather to the acceptance the principles and the language of another philosophy, such as—in particular Tischner's case—phenomenology and the philosophy of dialogue. The same is even more obvious in the case of "Wittgensteinian fideism" which formulates its critique of philosophical theology on the basis of Wittgenstein's philosophical philosophy. As John Paul II wrote, "were theologians to refuse the help of philosophy, they would run the risk of doing philosophy unwittingly and locking themselves within thought-structures poorly adapted to the understanding of faith."[16] It seems therefore that theology simply cannot get away from philosophy.

Theological Philosophy

Theological philosophy is the inversion of philosophical theology. As far as the latter adjusts the truths of faith to the language of the existing philosophy, the former attempts to adapt philosophy to faith. In the case of theological philosophy the dogmatic theological content inspires philosophical speculations, which apply concepts and principles formulated by theology in the broad philosophical domain.

The revealed religion, as was noticed in *Fides et Ratio*, undoubtedly expanded the scope of interest of pure philosophy. It seems however that the influence of theology on religion was even more deeper when it directly inspired philosophical theories based on theological principles and concepts. The clearest example of such a theory might be the Thomistic doctrine of

---

14. Gomułka, *Gramatyka wiary*.
15. Tischner, "Schyłek chrześcijaństwa tomistycznego."
16. John Paul II, *Fides et Ratio*, 77.

esse, which was primarily an attempt to draw metaphysical consequences from biblical sources. Charles Kahn famously claimed that in general

> the existence in the modern sense becomes a central concept in philosophy only in the period when Greek ontology is radically revised in the light of the metaphysics of creation; that is to say, under the influence of biblical religion.[17]

Aquinas's theory of soul has a similar character and Joseph Ratzinger argued that despite appearances it had little common with the ancient Greek concept of soul and was an original philosophical answer to the challenge posed by the idea of man presupposed by the revelation.[18] The other important example is undoubtedly the concept of person which appeared first as a discovery of theological investigations.[19]

How much philosophy is in revelation? Certainly the biblical message presupposes some philosophical principles and excludes others. First of all, the revelation is "metaphysical" in that sense that it contains claims which have realistic meaning.[20] Besides, it seems that it might suggest some particular ontological principles. Claims such as the personal character of God, contingency of the world, human freedom or immortality limit the revelation-based philosophy. Therefore one can speak about particular metaphysics included in biblical records. "The Bible—argued Vittorio Possenti—contains innumerable amount of ontological claims," and is "inexhaustible source of inspiration for Christian thought," which can be therefore labeled as "biblical metaphysics" or even "Christian metaphysics."[21]

It might be doubted however if the revelation really contains a particular, positive philosophy, which should be only extracted, refined and systematized. It seems that the supposed principles of "biblical metaphysics" are quite indeterminate and allow many possible interpretations. It might be seen in the example of the Thomistic doctrine of existence, which was obviously inspired by theology. Possenti suggested that it directly belongs to the very content of the revelation.[22] Aquinas was also convinced that his theory stemmed immediately from the Bible, where God introduced himself as "he, who is." (Ex 3:14) Aquinas wrote:

---

17. Kahn, *Essays on Being*, 62–63.
18. Ratzinger, *Eschatology*, 146–49.
19. Ratzinger, "Concerning the Notion of Person," Lobkowicz, "Was ist eine Person?"
20. John Paul II, *Fides et Ratio*, 82.
21. Possenti, *Philosophy and Revelation*, 25.
22. Ibid., 42.

His essence is . . . his being. This sublime truth Moses was taught by our Lord . . . Our Lord showed that his own proper name is *he who is*. Now, names have been devised to signify the natures or essences of things. It remains, then, that the divine being is God's essence or nature (*Contra Gentiles* I, 22).[23]

However the case is obviously not so easy. One might agree with Kahn's general opinion that the problem of existence might appear only due to the biblical revelation and at the same time deny that the only true account for it is the Thomistic doctrine of *esse*. Moreover, it is far from evident what exactly our Lord said to Moses.[24] It might be held that this passage of the Book of Exodus really contains some "metaphysics," but not necessarily in the sense which was suggested by Aquinas. For instance, Roger Scruton recently claimed, that God revealed to Moses not his essence, but rather his personal status and at the same time confirmed Scruton's argumentation.[25] All this indicates that revelation indeed presupposes a kind of metaphysics, but not a determinate one. There might be many different theories consistent with revelation.

Theological philosophy is theological in the sense that it draws some general concepts or principles from theology. It does not mean, however, that it becomes simple theology or is acceptable only for believers. The ultimate justification is the use of theological philosophy, which is evaluated in the same way as any other philosophy. Theological philosophy might simply work better than pure philosophy and from the theoretical point of view the provenance of concepts and axioms does not matter. The concept of formal distinction, for instance, originally introduced by Duns Scotus for analyzing the interrelations between divine attributes, has enjoyed a great career in contemporary analytic metaphysics. The idea of formal distinction, although formulated in theological context, might be successfully applied in other ones, most importantly in the theory of universals. The philosophers who use it not only need not be religious, but even might not realize its genealogy. The famous naturalistic realist David Armstrong for example is a declared atheist, whereas his anti-naturalistic critic James Moreland is a Christian apologetic; both refer to *distictio formalis* in their works on universals.[26]

---

23. Aquinas, *On the Truth of the Catholic Faith*.

24. For a survey of contemporary interpretations of Ex 3:14 see, for instance, LaCocque, Ricoeur, *Thinking Biblically*, 307–64.

25. Scruton, *The Face of God*, 51–53.

26. See Armstrong, *Nominalism and Realism*, 110; Moreland, *Universals*, 22.

In this short survey of the possible interrelations between philosophy and theology I wanted to stress that there are two general strategies for joining these two disciplines. The first one starts from the bottom, from the natural reality, and tries to reach the whole universe, including its ultimate source. The second one, conversely, starts from the top, from the divinity, and then embraces all of the remaining reality. Philosophy enters the domain of theology and theology descends into the arena of philosophy. If the first movement is usually called the "natural" or "philosophical" theology, the second one might be perhaps dubbed "graceful" or "theological" philosophy.

Now, the kinds of thinking distinguished here are definitely merely ideal types and perhaps no historical example fits any of them exactly. Nevertheless it seems that it is possible to find some tendencies in historical epochs and intellectual traditions which may approximate one of the ideal patterns. It seems convincing, for instance, that the philosophy of the Church Fathers was closer to the ideal of theological philosophy than late Scholasticism, which usually rather followed the pattern of philosophical theology. Likewise, the Western intellectual tradition in general seems to be closer to philosophical theology, whereas Eastern Christianity adheres more to theological philosophy. Yet these are certainly only general tendencies. As I pointed out, many of the ideas of Aquinas, a supposed paradigm of natural theology, might be understood as examples of philosophy inspired by theology. However, if these general attribution are true, we should expect good samples of theological philosophy from Orthodox theologians calling for the return to the Church Fathers. That is why I will turn now to Father Georges Florovsky.

Florovsky's Project of Theological Philosophy

Father Georges Florovsky was undoubtedly one of the most influential Orthodox theologians of the twentieth century. He is the main figure in the project of "neopatristic synthesis," which became the dominant paradigm of contemporary Orthodox theology. He started as a religious philosopher and positive scientist and in Odessa, where he lived and studied for the first years, he was the secretary of both the Philosophical and Scientists Associations. At the age of seventeen he corresponded with the great philosopher Pavel Florensky; at the age of twenty four he published research in English on the reflex salivary secretion which was praised by the famous psychologist Ivan Pavlov.[27] Exiled from Soviet Russia, he became involved in the

---

27. Obolevitch, *Filozofia rosyjskiego renesansu patrystycznego*, 63–87.

Eurasian movement seeking a cultural and political alternative both to the communist order and the *ancien régime*. In Prague he became a member of the Brotherhood of Saint Sophia, led by Father Sergey Bulgakov, who was also for a time his spiritual father.[28] After the split with the Eurasians he devoted himself entirely to theological studies and, shortly after, Bulgakov invited him to work as a lecturer of patristics in Paris. In 1932 he was ordained a priest. During the debate on Bulgakov's sophiology, Florovsky tried to remain aloof despite being quite critical of it. Pressed by Orthodox hierarchy, he signed a theological opinion condemning sophiology prepared by Father Sergey Chetverikov. In 1948 he moved to the US where he became the dean of St. Vladimir Theological Seminary, and afterwards a professor at Harvard and Princeton, being at the end of his life probably the most honorable Orthodox theologian in the world.

I would like to take a closer look here at Florovsky's original view on the relation between philosophy and theology. It seems that he tried to formulate an approach based on patristic experience and opposed to the dominating secular paradigm of philosophy. As Teresa Obolevitch aptly suggested, he wanted to replace the principle *fides quaerens intellectum* with the rule *intellectus quaerens fidem*.[29] It was faith which usually sought out reason; for Florovsky reason should seek out faith. In that first default case faith needs to be justified or proved by reason, in the second, unobvious one, faith has absolute priority and illuminates natural thought itself. Philosophy should not attempt to ground theology, formulating arguments for the existence of God or proving the coherence of theism, but should rather accept theology as a fundamental premise and then develop a new, non-secular account for the old philosophical topics.

I would like to focus here on the two Florovsky's papers, which brilliantly illustrate the way to the theological philosophy. The first one, scarcely known and rarely cited, entitled "Philosophy and Religion," has been written in 1923 for a Russian émigré journal *Logos*, which unfortunately ceased to appear soon after the submission. Anyway, the paper probably would not be accepted by its editor Boris Yakovenko, who had completely different philosophical views. The forgotten text has been recently discovered in Yakovenko's personal archive in Prague and published in Russian by Professor Oleg Ermishin.[30]

---

28. Gallaher, "Waiting for the Barbarians," 662, 685.

29. Obolevitch, "Faith and Knowledge in the Thought of Georges Florovsky," 210.

30. Florovskiy, "Filosofiya i religiya," for the history of the text see Ermishin, "Neizvestnaya stat'ya."

The second of Florovsky's papers, which is perhaps one of his most acknowledged and referred to texts, was presented (presumably in French) on June 29, 1931, at Karl Barth's theological seminary at the University of Bonn and provoked a fierce discussion.[31] Florovsky recalled that the debate with Barth "took two evenings, or rather one evening and a second night, because we parted at six in the morning, walking the streets, singing *Gaudeamus*."[32] However, despite this ecumenical spirit, Barth's opinion on Florovsky's paper was crushing. In a letter to Eduard Thurneysen he described it as "a formless Russian heap of thoughts, in which everything is allowed to blur into everything else."[33] Nevertheless Barth advised him to publish the text which appeared soon in German as "Revelation, Philosophy and Theology." At the same time the journal *Put'* published its Russian extended version, entitled simply "Theological Fragments."[34]

These two papers mark Florovsky's personal path from philosophy to theology. As was noticed by Oleg Ermishin, there are various links between them which indicate the development of Florovsky's thought.

> The last echo of the paper "Philosophy and Religion" in the later Florovsky's works we hear in a text from 1931 "Theological Fragments" . . . His theological investigations show that he finally moved from philosophy to theology, which he presented here as a higher type of knowledge.[35]

In 1923 Florovsky, although radically limited in terms of the possibility of rationally grounding faith, nevertheless would describe himself as a philosopher. In 1931 he clearly realized the need for a change to the whole existing paradigm of philosophy. He firmly called himself a theologian and moved towards a provocative project of the theological grounding of philosophy. I will try to show that these papers complement each other. The first one outlines an argument against old natural theology, the second one sketches

---

31. For details of the meetings see Baker, "Offenbarung, Philosophie, und Theologie."

32. Blane, *Georges Florovsky*, 69, cited after Baker, "Offenbarung, Philosophie, und Theologie," 305.

33. Barth to Thurneysen, July 2, 1931, *Karl Barth—Eduard Thurneysen Briefwechsel*, 3:160, as translated by Baker, "Offenbarung, Philosophie, und Theologie," 305.

34. Florovskiy, "Bogoslovskiye otryvki," Florowskij, "Offenbarung, Philosophie und Theologie." I will rest here on the English translation of German version and refer occasionally to Russian text. Notice that the German version is not a simple abridgement of Russian paper but contains some additional material. It is not determined which paper was an original version.

35. Ermishin, "Neizvestnaya stat'ya," 98.

a program of a new philosophy. Both papers make, as it seems, one of the clearest expositions of the idea of theological philosophy.

Against Philosophical Theology

The paper "Philosophy and Religion" is a hard attack on the traditional project of the natural theology. Florovsky argues that not only does faith need not be justified by reason, but also that attempts to do so are dangerous for faith itself. It is so because the religion is a matter of experience, not speculation. The paper starts as follows:

> The religion is an experience, a revelation. God manifests and reveals himself to believer in a religious perceptions. The believer perceives the Transcendence . . . directly, with obviousness, and self-evidence.[36]

Religious experience therefore has the same nature as the sensory one, the difference lies in the nature of the experienced object. Religious experience might also be compared with the experience of external things or other minds. Theology is only a description of religious experience. "The dogmatic statements—claims Florovsky—are the statements of experience, the descriptive expressions of the experienced."[37]

If it is so, it becomes clear why the religious faith need not be justified by any kind of reasoning. The case with religion is the same as with the experience of the world itself or other minds. We simply accept the existence of external reality and other persons on the basis of our experience. No additional arguments are needed. Although some philosophers might still think that the lack of a proof of the existence of the external world is a perennial scandal of philosophy, nobody else is embarrassed by it. Similarly, a believer need not seek a justification for that which he or she sees and feels. If somebody does not experience Transcendence, no arguments can fill that gap.

Florovsky argued, however, that attempts to justify religion are not only unnecessary, but also dangerous. He wrote: "The rational justification of the faith is its destruction: the faith justifies itself."[38] The reason is that natural theology needs to postulate a kind of causal connection between the world and God. The world is usually thought of as an effect of God's creative act. This way of thinking, Florovsky argues, involves God in the relation to

---

36. Florovskiy, "Filosofiya i religiya," 100.
37. Ibid.
38. Ibid., 102.

the world and undermines his absolute character. Moreover, such a natural connection between the world and God excludes divine freedom, which is the basis of religious experience. The science of creation is impossible since the creation was a voluntary act of God's mercy. To claim otherwise is to deny God's transcendence and make him an element of an immanent causal network.

Florovsky concludes for a moment that faith on the one hand and reason on the other are two distinct and separate human abilities. He writes:

> Religion and philosophy, faith and knowledge, are essentially different, and so they are mutually autonomous. The faith is the "the evidence of things not seen," whereas the knowledge is the evidence of the visible things; the faith is the experience of the Transcendent, whereas the knowledge is the experience of the Immanent.[39]

This passage, as it stands, suggests a sharp distinction between faith and reason. From this perspective Florovsky would be close to the Protestant tradition of limited natural reason and autonomous faith. Few commentators to this text seem to notice only this negative claim and find difficulty in rejoining it with the author's other statements.[40] The point is however that it is not the end of Florovsky's paper. Suddenly he makes an important turn towards a new direction. He continues:

> But here we have to make a reservation. The separation of the faith and reason is not absolute, is not in all respects . . . The experience of faith, of the real communion with God, of the transgressing the borders, of the religious transcensus, is not isolated in an individual human soul. The believer perceives the world in another way . . . Both the primary experience, and the creative work of philosophical imagination, are influenced by the religious experience.[41]

Religion, despite being unattainable for natural reason alone, might nevertheless shape the philosophical view of the world. Florovsky suggests that the great philosophical systems, such as Plato's theory of ideas, Aristotle's metaphysics, or even systems of Descartes, Kant and Hegel, were all philosophical expressions of the primary experience of the faith of their inventors.

---

39. Ibid., 104.

40. Ermishin, "Neizvestnaya stat'ya," Obolevitch, *Filozofia rosyjskiego renesansu patrystycznego*, 155; Obolevitch, "Gieorgija Fłorowskiego krytyka rosyjskiego renesansu religijno-filozoficznego."

41. Florovskiy, "Filosofiya i religiya," 103.

Even atheistic philosophies are influenced by religion, since "the negation of God is also a kind of religion, at least in the psychological sense."[42] Florovsky ended his short paper with the following summary:

> The believing thinker should faithfully guard the border between the divina and the humana, between the Transcendent and the Immanent, but he could not, should not and in fact cannot look at the world, think about it and explain it as if there were no God. Since God really exists, religious eyes directly perceives him everywhere, and the experience of religious freedom embraces all the nature of the believer. On the personal level, the faith . . . always enters into philosophy, and its banishing is impossible.[43]

It turns out that faith and reason are distinct, but not wholly separate. Although faith is autonomous from reason, reason is not autonomous from faith. The experience of faith might therefore change the attitude to the reality, but may also modify the whole worldview, and penetrate the system of philosophical beliefs. Indeed, such a philosophy would not be merely a justification of religion, but rather an expression of faith.

Oleg Ermishin attempted to compare Florovsky's ideas with the current views in analytical philosophy of religion in his commentary to the "Philosophy and Religion." He wrote:

> It can be said without any exaggeration, that if Florovsky's paper was published nowadays, it would cause a great academic scandal, since his basic thesis deny in fact the very principles of the contemporary philosophy of religion, as well as its general tendency.[44]

It would be so, according to Ermishin, because the mainstream of analytical philosophy of religion tries to give a rational justification of faith, and Florovsky, as we have seen, radically criticized any attempts at philosophical theology. Ermishin regrets that the paper has not been published in English, for instance after Florovsky's move to the US. Unfortunately, the only existing copy of it was then enclosed in Yakovenko's folder in Prague.

I think that Ermishin is right, but not for that reason he actually gave. Certainly a great part of the contemporary philosophy of religion still develops the program of natural theology and attempts to justify religious beliefs. But at the same time there is an influential group which put forward

---

42. Ibid.
43. Ibid.
44. Ermishin, "Neizvestnaya stat'ya," 93–94.

the thesis, exactly in Florovsky's spirit, that faith cannot and should not be justified in that way. John Hick in the seventies formulated an idea of "rational theistic belief without proofs,"[45] and Alvin Plantinga with Nicholas Wolterstorff in the eighties initiated the ambitious program of "reformed epistemology," holding that faith need not to be grounded by reason.[46] Their argumentation, based on religious experience, seems to be close to Florovsky's line. Now, his old paper might be of interest nowadays, not as a groundbreaking point, but as an early expression of the same intuitions.

The real scandal, or at least confusion which indeed could be started by Florovsky's paper, I believe, would be caused not by his claim on the experimental basis of faith, but rather by his final suggestion that religion might and should shape the philosophy. His last words were not about the autonomy, but the domination of theology over any other discipline of knowledge, including philosophy. This view, which breaks both with the stereotypical Catholic tradition of natural theology, and well as the conventional Protestant trend of independent theology, might indeed be a fresh inspiration for the contemporary philosophy of religion. And in fact that Florovsky's proposal raised a great debate. The strict formulation of the new Christian philosophy was given in his famous paper written in 1931.

Towards Theological Philosophy

Florovsky starts his "Revelation, Philosophy, and Theology" as if it was supposed to be a new version of his "Philosophy and Religion." The very first sentence of his second paper directly corresponds to the beginning of the earlier essay:

> There are two aspects of religious knowledge: *revelation* and *experience* . . . Revelation is theophany. God descends to man and reveals himself to man. And man sees and beholds God. And he describes what he sees and hears; he testifies to what has been revealed to him.[47]

Previously Florovsky was mainly concerned with the experience of faith, now he completes his account by the detailed analysis of revelation. These two categories are closely related. The revelation of God is not a series of remote events described in ancient documents, but an actual experience of the community of faith. Even the stories included in Scripture are not

---

45. Hick, *Arguments for the Existence of God*, 101–20.
46. Plantinga, Wolterstorff, *Faith and Rationality*.
47. Florovsky, "Revelation, Philosophy, and Theology," 21.

merely documents for inquiry but the present reality to be experienced by the believers. The revelation in a proper sense turns out to be a way of life of the religious community.

The revelation of God was completed in Jesus Christ. After the hearing the words of the prophets and seeing the actions of God in the history of Israel, we finally listened and witnessed the Son of God, who fully revealed the mystery of God. In this incarnation God descended and revealed himself to man. That was the fullest theophany. Now, to have a part in this revelation one need not only to hear the words of Christ, but first of all to live his own life. Revelation is therefore accessible only in the church, which is a mystical Body of Christ. The church renews human nature and makes the experience of God possible. Here man can truly see and behold God. Again, it turns out that the knowledge of God is possible only within the living community of faith.

Now, Florovsky argues that man is called to be a witness of his faith. The revelation of God, which is the experience of the life in the church, should be manifested, expressed, and described. Man realizes this vocation in many different ways: writing down Scripture, preaching the Word of God or creating religious art. One of the important ways of testifying our faith is the use of reason. Florovsky writes:

> Reason is summoned to the knowledge of God. The "philosophizing" about God is not just a feature of inquisitiveness or a kind of audacious curiosity. On the contrary, it is the fulfillment of man's religious calling and duty.[48]

All human capacities, including natural reason, are open for the operation of divine grace. To think otherwise, to ignore the call of reason for the expression of faith, is to fall into the heresy of Apollinarism. It was Apollinaris of Laodicea, Florovsky reminds, who denied in Christ the capacity for human reason. The rejection of his teaching by the church meant the fundamental justification of reason. It was acknowledged that human reason might be transformed to be able to grasp the revealed divine truths.

The vocation of reason is an expression of the experience of the faith. The spiritual vision given in the church should be translated into a discursive form. The first step in this project is the formulation of the dogmas of faith. Dogmas are therefore primarily the expressions of the religious experience.

> Dogma is the testimony of thought about what has been seen and revealed, about what has been contemplated in the experience of faith and this testimony is expressed in concepts and

---

48. Ibid., 31.

definitions. Dogma is an "intellectual vision," . . . the logical image, a "logical icon" of divine reality.[49]

The formulation of dogmas is only the beginning of the fully rational expression of the experience of faith. The principles of dogmatic theology primarily concern only the divine reality and the task of Christian philosophy is to develop theological dogmas into the complete philosophical system which could embrace every sphere of human experience. Florovsky claims:

> Revelation must unfold within human thought, must develop into an entire system of believing confession, into a system of religious perspective—one may say, into a system of religious philosophy and a philosophy of Revelation.[50]

Florovsky clearly picks up here an idea he sketched previously in the closing paragraphs of "Religion and Philosophy." He pointed out that the believer perceives the world in a new way. That what was previously taken as a mere inevitable result of individual conversion is now seen as the obligation of the community of faith. The aim of the believing philosopher is to elaborate a religious perspective for the whole world. The foundation of such a philosophical system should be the principles provided by theology.

> Dogmatic theology, as the exposition and explanation of divinely revealed truth in the realm of thought, is precisely the basis of a Christian philosophy, of a sacred philosophy, of a philosophy of the Holy Spirit.[51]

The Russian version of Florovsky's paper here makes some important clarifications. First, the bizarre expression "a philosophy of the Holy Spirit" turns out to be an unfortunate translation of "a philosophy of the transformed spirit."[52] Indeed, the system based on dogmas is a philosophy developed by a new creature, renewed and transformed by the life in Christ. Second, Florovsky adds in the Russian text a remark on the difference between the natural and Christian philosophies. He says:

> A Christian philosopher in his creative explorations should depart from the dogmas, that is from the concrete experience of faith in a determined absolute logical form, not from the problems of "natural thought." In some sense he would and should

---

49. Ibid., 29.
50. Ibid., 26–27.
51. Ibid., 35.
52. Florovskiy, "Bogoslovskiye otryvki," 17.

stay "on the other side" of that "natural" problems, arising from the limited, and now also outdated way of perceiving.[53]

This is perhaps the clearest formulation of the program of theological philosophy ever made. This new philosophy should start from heaven and then descend to the earth. It is a reversed way of the old philosophy which took off from the earth and was supposed to reach heaven. A philosopher, aimed at searching for the ultimate truth, cannot ignore revelation. A natural philosophy, that is a pure philosophy or philosophical theology, remains true, but baldly insufficient. Now we have a great philosophical upgrade provided in the experience of the church. Christian philosophy should therefore start, not end, with Christian dogmas.

The crucial question now is the relationship between the new Christian theological philosophy and the old natural philosophical theology. This is the true challenge for Christian philosophy. The revelation, if is to be understood, must be expressed in the available language. At the same time, it is something new and exceeds the existing conceptual categories. So, the experience of faith must and yet cannot be expressed in the old language. The categories of natural philosophy must therefore somehow be modified, adjusted and transformed for the new theological purposes.

Florovsky starts with a general remark on the relation between human words and the divine Word. He indicates that there is a kind of pre-established harmony between the human capacities and the divine revelation. "The Word of God—says Florovsky—can be expressed precisely and adequately in the language of man. For man is created in the image of God."[54] Man has been created in order to be able to accept and to express revelation. So, there is no surprise that the Word of God somehow fits the language of man. Father Georges admits, however, that human words might need to be adjusted for religious purposes. He says:

> The Word of God is not diminished while it resounds in human language. On the contrary, the human word is transformed and, as it were, transfigured because of the fact that it pleased God to speak in human language.[55]

And further on:

> When divine truth is expressed in human language, the words themselves are transformed. And the fact that the truths of the faith are veiled in logical images and concepts testifies to the

---

53. Ibid., 17–18.
54. Florovsky, "Revelation, Philosophy, and Theology," 22.
55. Ibid., 22–23.

transformation of word and thought—words become sanctified through this usage.⁵⁶

It seems therefore that the pre-established harmony really means that although human words in their current state are not quite suitable, they nevertheless might be adjusted and customized for the expression of the experience of faith. Human words might be—as Florovsky often repeats—"transformed," "transfigured," and "sanctified." In the Russian version of the paper he even spoke literally about the "transubstantiation" (*presushchestvleniye*) of the natural language.⁵⁷ Such expressions suggest that in the process of its adaptation for theological purposes one part of the meaning, presumably the essential one, undergoes a change while the other, which might be called accidental, remains the same. Revelation brings about a fundamental change, but nevertheless preserves some of the previous natural content.

This general view is then applied to the particular case of the transformation of Greek natural philosophy by the Church Fathers. Florovsky makes here his most famous statement:

> in establishing dogmas the church expressed revelation in the language of Greek philosophy . . . That meant, in a certain sense, a "Hellenization" of revelation. In reality, however, it was a "churchification" of Hellenism.⁵⁸

The "churchification" (Russian *votserkovleniye*, German *Verkirchlichung*) means for Florovsky both a partial transformation and a partial preservation. The transformation is necessary for the expression of the new kind of experience entailed by Christian faith whereas the preservation is possible due to the great potency of the concepts and categories of Hellenic thought. Florovsky constantly highlights the double nature of this process. He writes:

> particular themes of Hellenic philosophy are received and, through this reception, they change essentially; they change and are no longer recognizable. Because now, in the terminology of Greek philosophy, a new, totally new experience is expressed. Although themes and motives of Greek thought are retained, the answers to the problems are quite different; they are given out of a new experience.⁵⁹

---

56. Ibid., 33.

57. Florovskiy, "Bogoslovskiye otryvki," 4, cf. also "Revelation, Philosophy, and Theology," 31: "human thought changes, the essence of thought itself is transformed and sanctified."

58. Florovsky, "Revelation, Philosophy, and Theology," 31–32.

59. Ibid., 33.

Florovsky clarifies this place by claiming firmly in the Russian version: "There was a rupture in the history of thought. Hellenism was churchified by its transformation."[60] Then he proceeds in both versions:

> Hellenism, forged in the fire of a new experience and a new faith, is renewed; Hellenic thought is transformed. Usually we do not sufficiently perceive the entire significance of this transformation which Christianity introduced into the realm of thought. This is so, partially because we too often remain ancient Greeks philosophically, not yet having experienced the baptism of thought by fire.[61]

The "churchification" of pagan categories is therefore neither their total replacement nor its adaptation without change. The experience of faith has not been expressed in entirely new language, nor has it been fully covered by old concepts.

It is clear that Florovsky's thesis was directly opposed to the influential, mainly Protestant, tradition of suspiciousness to any philosophical influences to Christianity. Theologians such as Albrecht Ritschl, Adolph Harnack or Anders Nygren argued that the simple message of Jesus Christ has been distorted and corrupted by the intervention of Greek thought. That would be a disastrous "Hellenization" of revelation. Florovsky provocatively argues that it was rather the Christian faith which influenced and transformed Hellenic culture, not the other way round. We experienced not the hellenization of Christianity but Christianization of Hellenism.

Yet, it seems that strictly speaking Florovsky's was not an opposition of Harnack's view. Their views are usually rightfully contrasted and opposed, but sometimes it goes too far. Paul Gavrilyuk for instance claimed recently that their positions are "two opposite extremes" and "antipodes."[62]

> If Harnack demonizes the Hellenization of Christianity, Florovsky idealizes the Christianization of Hellenism. Harnack s theological purpose was to de-Hellenize contemporary Christian theology; Florovskys purpose was, in contrast, to re-Hellenize Russian Orthodox theology.[63]

---

60. Florovskiy, "Bogoslovskiye otryvki," 16, see also Florovsky, *Ways of Russian Theology*, 2:297: "The baptism of Hellenism marked a sharp cleavage in its time. And the criterion for measuring this break was the Good News, the historical image of Incarnate Word."

61. Florovsky, "Revelation, Philosophy, and Theology," 33–34.

62. Gavrilyuk, "Harnack's Hellenized Christianity or Florovsky's Sacred Hellenism," 323, 333.

63. Ibid., 333–34.

It seems however that the true logical opposition of Harnack's view would be a strict defense of Hellenism against Christian influences, to be found perhaps among some renaissance thinkers, not a vision of the transformation of Hellenistic categories. Florovsky did not want to go back to pagan philosophy, but to the "Christianized," "baptized" and "churchified" Hellenism. Gavrilyuk obviously notices it, but nevertheless continues to speak as if both authors represented "two limiting cases," and two different "ends" of "the spectrum."[64] Harnack indeed occupies one of the extreme points of the logical spectrum, but Florovsky stays perfectly in its middle, not at the opposite end.

The Russian Project of Theological Philosophy

I started this chapter with a general analysis of the possible relationships between philosophy and theology. It appears that there are two fundamental ways of combining them. The first one is a rational reconstruction of faith, which departs from natural premises and hopes to reach the mysteries of faith. Arguably, this project has dominated the Western philosophical and theological imagination for centuries. The second path moves in the opposite direction and starts with the evidence of faith and tries to understand the whole of reality in light of revelation. This way of doing philosophy, so clearly exposed by Georges Florovsky, is characteristic of the Church Fathers and although it has been preserved first of all in Eastern Orthodoxy, it belong to the common heritage of Christianity. Nowadays the latter strategy seems to be an invaluable alternative for the domination of secular reason, plausibly originated by the Western project of philosophical theology.

Now, I think that Florovsky, formulating the program of theological philosophy, which was supposed to be a reconstruction of a patristic view, also unwittingly expressed the fundamental aspiration of all Russian religious philosophy. It seems that since its very beginning original Russian thought was intended to reconcile faith and reason, but not under the terms of reason, but faith. Surprisingly enough, Florovsky himself seemed to do not realize it. He was curiously averse to the tradition of Russian philosophy, including his own former masters and teachers, such as Florensky and Bulgakov. He believed, apparently mistakenly, that his great predecessors had simply imitated the Western path and generally aimed in rational justification of religious faith. I believe that we should not trust Florovsky in this regard since no matter how emphatically he renounced the tradition of Russian philosophy, he nevertheless was formed by it and in fact he

---

64. Ibid., 334.

never extend its limits. Florovsky's "Revelation, Philosophy, and Theology" therefore should not be read as an accusation nor a correction of Russian religious philosophy, but rather as a perfect expression of its spirit.

Kireevsky's Program

To prove it, I would like to return for a moment to the very beginning of the Russian philosophy. The proper Russian philosophical tradition starts with the appearance of the first Slavophiles and a tremendous amount of original Russian philosophy began with the philosophical program outlined by them. Quite surprisingly, that program seems to be very close to Florovsky's project and it is particularly clear in the case of Ivan Kireevsky, the initiator of Slavophilism and arguably the first original Russian philosopher.

Kireevsky started as an admirer of Western culture, familiar with German romanticism and fascinated by idealistic philosophy. During his scholarly trip around Europe he studied under Hegel in Berlin and Schelling in Munich. After his return to Russia, he launched an intellectual journal in 1832 called notably *The European* (*Evropeyets*) which was instantly banned by the tsarist regime for its liberal tendencies. In 1834 Kireevsky married Natalia Arbeneva, a well educated and profoundly religious lady, the spiritual daughter of Saint Seraphim of Sarov. According to Aleksandr Koshelev, who recorded her memoirs, Kireevsky, far from religiosity at that time, started to give his wife some contemporary philosophers to read. She refused to read Voltaire, but agreed to Schelling. Koshelev reports:

> They began to read Schelling together and when they found some great and bright thoughts, Kireevsky expected her admiration, but she responded that she already had known them from the works of Saint Fathers . . . He was unpleasantly surprised, that she actually found in Fathers many thoughts, which he enjoyed in Schelling. He was not willing to admit it, but he borrowed her wife's books in secret and read them with enthusiasm.[65]

It seems that the influence of that faithful and patient woman changed the history of Russian philosophy. Shortly after this discussion Kireevsky returned to the church, started to meet with pious Orthodox monks, and begun serious studies in patristics. He realized that the Christian theology need not be justified by philosophy, as in the contemporary Western view, but conversely, rational speculation should be subordinate and determined by religious dogmas, as in the case of the Church Fathers.

---

65. Koshelev, "Istoriya obrashcheniya," 285–86.

At the end of his life Kireevsky outlined a program for the renewal of Christian philosophy, which might be considered as the agenda for all of the Russian religious philosophers who followed up to Florovsky. His seminal paper "On the Necessity and Possibility of New Principles of Philosophy" was published in 1856, shortly after his death. The new philosophy, intended by Kireevsky, was supposed to be based directly on the religious experience of the church. The Christian revelation, according to him, should complement the efforts of natural reason. It is possible, since, as he put it,

> faith is not a blind notion that is in the state of faith simply because it has remained undeveloped by natural reason, nor is it a notion that should be elevated by reason to the level of knowledge . . . It is, rather, a . . . higher reason that grants life to the mind. The developments of natural reason serves faith only as a series of step, and, by transcending the usual state of mind, faith informs reason.[66]

Faith is therefore a light that should illuminate reason. Theological dogmas should discipline, shape and inform philosophical doctrines. As a result, a new integral knowledge would unite theology and philosophy, but not like the German idealism, which was ultimately aimed at the rationalization of the mysteries of faith, but rather in the spirit of Greek patristics, subordinating the natural truth to the truth of revelation. In "Fragments," discovered and published by Ivan Aksakov, which was supposed to be a continuation of the previous paper, Kireevsky wrote:

> This new and vivifying thinking which . . . bring faith and reason into harmony, fill the emptiness that divides the two world requiring union, affirm spiritual truth in the human mind by its clear dominion over natural truth, and elevate natural truth by correcting its correlation to spiritual truth, tying together at last both truths into one living thought. For truth is one, as the human mind is one, created to strive toward One God.[67]

The natural reason should therefore accept the priority of the revelation, but this concession would not lead to the irrational faith, but on the contrary, to the improvement of reason itself. The unity of God, which is the ultimate goal of philosophy and theology, warrants the unity of truth and thus the possibility of adaptation of human reason to the revealed truth.

---

66. Kireevsky, "New Principles of Philosophy," 260–61.

67. Kireevsky, "Fragments," 282. Note that the very title of Florovsky's seminal paper in Russian—"Theological Fragments"—somehow recalls Kireevsky's work. It might be however a mere coincidence.

I believe that the program formulated first by Kireevsky and then undertaken by Florovsky, determined almost all of the original content of Russian philosophy. The Russian intellectual experiment was an impressive attempt to construct an alternative to the secular Western modernity model combining faith and reason. In this model, theology preserved its proper status as the ultimate discourse. At the end of his life Kireevsky wrote:

> The doctrine of Holy Trinity attracts my attention not only because it appears as the highest focus of the all holy truths, uncovered to us in the revelation, but also because, working on essay on philosophy, I came to the conclusion that the direction of philosophy depends in the first place on that concept which we have of the Holy Trinity.[68]

This great confession proves again that, according to Kireevsky, it is theology which should determine philosophy, not the other way round. The Trinitarian dogma in particular is seen here as the deepest source of all theology and philosophy. Both this general and other particular claims were developed by the subsequent Russian philosophers. Nikolai Lossky, who quoted Kireevsky's confession in his *History of Russian Philosophy*, noticed:

> This thought, at first paradoxical, acquires profound meaning if we read such works as Vladimir Soloviev's *Lectures on Godmanhood* . . . Father Paul Florensky's *Pillar and the Ground of Truth*, Father Sergey Bulgakov's *Tragedy of Philosophy*.[69]

Indeed, it might be argued that Soloviev, Florensky and Bulgakov, among many other Russian religious philosophers, implicitly accepted the methodological principles formulated by Kireevsky and finally systematized by Florovsky. Soloviev for instance tried to apply Trinitarian theology as an inspiration for social and political order and initiated Russian sophiology, rooted both in his personal religious experience and Christian tradition (though not always generally admitted).[70] Florensky, in his turn, saw the Holy Trinity as the fundamental principle of all philosophy, deepened sophiology by finding its liturgical and iconographical sources, and most of all formulated the philosophical outlook based on the premises of the onomatodoxy.[71] All these topics were taken up by Bulgakov, who for example

---

68. Kireyevskiy, *Polnoye sobraniye sochineniy*, 1:74. It seems that this confession is known only in the version recorded by Mikhail Gershenzon, the editor of Kireevsky's works.

69. Lossky, *History of Russian Philosophy*, 25–26.

70. See Rojek, "The Trinity in History and Society."

71. See Rojek, "The Logic of Palamism," and "Onomatodoxy and the Problem of Constitution."

applied sophiology to the problem of universals and worked on the philosophy of language inspired by onomatodoxy.[72] Arguably, all these authors worked in a framework of theological philosophy, not philosophical theology. Religion was for them not merely a phenomenon to investigate, but the source of illumination and inspiration. The seed planted by Kireevsky had grown into a great tree of Russian religious philosophy. Florovsky was definitely sitting on one of its branches. Nevertheless for some reason he wanted to cut it down.

Florovsky and the Russian Religious Philosophy

Florovsky, a great Russian theologian and philosopher, was at the same time a furious critic of Russian theology and religious philosophy. In his *Ways of Russian Theology* published in 1937, he accused Russian official theology of being influenced most of all by the Western way of thinking. Since the very beginning, according to Florovsky, Russian theologians instead of studying their own Byzantine sources, had simply imitated scholastic and reformed handbooks of theology.[73] There was in fact, he complained, no original Russian theology at all. The great patristic heritage was retained solely in some monastic communities which successfully shaped the faith of the simple people but had not attempted to express it in intellectual categories. That is why Florovsky called upon the revival of the theology of the Church Fathers aimed in "neopatristic synthesis."

Florovsky was even more radical in his criticism of Russian religious philosophy. He seemed to have no respect or sympathy for the celebrated Russian religious renaissance or the Silver Age of Russian philosophy. He believed that the great tradition of Russian religious thought was a kind of hidden transplantation of German idealism into the body of Russian Orthodoxy. The religious turn of Soloviev and his followers was for Florovsky merely an apparent revolution. In fact Russian religious philosophers stayed in the paradigm of secular reason and was striving to reconstruct the content of revelation in the natural philosophical categories. In 1930, a few years before publishing *Ways*, Florovsky wrote a quite moderate study on Russian contemporary philosophy, recently discovered and published in Russian by Paul Gavrilyuk. In this paper Florovsky addressed the methodology of Russian religious turn.

---

72. See Royek, "Sofiya i problema universaliy."
73. Florovsky, *Ways of Russian Theology*.

> Religious topics have always powerfully bothered Russian thought. The philosophical temptation often led it to the religious metaphysics... However, that was always a way towards patrictics, towards the church, not conversely. In other words, philosophy ascended to theology, not descended from it.[74]

It is clear, that Florovsky anticipated here his own program of the new Christian philosophy formulated one year later in his talk at Barth's seminary. The bizarre thing is that he firmly denied that this program could have any references to the tradition of Russian philosophy. On the contrary, he directly accused Soloviev's followers for doing exactly the opposite. Why did Florovsky wanted to cut the branch on which he was sitting?

It seems to me that Florovsky confused two different charges against Russian religious philosophy. Florovsky himself believed not only that philosophy should be subordinated to theology, but also that there is only one proper Christian philosophy, namely that one developed by Church Fathers. The former thesis has, one might say, methodological or formal character, whereas the latter is rather substantial or material. I argue that Florovsky was in fact in agreement with the core tradition of Russian religious philosophy on methodological issues. I suppose that the general disagreement in the material issue might have suggested to Florovsky that he also differed in formal matters.

Russian religious philosophers, in general, were quite open for different kinds of philosophy, including contemporary ones. They agreed that the Church Fathers still had something important to say, but they apparently believed that the religious truth might also be expressed in some new philosophical languages. Kireevsky respected the Fathers like nobody else but nevertheless allowed the development of their heritage with the help of contemporary philosophy, first of all German romantic thought. Soloviev adapted some concepts of German idealism, Florensky even used devices of contemporary formal logic. Florovsky took completely opposite attitude. He believed that the form of Christianized Hellenism which served to express Christian dogmas should remain the fundamental conceptual framework for Christian philosophy forever. He famously said that it would be "ridiculous" to try to express "traditional doctrine in terms of categories of a new philosophy, whatever this philosophy may be."[75] From this point of view any attempts to translate the experience of faith into contemporary philosophy would be a betrayal of a true perennial Christian philosophy, already

---

74. Florovskyi, "Russkaya filosofiya v emigratsii," 325. For the context of that paper see editor's note, Gavrilyuk, "Neizvestnaya stranitsa."

75. Florovsky, "Patristics and Modern Theology," 231.

found in Church Fathers. I think that it was the main reason he rejected his own tradition.

The points of agreement and disagreement between Florovsky and Russian religious philosophy are clearly seen when we compare his "Revelation, Philosophy, and Theology" and Bulgakov's paper "Dogma and Dogmatic Theology," published in 1937, which was perhaps intended as an indirect reply to Florovsky. Bulgakov clearly shared the general methodological position with Florovsky. He wrote:

> Philosophy and theology are tightly bound up with each other. Dogmas are truths of religious revelation that have a metaphysical content and therefore are expressed in the language of philosophy, as is only natural for this purpose. Dogmatic theology, therefore, is religious philosophy . . . There is no formal difference between philosophy and theology. They differ in the character of the life experience from which they originate: in the case of one it is something human . . . in the case of the other, it is the theoantropic.[76]

Some of these phrases looks like they have simply been borrowed from Florovsky, others could readily be used by Florovsky to express his own views. Obviously the methodological principles of theological philosophy were common to both thinkers. Nevertheless in the next paragraph Bulgakov argues that the experience of faith might be, and in fact should be, expressed in many different philosophical languages.

> The patristic period theologized with the language of ancient philosophy, which for us, even though we respect its unique and unsurpassed value, is no longer our philosophical language . . . There is thus a voluntary (or involuntary) inevitability of the influence of contemporary philosophical thought . . . It is a kind of translation into modern language of the lexicon of the early church.[77]

Florovsky would undoubtedly not accept this position. For him the contemporary loss of the language of ancient philosophy was a call for the return to it, not to learn some new languages. Bulgakov, although firmly advised to learn from the Fathers, nevertheless saw the necessity of speaking in a new philosophical languages. That was the crucial point of disagreement, not the shared idea of theological philosophy.

---

76. Bulgakov, "Dogma and Dogmatic Theology," 79.
77. Ibid.

The philosophical exclusivism of Florovsky is now considered as perhaps the weakest point of his theological outlook. It is commonly agreed that the return to the Fathers should be understand as the return to their spiritual and intellectual attitude, presumably including methodology, but not as an exclusive sanctification of their conceptual scheme. As Brandon Gallaher recently wrote,

> Florovsky has collapsed the Gospel into a specific cultural expression of the truth of Christ—call it, Byzantinism—which then devours all other incarnations of that reality, since it will not abide anything as properly proclaiming the Good News but a specifically Greek voice.[78]

The same has been noticed by Paul Gavrilyuk. "To conceive of the Christian message—he wrote—as being permanently petrified in one cultural form, be it Hellenism, Slavism, or Americanism, would be a serious failure of theological imagination."[79] This rightfully critical appraisal of Florovsky's philosophical exclusivism should not, however, extend to his methodological principles. To say that theology should shape philosophy is one thing, to affirm that it might be done in only one way is quite another.

By the way, it is not clear for me why Florovsky really insisted on Greek exclusivism. It seems that even on the grounds of his own premises he should hold a much more open attitude to other philosophical languages. In "Revelation, Philosophy, and Theology" he implicitly made a considerable space for various intellectual ways of understanding faith. He directly admitted that the revelation expressed already in some theological formulas does allow new words and new interpretations. "The unalterable truths of experience—he said—can be expressed in different ways."[80] He also stressed that the formulation of dogmas in the language of Greek philosophy does not mean an "eternalization of one specific philosophical system."[81] Finally, he acknowledged that the experience of the church is "more comprehensive and fuller than her dogmatic pronouncement"[82] and thus she "does not endeavor to crystallize her experience in a closed system of words and concepts."[83] All these remarks suggest a more generous attitude to different philosophies than Florovsky actually held. Even his ultimate theological

---

78. Gallaher, "Waiting for the Barbarians," 668.

79. Gavrilyuk, "Harnack's Hellenized Christianity or Florovsky's Sacred Hellenism," 344.

80. Florovsky, "Revelation, Philosophy, and Theology," 29.

81. Ibid., 33.

82. Ibid., 35.

83. Ibid., 35–36.

argument, according to which the Hellenes had simply been chosen by God for the revelation in the similar way as Israelites previously,[84] might be extended to cover also different and more contemporary "Gentiles." If there was no historical accident that revelation met Greek philosophy, perhaps there is also no accident in its meeting with German idealism or analytic philosophy.

I think that Florovsky's position would be much more plausible if he distinguished between two kinds of eternity of intellectual categories. He wrote explicitly that Greek concepts were "eternalized" by the very fact that they "expressed divine truth." "This means—he said—that there is a so-called *philosophia perennis* that there is something eternal and absolute in thought."[85] But there is an ambiguity here. Are these concepts perennial in the sense that they remain forever as the only possible way of expressing the truth, or that they merely must be always taken into account, as a notable way, but not the only one? In the first case we arrive at the implausibly exclusive view that only the transformed Hellenistic language may grasp the truth of revelation. In the second case, however, we get an inclusive idea of an organic Christian tradition with cannot remove any of its previous categories, but nevertheless might develop new ones. In this case, the Greek transformed Hellenism would also be really a "standing category of the Christian existence."[86] It could not be replaced by a new formulation, but every new language should depart from it. In the living tradition nothing is lost, even if we develop it in new ways. This interpretation is based on Florovsky's claim that theology is always historical. "To theologize in the church—he wrote—means to theologize in the historical element, for the life of the church is tradition."[87] This path to overcome Florovsky's exclusivism was outlined in Adrian Pabst's and Christoph Schneider's criticism:

> Although theology is not dependent on any philosophy, it is neither in possession of a timeless "essence" of Christian faith, articulated in eternally fixed dogmas that can be "applied" in ever new circumstances. Rather, this "essence" is only present and accessible in the series of historical manifestations successively generated by the tradition.[88]

---

84. Ibid., 33.
85. Ibid.
86. Florovsky, "Patristics and Modern Theology," 232.
87. Florovsky, *Ways of Russian Theology*, 2:296.
88. Pabst, Schneider, "Transfiguring the World through the Word," 13.

It is worth noticing that this organic approach to the development of Christian philosophy would be similar to Florovsky's own view on the translations of the Scripture.

> The Gospel is given to us all and for all time in the Greek language. It is in this language that we hear the Gospel in all its entirety and fullness. That does not and cannot, of course, mean that it is untranslatable—but we always translate it from the Greek.[89]

The experience of the church was first expressed in the transformed categories of Hellenistic philosophy, meaning that every new attempt to express it in different categories should start with the first Greek version. It this sense it remains *philosophia perennis* but it does not exclude, however, the possibility of new formulations. I believe that it is a way to make Florovsky's claims consistent and plausible.

There is a growing literature on the relationships between "neopatristic synthesis" and the Russian religious philosophy undermining the official version created by Florovsky and his followers.[90] Florovsky formulated his own theological program in direct opposition to the Russian philosophical tradition on the one side and the Western tradition on the other; additionally, he believed that Russian tradition was influenced by the Western one. Nowadays, however, it is clear that we should not easily accept Florovsky's self-description. It has been shown that the program of "neopatristic synthesis" draws on the background of the Russian tradition on the one hand, and was itself inspired by some hidden Western ideas on the other. Teresa Obolevitch, in her book on the Russian patristic renaissance, indicated that it was precisely Russian philosophy which made way for neopatristic synthesis. Moreover, that was Bulgakov, the bad guy of Florovsky's own story, who invited him as a lecturer of patristics to Paris. Obolevitch reminds us that

> Bulgakov (as well as his friend Florensky) was in some sense a patrologist. Moreover, he was a specific forerunner or the godfather of neopatristic synthesis . . . Both trends are not so radical different as Florovsky claimed . . . The neopatristic synthesis was

---

89. Florovsky, "Revelation, Philosophy, and Theology," 32.

90. See for instance Gavrilyuk, *Georges Florovsky and the Russian Religious Renaissance*, Gallaher, "Waiting for the Barbarians," Obolevitch, *Filozofia rosyjskiego renesansu patrystycznego*, "Faith and Knowledge in the Thought of Georges Florovsky," and "Gieorgija Fłorowskiego krytyka rosyjskiego renesansu religijno-filozoficznego," Asproulis, "Creation and Creaturehood," for a brief survey see Chernyaev, "Retseptsiya idey G. V. Florovskogo."

not a negation, but rather a kind of correction of the philosophy of All-Unity.[91]

I would add to this that it was Florensky, another villain of the official neopatristic story, who first discovered and popularized the teachings of Gregory Palamas, which subsequently became a pillar and the ground of truth of renewed Orthodox theology.[92]

On the other hand, Brandon Gallagher argued that the crucial ideas of Florovsky's program were borrowed directly from the German idealists, primarily Adam Möhler. "Florovsky's idea of Christian philosophy—he wrote—echoes the Romantics in its talk of a 'philosophical synthesis' or total 'system' of the Christian faith."[93] If it is true, it establishes an additional connection between neopatristic synthesis and slavophilism, which draw on the same sources. All these findings fundamentally undermine the myth of perfectly original and the purely Eastern character of Florovsky's program, which now fortunately seem to be rather a common formulation of the Russian and simply Christian approach to the relationship between philosophy and theology.

Conclusions

Philosophy and theology differ in their point of departure. Philosophy starts from the natural world, theology begins from the revealed Word. Both disciplines have the same goal, namely the universal and ultimate truth. However, if there is God, if revelation gives us some new truths, if the incarnation transformed our own nature, then theology has obvious priority over philosophy. In some sense theology becomes true philosophy. There remains, nevertheless, great work to be done, an interpretation of the natural world in the light of the revealed Word. This is a proper task of the Christian philosophy after the First and before the Second Coming.

In this chapter I tried to analyze the Russian project of theological philosophy, originating first with Kireevsky as result of his nuptial encounter with Church Fathers, then developed by the mainstream of Russian religious philosophy, which modified the existing philosophical categories according to the experience of faith, and finally summed up and generalized by Florovsky, who clearly realized the difference between natural theology

---

91. Obolevitch, *Filozofia rosyjskiego renesansu patrystycznego*, 152–54, see also her "Gieorgija Florowskiego krytyka rosyjskiego renesansu religijno-filozoficznego," 64–66.

92. See Lur'ye, "Poslesloviye," 340.

93. Gallaher, "Waiting for the Barbarians," 673.

and Christian philosophy. This picture would obviously be much clearer if Florovsky did not surprisingly deny his own connection with this great company. I believe that the Russian proposal is the clearest, most elaborated and the most self-conscious version of theological philosophy. Every attempt to develop it, to my opinion, must draw on their results.

I think that the considerations in this chapter might help in re-evaluation of the heritage of Russian philosophy. Nikolai Berdyaev in his influential survey of Russian philosophy marked the deeply religious character of the Russian thought. Indeed, it was religious, but in a completely different way than is usually thought. For Berdyaev, Russian philosophy was such due to its "religious excitation."[94] It is true, but it does not grasp its most important feature. Russian philosophy was religious rather because of religious inspirations which were developed into highly rational and sophisticated philosophical theories. The peculiarity lies therefore not in the intensity of emotions but in the direction of the reason.

It seems that we are increasingly aware of the value of Russian religious philosophy. From the contemporary perspective the differences and debates within it seems to be less important than the general paradigm of doing philosophy with a close connection to the experience of faith and theology. Recently Artur Mrówczyński-Van Allen and Sebastián Montiel argued for the importance of Russian experience for contemporary post-secular philosophy and theology.[95] Characteristically, they simply neglected the differences between Florensky and Bulgakov, taking them both as opposition for Alain Badiou. In contrast with contemporary secular thought, all the controversies inside the Russian religious philosophy are decaying. The greatest value of Russian philosophy as a whole lies in the overt rejection of the secular model of philosophy. Kireevsky, Soloviev, Florensky, Bulgakov and Florovsky did not do philosophy as if there was no God. They simply lived a Christian life and let it shape their worldview, including their philosophical views. They tried to express in an intellectual way their experience of faith. This is the most radical challenge, not only to the secular reason, but also to the secular faith. For Mrówczyński-Van Allen and Montiel it is the most important lesson we can learn from Russian religious philosophy.

> We must accept as normal that the separation between theology and philosophy is superficial . . . This necessary assertion

94. Berdyaev, "O kharaktere russkoy religioznoy mysli," 321. The English translation of this paper is inadequate in this place, but surprisingly agrees with my thesis. Fr. Stephen Janos translated Berdyaev's "religioznaya vzvolnovannost'" as "religious stimulation," see Berdyaev, "Concerning the Character of the Russian Religious Thought."

95. Mrówczyński-Van Allen and Montiel, "Aspects of the Russian Tradition," see also Mrówczyński-Van Allen *Between the Icon and the Idol*, xxi-xxii.

makes the development of Christian thought in the post-secular context possible—a development in the direction defined by Fr. Florovsky as the "new Christian philosophy," which must grow with strong roots in the experience of faith and its dogmatic expression.[96]

In other words, Russian religious philosophers were not playing an allegedly neutral game with secular reason, but simply intended to change the rules of the game. Instead of shyly hiding their religious inspirations, they simply proudly made them explicit. Theology for them was not a hidden ugly dwarf, as in the famous metaphor of Benjamin's, recalled by Mrówczyński-Van Allen and Montiel; they were rather standing on the shoulders of a giant.

Bibliography

Aquinas, Thomas. *Faith, Reason, and Theology, Questions I–IV of the Commentary on Boethius' De Trinitate*. Translated by Armand Maurer. Toronto: Pontifical Institute of Mediaeval Studies, 1986.

———. *On the Truth of the Catholic Faith: Summa Contra Gentiles*. Vol. 1. Translated by Anton C. Pegis. New York: Hanover House, 1955.

Armstrong, David M. *Universals and Scientific Realism*. Vol. 1, *Nominalism and Realism*, Cambridge: Cambridge University Press, 1978.

Asproulis, Nikolaos. "Creation and Creaturehood: The Neo-Patristic Alternative Worldview to the Metaphysics of All-Unity? A Brief Approach of G. Florovsky's Theology." *Solov'yevskiye Issledovaniya* 27 (2010) 134–41.

Baker, Matthew. "Offenbarung, Philosophie, und Theologie: Karl Barth and Georges Florovsky in dialogue." *Scottish Journal of Theology* 68 (2015) 299–326.

Barth, Karl. *Church Dogmatics*. Vol. 1/1. Translated by G. W. Bromiley. Edinburgh: T&T Clark, 1975.

———, and Eduard Thurneysen. *Karl Barth—Eduard Thurneysen Briefwechsel*. Vol. 3, *1930–1935*. Zurich: Theologischer Verlag, 2000.

Berdyaev, Nikolay A. "Concerning the Character of the Russian Religious Thought of the XIX Century." Translated by Stephen Janos. Online: http://www.berdyaev.com/berdiaev/berd_lib/1930_345.html.

———. "O kharaktere russkoy religioznoy mysli XIX veka." *Sovremennyye Zapiski* 63 (1936) 309–43.

Blane, Andrew, editor. *Georges Florovsky: Russian Intellectual and Orthodox Churchman*. Crestwood, NY: St. Vladimir's Seminary Press, 1993.

Bulgakov, Sergius. "Dogma and Dogmatic Theology." Translated by Peter Bouteneff. In *Tradition Alive: On the Church and Christian Life in our Time. Readings from the Eastern Church*, edited by Michael Plekon, 67–80. Lanham, MD: Sheed & Ward, 2003.

---

96. Mrówczyński-Van Allen and Montiel, "Aspects of the Russian Tradition," 22–23.

Chernyaev, Anatoliy V. "Retseptsiya idey G.V. Florovskogo: sovremennyy kontekst." *Filosofskie Nauki* 10 (2013) 71–76.
Ermishin, Oleg T. "Neizvestnaya stat'ya G.V. Florovskogo v kontekste sovremennoy filosofskoy teologii." *Filosofskie Nauki* 10 (2013) 93–99.
Florovskiy, Georgiy V. "Bogoslovskiye otryvki." *Put'* 31 (1931) 3–29.
———. "Filosofiya i religiya." *Filosofskie Nauki* 10 (2013) 100–05.
———. "Russkaya filosofiya v emigratsii." In *Istoriko-filosofskiy ezhegodnik 2013*, edited by Mariya A. Solopova, 314–37. Moscow: Kanon, Reabilitatsiya, 2014.
Florovsky, Georges. *Collected Works of Georges Florovsky*. Vol. 1, *Ways of Russian Theology*. Part 2. Vaduz: Büchervertriebsanstalt, 1987.
———. "Patristics and Modern Theology." *Diakonia* 4/3 (1969) 227–32.
———. "Revelation, Philosophy and Theology." Translated by Richard Haugh. In *Collected Works of Georges Florovsky*. Vol. 3, *Creation and Redemption*, 21–40. Belmont, Mass.: Nordland, 1976.
Florowskij, Georgij. "Offenbarung, Philosophie und Theologie." *Zwischen den Zeiten* 9 (1931) 463–80.
Gallaher, Brandon. "Waiting for the Barbarians: Identity and Polemicism in the Neo-Patristic Synthesis of Georges Florovsky." *Modern Theology* 27 (2011) 659–91.
Gavrilyuk, Paul L. *Georges Florovsky and the Russian Religious Renaissance*. Oxford: Oxford University Press, 2013.
———. "Harnack's Hellenized Christianity or Florovsky's Sacred Hellenism: Questioning two metanarratives of early Christian engagement with late Antique culture." *St. Vladimir's Theological Quarterly* 54 (2010) 323–44.
———. "Neizvestnaya stranitsa istoriko-filosofskogo naslediya G.V. Florovskogo." In *Istoriko-filosofskiy ezhegodnik 2013*, edited by Mariya A. Solopova, 304–13. Moscow: Kanon, Reabilitatsiya, 2014.
Gomułka, Jakub. *Gramatyka wiary. Dziedzictwo Wittgensteinowskiego fideizmu*. Krakow: Instytut Myśli Józefa Tischnera, 2011.
Hick, John. *Arguments for the Existence of God*. London: Macmillan, 1971.
John Paul II. Encyclical Letter *Fides et Ratio*. September 14, 1998.
Kahn, Charles H. *Essays on Being*. Oxford: Oxford University Press, 2009.
Kireevsky, Ivan. "Fragments." Translated by Robert Bird. In *On Spiritual Unity. A Slavophile Reader. Alexei Khomiakov. Ivan Kireevsky*, edited by Boris Jakim and Robert Bird, 275–92. Hudson, NY: Lindisfarne, 1998.
———. "On the Necessity and Possibility of New Principles of Philosophy." Translated by Peter K. Christoff. In *On Spiritual Unity. A Slavophile Reader. Alexei Khomiakov. Ivan Kireevsky*, edited by Boris Jakim and Robert Bird, 233–273. Hudson, NY: Lindisfarne, 1998.
Kireyevskiy, Ivan V. *Polnoye sobraniye sochineniy*. 2 vols. Moscow: Tipografiya Imperatorskago Moskovskago Universiteta, 1911.
Koshelev, Aleksandr I. "Istoriya obrashcheniya Ivana Vasil'yevicha." In *Ivan V. Kireyevskiy. Polnoye sobraniye sochineniy v dvukh tomakh*. Vol. 1, edited by Mikhail O. Gershenzon, 285–86. Moscow: Tipografiya Imperatorskago Moskovskago Universiteta, 1911.
LaCocque, André and Paul Ricoeur. *Thinking Biblically: Exegetical and Hermeneutical Studies*. Translated by David Pellauer. Chicago: University of Chicago Press, 1998.
Leo XIII. Encyclical letter *Aeterni Patris*. August 4, 1879.

Lobkowicz, Nikolaus. "Was ist eine Person?" In *Sozialethik und politische Bildung: Festschrift für Bernhard Sutor zum 65. Geburtstag*, edited by Karl Graf Ballestrem, Hans Buchheim, Manfred Hättich, Heinz Hürten, 39–52. Paderborn: Ferdinand Schöningh, 1995.

Lossky, Nikolai O. *History of Russian Philosophy*. New York: International Universities Press, 1951.

Lur'ye, Vasiliy M. "Poslesloviye." In Ioann Meyyendorf. *Zhizn' i trudy svt. Grigoriya Palamy. Vvedeniye v izucheniye*. Translated by G. N. Nachinkin, 327–61. Saint Petersburg: Vizantinorossika, 1997.

Luther, Martin. *A Commentary on Saint Paul's Epistle to the Galatians*. London: James Duncan, 1830.

MacIntyre, Alasdair. *God, Philosophy, Universities: A Selective History of the Catholic Philosophical Tradition*. Lanham, MD: Rowman & Littlefield, 2009.

Moreland, James P. *Universals*. Chesham: Acumen, 2001.

Mrówczyński-Van Allen, Artur. *Between the Icon and the Idol. The Human Person and the Modern State in Russian Literature and Thought: Chaadayev, Soloviev, Grossman*. Translated by M. P. Whelan. Eugene, OR: Cascade, 2013.

———, and Sebastián Montiel Gómez. "Aspects of the Russian Tradition of Philosophical-Theological Synthesis in the Post-Secular Context. Georges Florovsky, Sergey Bulgakov, Alain Badiou, and the Theology Dwarf." In *Beyond Modernity: Russian Religious Philosophy and Post-Secularism*, edited by Artur Mrówczyński-Van Allen, Teresa Obolevitch and Paweł Rojek 13–24. Eugene, OR: Pickwick Publications, 2017.

Obolevitch, Teresa. "Faith and Knowledge in the Thought of Georges Florovsky." In *Faith and Reason in Russian Thought*, edited by Teresa Obolevitch and Paweł Rojek, 197–218. Krakow: Copernicus Center, 2015.

———. *Filozofia rosyjskiego renesansu patrystycznego: o. Gieorgij Florowski, Włodzimierz Łosski i inni*. Krakow: Copernicus Center, 2014.

———. "Gieorgija Florowskiego krytyka rosyjskiego renesansu religijno-filozoficznego: próba oceny." *Logos i Ethos* 38 (2015) 59–80.

Pabst, Adrian and Christoph Schneider. "Transfiguring the World through the Word." In *Encounter between Eastern Orthodoxy and Radical Orthodoxy*, edited by Adrian Pabst and Christoph Schneider, 1–25. Burlington, VT: Ashgate, 2009.

Plantinga, Alvin and Nicholas Wolterstorff, editors. *Faith and Rationality: Reason and Belief in God*. Notre Dame: University of Notre Dame Press, 1983.

Possenti, Vittorio. *Philosophy and Revelation: A Contribution to the Debate on Reason and Faith*. Translated by Emanuel L. Paparella. Aldershot: Ashgate, 2001.

Ratzinger, Jospeh. "Concerning the Notion of Person in Theology." Translated by Michael Waldstein. *Communio* 17 (1990) 439–54.

———. *Eschatology: Death and Eternal Life*. Translated by Michael Waldstein. Washington, DC: The Catholic University of America Press, 1988.

Rojek, Paweł. "The Logic of Palamism." In *Logic in Orthodox Christian Thinking*, edited by Andrew Schumann, 38–80. Hausenstamm: Ontos Verlag, 2013.

———. "Onomatodoxy and the Problem of Constitution: Florensky on Scientific and Manifest Images of the World." In *Faith and Reason in Russian Thought*, edited by Teresa Obolevitch and Paweł Rojek, 127–59. Krakow: Copernicus Center, 2015.

———. "Rosyjska filozofia teologiczna." In *Rosyjska metafizyka religijna*, edited by Teresa Obolevitch and Wojciech Kowalski, 23–44. Tarnow: Biblos, 2009.

———. "The Trinity in History and Society: The Russian Idea, Polish Messianism, and the Post-Secular Reason." In *Apology of Culture: Religion and Culture in Russian Thought*, edited by Artur Mrówczyński-Van Allen, Teresa Obolevitch and Paweł Rojek, 24–42. Eugene, OR: Pickwick Publications, 2015.

Royek, Pavel. "Sofiya i problema universaliy." In *Sofiologiya*, edited by Vladimir N. Porus, 178–95. Moscow: Bibleysko-Bogoslovskiy Institut Sv. Apostola Andreya, 2010.

Scruton, Roger. *The Face of God: The Gifford Lectures 2010*. London, New York: Continuum, 2012.

Tillich, Paul. *Systematic Theology*. Vol. 1. Chicago: The University of Chicago Press, 1973.

Tischner, Józef. "Schyłek chrześcijaństwa tomistycznego." *Znak* 1 (1970) 1–20.

8

Sergey Bulgakov's Trinitarian Anthropology

*Meaning, Hope, and Evangelizing
in a Post-Secular Society*

Walter Sisto

In a recent homily Pope Francis related human existence to the constant question for "something capable of fully quenching our thirst."[1] This imagery of "thirst" is apropos to the current state of post-secular societies, particularly the United States of America. In the aftermath of militant secularism that has pushed the Judeo-Christian God out of the public realm and attempted to replace God with half-baked, inchoate materialism and philosophical relativism, secularism has yielded surprising results. While the majority of Americans remain Christian and religion has a visible role in politics and culture, Americans are opting out of organized religion at an alarming rate. These persons select "none" when asked about religious affiliation on surveys and are therefore categorized as "the nones." Nevertheless "the nones" are primarily theists, and atheism remains a minority. Further investigation of the "the nones" reveals that millennials, or young adults, constitute the largest identifiable grouping. Yet rise of "the nones" and their individualistic question for spiritual truth without the Christian tradition[2] has as of yet not revealed positive results, as suicide remains a leading cause of death amongst millennials.[3] Unfortunately, based on Center for Disease Control's recent study, around 20 percent of these millennials (persons be-

---

1. Pope Francis, "Homily."
2. More than half of "the nones" formerly identified as Christian.
3. "Facts and Figures: Suicide Deaths."

tween 15–24) kill themselves annually.[4] The rise of "the nones" as well as the rise in suicide amongst American youth is evidence of a troubled society that is "thirsting" for God.[5]

With this in mind, my essay explores Sergey Bulgakov's insight that "God is love—not love in the sense of a quality or a property peculiar to God, but as the very substance and vigor of his life" and the implication of this thought for evangelization in a post-secular context.[6] For Bulgakov, God encompasses love as a phenomenon of interpersonal relationships but also as loving action involving persons. Love is the starting point of Bulgakov's reflection on God but also humankind. The result is that humankind is made in the image of Divine Love. This insight offers an operative analogy for persons living in post-secular societies that "thirst" for God, as Bulgakov's thought on God and humankind is based on the shared human experience and need for love.

For the purpose of clarity this paper will first briefly examine how "God is Love" informs his Trinitarian thought. Afterwards it will examine the implications of his Trinitarian thought for his anthropology. The final section demonstrates how his theological anthropology could inform good evangelization practices.

God as Love

For Bulgakov *kenosis* is the mediating principle of God's love. By *kenosis* he means the sacrifice and self-depleting of self for another.[7] His biblical warrant for making *kenosis* a central idea about Divine Love is Philippians 2:6 but also the paschal mystery. The crucifixion and death of Christ are the penultimate expressions of God's love; this for Bulgakov reveals an important insight about the immanent Trinity, for God's Love must also "have the character of the cross"; otherwise the formula of Chalcedon cannot be respected and Christ would suffer and love only in his humanity, resulting in nestorianism, Therefore Divine Love is kenotic love or what he calls love as an "Eternal Cross."[8] This cross is evident in Father's begetting of the Son. Bulgakov writes:

4. "Suicide: Facts at a Glance."

5. A recent 2015 study by the Pew Research Center, who initially discovered the "rise of the nones," projects that "the nones" will decline worldwide, see Lipka, "Why people with no religion are projected to decline."

6. Bulgakov, *Sophia*, 34.

7. See Oravecz, *God as Love*, 322.

8. Bulgakov, *Churchly Joy*, 3.

> The intimate connection of the Holy Trinity is the connection of love. And this love is trihypostatic love . . . There is, however, a common feature that characterizes love *as such* and thus all the forms of love. This is sacrificial self-renunciation, for the axiom of *personal* love is that *there is no love without sacrifice*. But this sacrificialness is realized in a triple manner in the life of the Holy Trinity. The Father and the Son are in a relation of mutual self-renunciation.[9]

Bulgakov is not speaking equivocally about sacrifice; nevertheless just as the Son exhausts himself to death for the love of the Father and humankind in his crucifixion, so too does the Father eternally exhaust Himself, making Himself vulnerable to the Son in his begetting the Son. Yet this love is reciprocated in the Son's love and eternal sacrifice for the Father.

Bulgakov's Christological love-analogy reveals a second aspect of love, as Jesus's love did not end in sacrifice but continues in the resurrection. Thus the Father's "eternal cross" also entails an "eternal resurrection" inasmuch as the Father is resurrected in the Son's love for him. This resurrection-love illustrates the second aspect of love, or the life giving aspect of love associated with the experience of joy and bliss. Bulgakov writes: *"there is no love without joy and bliss*; and in general there is no bliss other than love. Being tragic, love is also the overcoming of tragedy; and the *power* of love consists in this overcoming."[10] This overcoming of tragedy is personified in the Holy Spirit who is "hypostatic Love" or "hypostatic Joy."[11] Just as the Holy Spirit descends to earth on Pentecost to comfort and renew the church, the Holy Spirit proceeds from the Father onto the Son in the Father's love for the Son, but also from the Son to the Father, giving the Father renewed life and joy in the generation of the Son. Antinomy between temporal concepts and eternal reality is encountered, as generation as sacrificial-love and procession as joy and bliss-love are one event, and the Holy Spirit is the "transparent medium" by which the bliss of Love exists eternally in the Trinity. Nevertheless, the Holy Spirit is in a sense the resurrection of Father in generating the Son and the Son's resurrection in the Son's love for Father. But this is also a kenotic relationship, as the Holy Spirit exhausts himself completely for the Father and the Son. This "self-dying" of the Holy Spirit, if you will, is realized in the bliss of Love between the Father and Son. These relationships of God's kenotic love as both sacrifice and bliss are eternal and simultaneous actions. To be made in this image of God who is a ceaseless movement of

---

9. Bulgakov, *Comforter*, 65.
10. Ibid., 66, cf. Bulgakov, *Bride of the Lamb*, 49.
11. Bulgakov, *Comforter*, 66.

kenotic love between persons provides important insight into what is means to be human.

Made in the Image of Trinitarian Love

Humankind is unique because it alone images the inner-life of God; however humankind, as Bulgakov notes, is a dyad as opposed to a Trinity of persons.[12] For Bulgakov this is appropriate for two reasons: first, in Sacred Scripture, the Son and the Holy Spirit act in history directly; the Father, Who is the revealer, does not enter salvation history directly. Second, God created humankind as a dyad, male and female.[13] Based on the role and function of the dyad of the Son and Holy Spirit in salvation history, Bulgakov argues for a complementarity of the sexes. Thus to be made male and female is to be made in the image of the revealing hypostases, the Son and the Holy Spirit. The upshot is that human persons are not only hardwired to be in loving relationships with other human persons, but this love must involve the elements of how the Son and Holy Spirit love in the immanent and economic Trinity, i.e. involving sacrifice, joy and bliss.

This is not simply a metaphor for Bulgakov, as Bulgakov postulates the ontological dimensions of what this human dyadic relationship entailed in the prelapsarian state. He postulates that Adam was an individual without individuality, a "hypostasis, which is a center of love, an intelligent ray of Sophia."[14] Bulgakov appropriates Trinitarian kenotic love to human relationships. Like the persons of the Trinity, Adam was a penetrable center who had the ability to penetrate other human centers. Just as the Son and Holy Spirit are present to one another in their shared Divinity, Adam could be present to other created hypostases in his humanity.[15] Moreover, Adam "was completely accessible to Divine action on him."[16] What follows is that the love of God for Adam and Adam's love for God nourished his love for other persons.

After the original sin, this incipient Trinitarian-like existence that is immersed in the love and joy of God's love was lost, yet the empirical unity as expressed as human heredity is retained.[17] The result is that a "bad

---

12. See Bulgakov, *Orthodox Church*, 105; Bulgakov, *Comforter*, 254–54.
13. Ibid., 212.
14. Bulgakov, *Burning Bush*, 23.
15. See Crum, *The Doctrine of Sophia*, 56.
16. Bulgakov, *On Original Sin*, 15.
17. See Bulgakov, *Burning Bush*, 23.

multiplicity" emerges[18] at the metaphysical level, and rather than constituting a single I, interpenetrating one another[19] or a multi-hypostatic being like the Trihypostatic being of God, individualism emerges. But this individualism is a false perception that is ennobled by "nothing" or absence of God's love. This false perception is perpetuated by generations and thus human beings are born predisposed to selfishness and loneliness. It should not be surprising that American society which reifies false individualism also has high rates of depression and suicide, as concern for self is a dead end that ultimately leads to tragedy.

Nevertheless not all is lost, as the original sin simply creates a new situation for humanity. Bulgakov writes that just as there is "one common world for all humanity, so too human nature, realizing itself in different hypostases, remains one and does not reconstitute itself."[20] This is important for Bulgakov because Jesus Christ as the New Adam, does not constitute a new type of human being, but rather a human being that has the original prerogatives of prelapsarian Adam. Bulgakov always conscious of the Chalcedonian formula stresses that when we talk about Jesus we are talking about a person in whom the Trinitarian-like potential existence of humanity is fully realized. Bulgakov is apt to stress the causes of Jesus's miracles, foreknowledge, and ability to read and be present to people are the result of his humanness.[21] At the same time his humanity is "completely accessible to Divine action on him," thus Jesus credits God the Father as the cause of his amazing deeds.

Christ recapitulates the image of God and its potential prelapsarian existence for humanity in founding the church. Churchly existence is then the means to unlock the human potential. The church is a training ground for being more human: to learn what true love is; humans are made in the image of Love; and how to love others in a meaningful and healthy manner. Specifically, to learn that human beings are made in the image of a God Who is Love, and human beings can only find true joy and bliss in their lives if they are willing to love their neighbor and God to the point of sacrifice.

Evangelization and Trinitarian Anthropology

In 2012, the Catholic Bishops in *Instrumentum Laboris*, a document that offers instruction on how to evangelize, wrote the "recurring appeal is that

---

18. Crum, *The Doctrine of Sophia*, 36.
19. Bulgakov, "Die christliche Anthropologie," 227.
20. Bulgakov, *Burning Bush*, 23.
21. See Bulgakov, *On the Gospel Miracles*, 56–77.

our communities, in proclaiming the Gospel, might better know how to attract people's attention today and interpret their questioning and search for happiness."[22] This succinct statement captures the greatest challenge Christians face in proclaiming the gospel to millennials, particularly finding a meaningful expression of the Christian tradition for persons living in a post-secular culture. We need only to look to American popular culture, particularly the highest grossing songs and movies,[23] to find opportunities for preaching the gospel message. What I have found is that the theme of love, particularly the loss of love, desire to be loved, and the sacrifice for love, dominates American popular culture.[24]

In this context, Bulgakov's interpretation of the Christian tradition is relevant and may provide an opportunity for evangelization since his thought is an explication of love.[25] Specifically, Bulgakov's reflection on the *Imago Dei* provides an important opportunity to interpret the desire for love within a Christian context so as to offer a meaningful explanation of this basic human experience. As the desire to love is in Bulgakov's terminology sophiological, or it is a function of what it means to be human, for God does not simply love us, but rather humankind is made in the image of Love Itself, or a community of persons who perfectly give of themselves and experience perfectly the intimacy and joy of a loving relationship. For when looking to the Trinity we discover that not only does love involve mystery, as we can never fully comprehend it, but love moves us beyond abstraction and requires the lover to not only give of themselves, but to hope in the joy of this giving and reciprocation of this love. Bulgakov's provides a framework to interpret and explain the high rates of divorce and failed relationships in the US, as in these relationships there is either lack of joy, too much concern for self or failure to rightly order their love.

22. *Instrumentum Laboris*, no. 138.

23. The recent theatrical rendition of *Anna Karenina* (2013) that was nominated for several academy awards is one of many examples. This tale along with other western classics including *Romeo and Juliet*, and *Tristen and Isolde* remind us of the need for true love; however, in each of these novels/recent films, true love, as defined as human love, ends in tragedy.

24. This theme resonates in all genres of entertainment including action films. For instance, in Marvel Comics's *The Avengers* (2012), which was one of the highest grossing films of all time, the hero, Iron Man sacrifices himself to save his city. Here is an example of love as sacrifice.

25. Bulgakov's conversion from atheism to spiritualism to Orthodoxy was in a large part due to his inability to reconcile his experience and desire to love with materialistic and popular philosophical ideologies. Not only did his quest for God begin with his partial realization that nature was "the vesture of his [God's] love and glory," but at the end of his life in 1939 he was enraptured by the love of God in his near-death experience. See Bulgakov, *Autobiographical Notes*, 10, 24.

Moreover, Bulgakov has a pertinent insight that love is a strange phenomenon, as it always goes outward and beyond itself. This is the necessity of love, which is fully on display in God's creation of the world, as God creates not out of external compulsion but rather out of Divine Love to share God's love with other beings.[26] For the potential convert this means that love has inertia; it cannot rest in/with a created being. Just as God continually outpours Godself within God but also outside of God, love requires human beings constantly go outside their self to love another person. Ultimately, love for other human beings will leave a person unfulfilled since it must overflow into a love of Love, a love for Love Itself or love for God. Here we should be reminded that Jesus commands, not simply to love your neighbor as yourself, but to love God (Matt 22:36–44). This is another important point to bring to the attention of a potential convert; love cannot be satisfied unless the object of our love is God, and God creates us with the ability to freely communicate our love to Godself through Jesus Christ. When we return to the source of our human love, our love is sustained and raised to a new level.

Interestingly, after properly ordering our love to God, our love, now deified by God's love, does not remain in a stasis but rather participates in God's love for humankind and creation. Thus the saints in heaven and earth participate in God's love. True love is always cyclical involving not only relationships between persons, but God, and then participates in God's love for persons and creation. The effect of this is that you become less inclined to sin and more fully human by loving God. But this is of course the importance of the Christian message for a culture that is sick with individualism and suicide. Moreover, in pluralistic societies, such as the American society, that tend to discount Christianity as a unique voice amongst the world religions, it is important to illustrate the unique message of the Christian tradition: unlike Islam, Judaism, Hinduism, or Buddhism, or any other world religion, to return to Bulgakov's insight about Divine Love, love is not only an attribute of God but God's nature and life; only after embracing this love can a person experience the joy and bliss for which they "thirst." The church is the beginning of this encounter with not only loving persons but also the loving God. Nevertheless it is incumbent upon members of the church to demonstrate this love in their actions. This is a challenge, as attempting to love as the Son loves us, leads to vulnerability and perhaps rejection and death, but is it in these cases that Christian martyrs and saints are born. If God is open in love to all people, then we, who are made in the image of Divine Love, must always demonstrate openness to others and a longing to grant to them

---

26. See Bulgakov, *Bride of the Lamb*, 49.

the ability to experience true and everlasting love as a member of the body of Christ himself, the church.

If there is any doubt the importance of placing love as the priority in churchly existence and evangelical activity in post-secular societies, we need only look to the example of Pope Francis and his emphasis on love in North America which properly known as the "Francis Effect." Pope Francis stress on the love of God in his preaching and example are not only credited with the new positive image of Catholicism in North America but has curtailed the exodus of Catholics in the North American Catholic Church.[27] Bulgakov's thought offers meaningful insights on God and humankind that can perhaps help further express and aid in the evangelization and conversion of many Americans. Perhaps it is time for the Orthodox and Catholic Churches to examine Bulgakov's thought anew to help further strengthen its witness to the world and re-establish itself as the antidote to negative trends amongst American youths that lead to lives without eternal bliss and joy of the Holy Spirit.

Bibliography

Bulgakov, Sergey. *Autobiographical Notes*, 3–27. In *A Bulgakov Anthology*. Philadelphia: The Westminster, 1976.

———. *The Bride of the Lamb*. Translated by Boris Jakim. Grand Rapids, MI: Eerdmans, 2002.

———. *The Burning Bush: On the Orthodox Veneration of the Mother of God*. Translated by T. A. Smith. Grand Rapids, MI: Eerdmans, 2009.

———. "Die christliche Anthropologie." In *Kirche, Staat und Mensch: Russisch-Orthodoxe Studien*, 209–55. Genf: Russisch-Orthodoxe Studien und Forschungen des Oekumenischen Rates für Praktisches Christentum, 1937.

———. *Churchly Joy: Orthodox Devotions for the Church Year*. Translated by Boris Jakim. Grand Rapids, MI: Eerdmans, 2008.

———. *The Comforter*. Translated by Boris Jakim. Grand Rapids, MI: Eerdmans, 2004.

———. "On Original Sin." *Journal of St. Alban and St. Sergius* 7 (1929) 15–26.

———. *The Orthodox Church*. Translated by Lydia Kesich. Crestwood, NY: St. Vladimir's Seminary Press, 1988.

———. *Relics and Miracles*. Translated by Boris Jakim. Grand Rapids, MI: Eerdmans, 2011, Kindle e-book.

———. *Sophia: The Wisdom of God*. Translated by Patrick Thompson. Hudson, NY: Lindisfarne, 1993.

Crum, Winston Ferris. *The Doctrine of Sophia According to Sergius N. Bulgakov*. PhD diss., Harvard University, 1965.

"Facts and Figures: Suicide Deaths." *American Foundation for Suicide Prevention* 2015. Online: https://www.afsp.org/understanding-suicide/facts-and-figures.

---

27. Last year was the first year since the fifteenths that Catholic population in the United States has not decreased, see Reese, "The Francis Effect."

Francis, Pope. "Homily of His Holiness Pope Francis." Vatican City, January 25, 2015. Online: https://w2.vatican.va/content/francesco/en/homilies/2015/documents/papa-francesco_20150125_vespri-conversione-san-paolo.html.

Instrumentum Laboris. The New Evangelization for the Transmission of the Christian Faith. Vatican City 2012. Online: http://www.vatican.va/roman_curia/synod/documents/rc_synod_doc_20120619_instrumentum-xiii_en.html.

Lipka, Michael. "Why People with no Religion are Projected to Decline as a Share of the World's Population." *Pew Research Center*, April 3, 2015. Online: http://www.pewresearch.org/fact-tank/2015/04/03/why-people-with-no-religion-are-projected-to-decline-as-a-share-of-the-worlds-population/.

Oravecz, Johannes. *God as Love: The Concept and Spiritual Aspects of Agape in Modern Russian Religious Thought.* Grand Rapids, MI: Eerdmans, 2014.

Reese, Thomas. "The Francis Effect." *National Catholic Reporter*, March 6, 2014. Online: http://ncronline.org/blogs/faith-and-justice/francis-effect.

"Suicide: Facts at a Glance." Centers for Disease Control and Prevention, 2012. Online: http://www.cdc.gov/violenceprevention/pdf/suicide-datasheet-a.pdf.

PART III

Historical Focuses

11

Friedrich Nietzsche as a Christian Thinker

The Philosophy of Nietzsche in the Context of the Russian Religious Philosophy of the Nineteenth and Twentieth Centuries[1]

Igor Evlampiev

From the early days of the twentieth century, there appeared a great interest in the philosophy of Friedrich Nietzsche among Russian philosophers. Regarding Nietzsche's philosophy as an example of atheism and a consistent critique of Christianity, some Russian philosophers disapproved of his ideas. Evgeni Trubetskoy, Sergey Bulgakov, Nikolai Fyodorov disputed with Nietzsche particularly fiercely, believing that Nietzsche's ideas were incompatible with the tradition of Russian religious thinking. Nevertheless, more thoughtful philosophers such as Semen Frank, Nikolai Berdyaev, Lev Shestov and Andrei Bely evaluated Nietzsche's creative work in a different way. Frank found in his philosophy deep insight into the highest spiritual demands of humanity. Shestov thought that in the situation when old forms of religion are no longer capable of complying with the aspirations of humanity, Nietzsche was a frank searcher of new forms of religion. However, Bely, who found it possible to juxtapose Nietzsche with Jesus Christ himself, went farther than anyone in "rehabilitation" of Nietzsche. On Bely, Nietzsche had the true Christian point of view and understood the glad tidings of Jesus Christ much deeper than many adherents of Christianity understood. "Only Christ and Nietzsche knew all power and greatness of a man," writes Bely.[2]

---

1. The project of Saint Petersburg University "University philosophy in the context of social processes," No. 23.38.328.2015.

2. Belyy, "Fridrikh Nitsshe," 885.

This paradoxical view is sufficiently well known, but it is more often regarded to be the result of a very subjective interpretation that does not reflect the authentic intention of Nietzsche's philosophy. This is why those who professionally study Nietzsche's philosophy do not consider this standpoint as serious.

At present, we can confidently state that the opinion of Russian philosophers of the early twentieth century on the Christian nature of Nietzsche's philosophy was not their invention or the result of their "loose interpretation." Russian philosophers were correct in realizing the trend that can be found as an objective verity in Nietzsche's creative work. Moreover, these ideas can clearly be read from a work usually considered to have a far from positive attitude to Christianity, i.e. *The Anti-Christ*.

If read attentively, Nietzsche's notebooks of the period when he worked on *The Anti-Christ* (end of 1887–beginning of 1888) show that immediately before Nietzsche started to write this work he had read the book *What I Believe?* by Leo Tolstoy and the novel *The Devils* by Fyodor Dostoevsky. Both books had a significant influence on Nietzsche, something which can easily be traced in his treatise. Since the ideas of the two great religious thinkers influenced Nietzsche considerably, it is not surprising that at that moment he could not take an undisguised anti-Christian point of view—as many researchers put it. A scrupulous reading of *The Anti-Christ* and of the excerpts Nietzsche quoted from the works by Tolstoy and Dostoevsky helps us clearly understand both the extent of the influence on Nietzsche by these Russian thinkers and the Christian nature of his own viewpoint.

Nietzsche and Tolstoy

We will start with the influence of Tolstoy (Nietzsche read his book prior to the reading of the novel by Dostoevsky). Let us convey the essential ideas of *What I Believe?* by Tolstoy before we start analyzing the texts by Nietzsche. Tolstoy's main idea is that there is a stiff opposition between the original doctrine of Jesus Christ and the doctrine propounded by the Christian Church in the course of its own history. Tolstoy argues that there is a severe *distortion* of the original doctrine of Jesus Christ in history.

Tolstoy sees the essence of this distortion in three key aspects. Firstly, the original doctrine of Jesus Christ was directly opposed to Judaism and, thus, repudiated its basic principles—and above all it refuted the necessity of the church as a way to regulate the lives of believers. Secondly, the original doctrine of Jesus Christ was focused on finding conditions for man to achieve *absolute perfection of his life* directly during his mortal life. However, the historical Christianity states the utter imperfection both in human nature and in human life (the idea of deep sinfulness borrowed from Judaism). As a result, perfection is understood here as possible only in a transcendent, afterlife reality. Thirdly, in Tolstoy, while the idea of immortality of soul is adopted in ecclesiastical doctrine, Christ himself did not implied any individual immortality of soul. According to Tolstoy, the eternal life Christ spoke about is a universal human life, i.e. life in succession of human generations. Christ did not think of the immortality of a single soul.

In Nietzsche's notebook dating from the end of 1887 we can find a number of extracts from the book by Tolstoy *What I Believe?* and an exposition of its fragments. It is interesting to compare Nietzsche's judgments about Christianity written before he started to study *What I Believe?* to his judgments concerning Christianity which he borrowed from Tolstoy and then treated them as *his own* and after that introduced into the text of *The Anti-Christ*. In a number of aspects we can observe a *fundamental* change of Nietzsche's point of view. Moreover, it is obvious that this happened after he had read attentively the book by Tolstoy.

Primarily one should take into consideration that almost about dozen pages before the extractions from the book *What I Believe?* Nietzsche states his attitude to Tolstoy. It is clear that this attitude is extremely negative. Nietzsche has not studied the works by Tolstoy yet and he uses the widespread stereotype that Tolstoy is the epitome of the standpoint of "compassion," which is common for all Christians. After regarding pessimism as the disposition which hinders to achieve the true power of man (his "will to power") Nietzsche reflects on some forms of pessimism, and, finally, he refer them to the category of "corruption and sickness":

> But where is Pascal's *moral pessimism*? The *metaphysical pessimism* of Vedanta philosophy? *The social pessimism* of the anarchists (or Shelley's)? *The compassion-pessimism* (like Tolstoy's, Alfred de Vigny's)? Are not all equally decay and morbidity phenomena? The excessive important business of moral-values, or "beyond" fictions, or social calamities and *sufferings* of all: each such *exaggeration of a single* viewpoint is in itself a sign of disease. Likewise, the preponderance of the *No* on the *Yes*![3]

At this stage and from Nietzsche's viewpoint, Tolstoy is a typical Christian moralist who shares generally known Christian conception, particularly about "'beyond' fictions." Nietzsche's judgments about Christianity made before he started to work on the book by Tolstoy are purely negative. Moreover, Nietzsche does not see any difference between historical

3. Nietzsche, *Notebook*, 59.

Christianity and Christ's doctrine itself. Reflecting on the typical preacher, Nietzsche claims that this is a model of "great mediocrity." He even refers Jesus Christ himself to this type.[4] Nietzsche incessantly repeats that his aim is the struggle with Christian ideal of man which is connected with the Sermon on the Mount and with the belief in individual immortality of soul.

However, here Nietzsche starts working on the book by Tolstoy. Reading his judgments attentively, we realize with amazement that he *deeply changes* his views on the history of Christianity and, what is the main point, his evaluation of the doctrine of Christ. Now following Tolstoy, he considers the doctrine of Christ to be a bitter opposition to the ecclesiastical doctrine! Nietzsche copies out a number of phrases from the French edition of the book by Tolstoy (in his own version) rendering exactly this thought. The first of those phrases reads follows: "the church is precisely that against which Jesus preached—and fight against what he taught his disciples."[5] It is possible to compare this phrase with following words of Tolstoy: "though the church calls its teaching a Christian doctrine, it is in truth the very darkness against which Christ strove and enjoined his disciples to strive."[6]

It is significant that Nietzsche does not stop at this thesis and strengthen its meaning, and now this is definitely his own judgment: "the church is not only the caricature of Christianity, but *the organized war against Christianity*."[7] Then we find Nietzsche's completely independent judgment which is important that it will be repeated with small changes in the text of *The Anti-Christ* (Chapter 27):

> I am unable to determine what was the target of the insurrection said to have been led (whether rightly or *wrongly*) by Jesus, if it was not the Jewish church—"church" being here used in exactly the same sense that the word has today.[8]

The ideas of the Russian writer are still can be observed in these words, as Tolstoy devotes a whole part of his book to demonstrate the thesis that Christ completely rejected both Law of Moses and all of the institutions of church, state and culture.

The most evident consequence that there was a revolution in Nietzsche's viewpoint is the bifurcation in his notion of Christianity. After all, if the church is "war against organized Christianity," one should doubtlessly

---

4. Nietzsche, *Nachgelassene Fragmente 1887–1889*, 32.
5. Nietzsche, *Notebook*, 65.
6. Tolstoy, *What I Believe?*, 202; Nietzsche, *Nachgelassene Fragmente*, 276.
7. Nietzsche, *Notebook*, 70.
8. Nietzsche, *The Anti-Christ*, 53; see also *Notebook*, 71–72.

differentiate between two forms of Christianity and oppose ecclesiastical Christianity to true Christianity. Now Nietzsche evaluates true Christianity in a completely different way than before. Now he ascribes all his previous judgments to ecclesiastical Christianity. But true Christianity connected with the doctrine of Christ is now regarded by Nietzsche as close to his own views on the significance and purposes of human life; true Christianity is directed not to the "corruption and sickness" (as he had thought before), but to the "rise" of man.

One more judgment of Tolstoy that Nietzsche copied out from French edition of *What I believe?* acquires extreme importance:

> The explanations of the church which pass for faith, and the true faith of our generation, which is in obedience to social laws and the laws of the State, have reached a stage of sharp antagonism. The majority of civilized people have nothing to regulate life but faith in the police. This state of things would be awful, were it universal. Fortunately, there are men in our days, the best men of our time, who, dissatisfied with such a creed, have a creed of their own concerning the life that we ought to lead. These men are considered as pernicious and dangerous unbelievers; and yet they are the only believers. They are believers in the doctrine of Christ, or at least in a part of it. These men often do not know the whole doctrine of Christ. They do not properly understand it, and indeed they often reject the chief basis of the Christian faith, which is non-resistance of evil; but their faith in what life ought to be is derived from the doctrine of Christ. However these men may be persecuted and slandered, they are the only men who do not passively submit to all that they are ordered to do, and therefore they are the only men who do not vegetate, but lead a rational life, and they are the only true believers.[9]

Nietzsche does not express his attitude to this opinion directly. Nevertheless, his view on it is quite clear. Now following Tolstoy, he understands true Christianity based on undistorted doctrine of Christ as a viewpoint of "the best people," i.e., the people whom he addresses to with his philosophy. Now one of the *crucial* theses of *The Anti-Christ* does not seem to be surprising in the light of this idea of Tolstoy's which was borrowed by Nietzsche:

> It is an error amounting to nonsensicality to see in "faith," and particularly in faith in salvation through Christ, the distinguishing mark of the Christian: only the Christian *way of life*, the life *lived* by him who died on the cross, is Christian . . . To this day

---

9. Tolstoy, *What I Believe?*, 215; see Nietzsche, *Nachgelassene Fragmente*, 277.

> *such* a life is still possible, and for *certain* men even necessary: genuine, original Christianity will remain possible in all ages.[10]

It is beyond question that *"certain* men" in this context are those who follow Zarathustra's precepts and the *"way of life"* (Christian!) is what Nietzsche appeals to in his philosophy.

In this connection, Nietzsche's viewpoint on Christian ideal of man, against which he intended to struggle before, dramatically changes. Now his struggle solely concerns the *ecclesiastical* ideal, although he evaluates his views on man in the doctrine of Christ as quite positive. He puts Tolstoy and Christ himself beyond the limits of "pessimism" which hinders the realization of the will to power in man. Now Nietzsche connects pessimism with the ecclesiastical distortion of the doctrine of Christ: "The 'Christianity' has become something fundamentally different from what its founder and that would . . . it is the rise of pessimism, while Jesus wanted to bring peace and happiness of the Lambs"[11] ("peace and happiness" are key notions employed by Tolstoy to describe the way of life Jesus Christ appealed to). It will be recalled that explaining his own (i.e. true) view on the doctrine of Christ, Tolstoy does not enunciate any unachievable "ideal," but he appeals to change our *false* way of life and turn to the *true* one:

> Christ does not consider his teaching as some high ideal of what mankind should be but cannot attain to, nor does he consider it as a chimerical, poetical fancy, fit only to captivate the simple-minded inhabitants of Galilee; he considers his teaching as work—a work that is to save mankind. His suffering on the cross was no dream; he groaned in agony and died for his teaching.[12]

As it has already been said, while ecclesiastical Christianity puts the ideal into the "supernatural" reality, Tolstoy puts the ideal into the real life. This idea appears to be the most important point for the coincidence of Tolstoy's and Nietzsche opinion. We can surmise how it was unexpected for Nietzsche to realize that Tolstoy was not at all a supporter of the "beyond" fancies, as he had put it before. Moreover, now Nietzsche admits that there is not this idea in the doctrine of Christ itself.

In this connection Nietzsche must think on what the true glad tidings brought by Christ are. This is the most important part of his treatise. Although this part does not take a lot of space (Chapters 29–39), it has immense significance for understanding Nietzsche's philosophy. As a

---

10. Nietzsche, *The Anti-Christ*, 66.
11. Nietzsche, *Notebook*, 76.
12. Tolstoy, *What I Believe?*, 43.

result, Nietzsche can be called a *Christian* thinker. While in criticism of historical and false Christianity Nietzsche follows Tolstoy, in his account of true Christianity (the doctrine of Christ himself) he employs the ideas of Dostoevsky.[13]

Nietzsche and Dostoevsky

Nietzsche's notebooks dating from November 1887–March 1888 comprise large excerpts from the novel *The Devils*. Moreover, the most important of them concern Kirillov who is the key character-ideologist of the novel. Unlike the overwhelming majority of Dostoevsky's contemporaries, Nietzsche clearly understood the sense of Kirillov's story. He understood that by means of it Dostoevsky showed his unusual conception of Christ. According to Kirillov, Christ was mistaken in his thought that man achieves perfection and plenitude of existence after his death. Contrary to this thought Kirillov holds that man must achieve perfection and plenitude of existence in every moment of his mortal life.

Almost after several pages from those excerpts Nietzsche enunciates his understanding of the image of Christ. The first excerpt shows Kirillov's paradoxical view on the story of Christ. In *The Devils* it begins with the following words:

> Listen to a great idea: there was a day on earth, and in the midst of the earth there stood three crosses. One on the Cross had such faith that he said to another, "To-day thou shalt be with me in Paradise." The day ended; both died and passed away and found neither Paradise nor resurrection. His words did not come true.[14]

This excerpt is not in Nietzsche's text, but it seems to be quoted here as the first drafts of *The Anti-Christ* contained exactly this image—Christ and the thief crucified together with him.

Slightly changing the word order and abridging some phrases, Nietzsche copies out from the novel by Dostoevsky the following text:

> If nature has not spared even its masterpiece when they let Jesus live in the midst of falsehood and a lie (and he owes the world everything he has let live) without him, the planet, with all that it is mere folly, now, the planet rests on a lie, a mockery of stupid. Consequently, the laws of nature itself one imposture and a

---

13. Evlampiev, "Dostoevsky and Nietzsche," 15–32.
14. Dostoevsky, *The Devils*, 637.

diabolical farce. Why is life so if you're a man?... "Feel that God is not at the same time and not feel that it's just become so God is an absurdity: otherwise you would not fail to kill themselves. If you feel that you're tzar, and, away to kill them yourself, you will live on the summit of glory."[15]

The second excerpt copied by Nietzsche is also important. Nietzsche copies out the words of Kirillov about specific states when he feels "joy," mystical plenitude of his existence, merge with the whole universe:[16]

> Five, six seconds and no more: because it suddenly feels the presence of eternal harmony. A person can, in his mortal shell that does not endure, and he has to physically transform or die ... During these five seconds I live a whole human existence, for them I would give my whole life, it would not have paid too dear. In order to endure it longer, one would have to transform them physically. I think the man listens to testify on. *Why children, if the goal is reached?*[17]

As it has already been said, immediately after these excerpts Nietzsche formulates his view on Christ for the first time that would be the key point of *The Anti-Christ*:

> *The thief on the cross*—when the criminal himself who suffers a painful death condemned, "as this Jesus, without revolt, without hostility, kind, faithful, suffers and dies, but it's the right thing": he has the gospel in the affirmative, and thus *he is in paradise* ... The Kingdom of Heaven is a state of the heart (is said of children "for theirs is the Kingdom of Heaven"), nothing that is "above the earth." The kingdom of God "is" not arranged chronologically and historically, not by the calendar, something that would one day since the day before and not, but it is a "mindchange in the individual," something that comes every time and every time is not yet there is.[18]

In the final text of *The Anti-Christ* this thought is expressed more compactly and brightly; it hints at the story of Christ and thief told by Kirillov:

> The whole evangel is contained in the words to the *thief* on the cross. "That was a truly *divine* man, a child of God," said the

---

15. Nietzsche, *Notebook*, 97; see Dostoevsky, *The Devils*, 637.
16. Evlampiev, "The Concept of *Joy*," 140–45.
17. Nietzsche, *Notebook*, 97–98, see Dostoevsky, *The Devils*, 610.
18. Nietzsche, *Notebook*, 103.

thief. "If this is how you feel," the redeemer replied, "*then you are in paradise*, then you too are a child of God . . . "[19]

The true belief in Christ is a capability for man to feel his own perfection and overcome the shortcomings of his mortal life together with all its sufferings *at any moment of it* (even being crucified!).

It is completely obvious that here the image of Christ is treated under the badge of the impression made on Nietzsche by Kirillov's words about "five seconds." The state of joy Kirillov speaks about is what Nietzsche apprehends to be the true experience of the Kingdom of Heaven. In addition, that experience, i.e., experience of *this-worldly and fleeting bliss*, is what he understands as the main point of the doctrine of Christ and the main sense of the true Christianity: "Our nineteenth century finally has the prerequisite for understanding something that nineteen centuries have misunderstood the reason—Christianity."[20]

The conception that in this state of the Kingdom of Heaven, "the paradise," Christ directly feels his indissoluble unity with God becomes the crucial idea in *The Anti-Christ*, though for both Nietzsche and Dostoevsky God is not "external" and transcendent existence but some kind of mysterious and inner profundity in man. Finding this profundity, Christ shows his absoluteness and deity. In addition, it is that practice of finding the absolute life in our own personality which becomes main and only postulate of the doctrine of Christ and it is that only practice which is true and original Christianity. With respect to it, all notions of sin, expiation and salvation appear to be the distortions just as the whole conception of church as "saving" organization ensuring connection between "mythological" God and weak man.

> In the whole psychology of the "Gospels" the concepts of guilt and punishment are lacking, and so is that of reward. "Sin," which means anything that puts a distance between God and man, is abolished—this is *precisely the "glad tidings."* Eternal bliss is not merely promised, nor is it bound up with conditions: it is conceived as the *only* reality—what remains consists merely of signs useful in speaking of it . . . *Not* by "repentance," *not* by "prayer and forgiveness" is the way to God: *only the Gospel way* leads to God—it is *itself* "God"!—What the Gospels *abolished* was the Judaism in the concepts of "sin," "forgiveness of

---

19. Nietzsche, *The Anti-Christ, Ecce Homo, Twilight of the Idols and Other Writings*, 32.

20. Nietzsche, *Notebook*, 105.

sin," "faith," "salvation through faith"—the whole *ecclesiastical* dogma of the Jews was denied by the "glad tidings."[21]

That is what offers the main conclusion of the whole treatise *The Anti-Christ*. And the simultaneous presence of the ideas of both Tolstoy (in what is rejected) and Dostoevsky (in what is taken as a supreme Christian truth) can clearly be seen in this conclusion.

Vladimir Bibikhin about Crisis of Modern Civilization

At the end of the twentieth century Vladimir Bibikhin (1938–2004), the most prominent religious thinker of the new Russia, continued the tradition of the Russian religious thinking of the early twentieth century. Owning to his research of the Italian Renaissance, to his translations of Gregory Palamas, Francesco Petrarca, Nicholas of Cusa and Martin Heidegger (including *Being and Time*) and of many other representatives of the modern and ancient philosophy Bibikhin became famous. *New Renaissance*, which is one of his main books, is formally devoted to research of the Italian Renaissance. However, in its contents the book goes beyond this narrow topic. Analyzing the Renaissance, Bibikhin formulates a theory explaining the whole history of Europe. The main thought of this theory compels us to recall Nietzsche's idea of eternal return. On Bibikhin, the essence of history consists in the constant returns to past and efforts to enliven the most valuable achievements of the past culture. That is why the notion of the Renaissance is not the description of a definite historical epoch but it renders the essence of history:

> renaissance is not a past period of our history but the essence of history. Every feeling the sense is a step towards Renaissance which with respect of its purpose is the same now and in last centuries.[22]

Bibikhin holds that there was a number of "renaissances" and each of them was a new historical source giving a new impulse for history. Taking already discovered cultural forms as models for creative work and life, people try to go further. However, the result is not the strict imitation of the past but the appearance of new culture.

Bibikhin strongly disapproves of the contemporary epoch and its prevailing ideology of liberalism. Such key concepts of this epoch as *modernity*

---

21. Nietzsche, *The Anti-Christ*, 59–60.
22. Bibikhin, *Novyy renessans*, 23.

and *post-modernity* presuppose the full rupture with the past. Contemporary western society considers itself so "up-to-date" and "progressive" that it denies the need to take into account in its own progress the past, which as thought to become antiquated. However, without taking into consideration the cultural heritage the civilization has been regressing and this deterioration has reached so degree that it threatens to destroy it.

> The end of history is sorrowful. There is neither art nor philosophy. The museum of culture guarded with tiresome efforts is everywhere. Among the cautionary and rich welfare in the very center of contemporary civilization of shop windows and TV-screens man pines for the past when, as he remembers, the readiness to risk the life for the sake of pure idea, courage, imagination and idealism set the tone.[23]

Like other Russian critics of Western society and its liberal ideology, Bibikhin sees the whopping lie of this ideology in the idea that individual being is primary with respect to society. This leads to "atomization" of society and its cultural regress. This fact in its turn leads to the regress of man as he loses the cultural basis for his own evolution. According to Bibikhin "unity" of the person with other persons, with society and the whole existence is primary with the respect to division and independence. Man can acquire his true individuality only in the act of unity with world and society: "individuality . . . has nothing to be based on but the whole and in the end the universal."[24] On the contrary, if the man considers division and independence the high values, he loses his creative essence and his life changes into the range of common roles, "masques." That is what we can see in contemporary society.

Nietzsche's influence is evident in such a critique of Western liberal civilization. Nevertheless, it becomes more evident in Bibikhin's analysis of the history of Christianity. Just as Nietzsche Bibikhin maintains that the original doctrine of Christ was distorted in the course of history. It has led to regress of European culture and has caused such phenomena as atheism, mechanicism and irreligious humanism of Enlightenment.

Bibikhin finds the essence of the Italian Renaissance not in the return to Antiquity. In his opinion, the Humanists tried to revive and "correct" Christianity, make it a living basis for European culture. At the same time, they considered the idea of unity of man and God the main thought in Christianity. However, Renaissance appeared to be the tragic epoch. Its intention did not turn out well. This resulted in returning of the European culture to

---

23. Ibid., 14.
24. Bibikhin, *Uznay sebya*, 148.

medieval, archaic viewpoint. Its crucial idea is insignificance of man. This idea became the basis of Enlightenment (in spite of all its bright slogans). It is fully expressed in the book *Man a Machine* by Julien Offray de La Mettrie. In this respect Enlightenment is not the continuation of Renaissance (as it is generally accepted) but it is its opposite—like the idea of "man a machine" is the opposite of the notion of man who is equal to God. It was the Enlightenment what has become the starting point of subsequent negative trend in European culture and what has caused its present regress.

The Christian Church in all its confessions was not capable of opposing that negative trend as the same idea of insignificance of man predominated in it. That is why both Nietzsche and Bibikhin (who was deeply religious orthodox believer) blame Christian Church for predominance of the "nihilism" in the history of Europe.

> From naïve point of view Modern Christianity teaches morality, tradition and participation in history. In practice, the situation is not so simple. Christian Church is the source of the whole historical evil of modern nihilism, although it is not the only culprit. The main mistake of the church is that it put God in too transcendent distance. If God does not exist, everything is allowed. But it would be more precise to say that if God is inaccessible in his eternity, cold loneliness falls to man's lot . . . If everything is equally far from God's infinity, everything is equally worthless.[25]

Overcoming the crisis is only possible if true religiosity and capability for spiritual creative work would return into the society and culture. As regards this idea, Bibikhin holds that we need a *new renaissance*, which is similar to that of the fiftieth–sixtieth centuries. The mentioned religiosity must be based not on the idea of human sinfulness and admittance that God is far from man but on the idea of *unity-identity* of man and God and on the admittance of the divine nature of man. Only in this case will man return his spiritual profundity and capability for the creative work. It is how in *The Anti-Christ* Nietzsche treated the doctrine of Christ. Moreover, before him Joachim of Fiore, Meister Eckhart, Nicholas of Cusa, Giordano Bruno, Gottfried Wilhelm von Leibniz, Johann Gottlieb Fichte, Martin Heidegger understood Christianity in the same way—just as the majority of Russian religious thinkers from Alexei Khomiakov and Fyodor Dostoevsky to Vladimir Bibikhin.

---

25. Bibikhin, *Novyy renessans*, 219–20.

Bibliography

Belyy, Andrey. "Fridrikh Nitsshe." In *Nitsshe: pro et contra*, edited by Yuliya V. Sineokaya, 878–903. Saint Petersburg: Izdatel'stvo Russkogo Khristianskogo gumanitarnogo instituta, 2001.

Bibikhin, Vladimir. *Novyy renessans*. Moscow: Nauka, Progress-traditsiya, 1998.

———. *Uznay sebya*. Saint Petersburg: Nauka, 1998.

Dostoevsky, Fyodor. *The Devils*. Translated by Constance Garnett. London: Wordsworth Editions, 2009.

Evlampiev, Igor. "The Concept of *Joy* in the Context of F. Dostoevskij's Understanding of the Essence of Religious Belief." *Studies in East European Thought* 66 (2014) 139–48.

———. "Dostoevsky and Nietzsche: Toward a New Metaphysics of Man." *Russian Studies in Philosophy* 41 (2002) 7–32.

Nietzsche, Friedrich. *The Anti-Christ*. Translated by Reginald J. Hollingdale. Radford, VA: Wilder Publications, 2008.

———. *The Anti-Christ, Ecce Homo, Twilight of the Idols and Other Writings*. Translated by Judith Norman. Cambridge: Cambridge University Press, 2005.

———. *Nietzsche's Notebook of 1887–1888*. Translated by Daniel Fidel Ferrer. Online: https://archive.org/stream/NietzschesNotebookOf1887-1888.ByFredrick Nietzsche1844-1900_650/NietzscheNote1887to1888#page/n13/mode/2up.

———. *Sämtliche Werke. Kritische Studienausgabe*, edited by Giorgio Colli and Mazzino Montinari. Vol. 13, *Nachgelassene Fragmente 1887–1889*. Berlin: Walter de Gruyter, 1967.

Tolstoy, Leo. *What I Believe?* Translated by Constantine Popoff. New York: Cosimo Inc., 2009.

10

Eschatology or Progress?

Vladimir Soloviev and his Criticism of St. Philaret of Moscow's Ecclesiology

Fr. Pavel Khondzinskiy

It would be no exaggeration to call the first two thirds of the nineteenth century in the Russian spiritual tradition a "Philaret era," while the last third of the century had no figure that would be equivalent to St. Philaret in theology. However, on the philosophical horizon, Vladimir Soloviev emerges as a person of a comparable scale for the *fin de siècle*. This shift in priorities, from theology to philosophy, could be a subject of a special study. At the same time, it is important to point out that Soloviev, the philosopher *par excellence*, especially by the way he thought, didn't hold himself aloof from theology. In particular, he showed interest in ecclesiological issues throughout his life, which comes as no surprise, as in his young years he set out to serve a transformation of humanity based on true Christian principles.[1]

In his ecclesiological reflections, Soloviev could not avoid a meeting with his great predecessor. His texts show that this meeting occurred, with the distant polemics with St. Philaret taking an important place. It perhaps then strange that this has not attracted researchers' attention thus far and I know of only one study on this topic, by Natalia Soukhova, the renowned contemporary scientist and expert in Russian spiritual education history.[2] However, her paper focuses only on the differences and similarities in the

---

1. See Soloviev's letter to Ekaterina Selevina, August 2, 1873, Solov'ev, *Pis'ma*, 3:88.

2. Sukhova, "Vselenskaya Tserkov' i Russkoye pravoslaviye."

positions of both authors without revealing their genesis and sense. On the contrary, I will focus on this below.

Firstly, I would say a few introductory words on Soloviev's ecclesiology in general. It can be divided into three periods: (1) "Philosophical" (*The Critique of Abstract Principles, Lectures on Divine Humanity, Three Speeches on Dostoevsky*), "Khomiakovian" (*The Spiritual Foundations of Life, The History and Future of Theocracy*), and finally "deMaistrean" (*Russian Idea, Russia and Universal Church*). Although this division is rather nominal and some of the works can be referred to "their own," as well as to a later period, nevertheless in my opinion it reflects an objective evolution of Soloviev's ideas.

In the first period, Soloviev predominantly gives a definition of the church beyond any confessional or historical context. In his speculations, he describes the church as "an ideal humankind," "the body of the Logos incarnate."[3]

In the second period, Soloviev builds on the base of theological texts a concept of church as a universal body of love. This concept is similar to the one put forward by Khomiakov, but with a few differences. Khomiakov attaches importance to natural connections and the internal unity of interaction, while Soloviev focuses on the very possibility of organic growth and development. Besides, Khomiakov moves from the church as *body* to the church as *community*, while Soloviev moves in the opposite direction, to the church as *organization*.[4]

In the end, Soloviev comes to the third, "deMaistrean," period, where repeating the arguments given by the author of *Du pape* he makes an obvious choice in favor of Rome, in the literal and figurative sense.

At the same time, we can highlight the recurring themes that are common to all periods. Firstly, it is the principle of positive development or progress, expressed for instance in *The History and Future of Theocracy*;[5] secondly, a corresponding principle of dialectical trinity of definitions, stages, functions, events, etc.[6] In the early studies, for example in the paper *Three Forces*, the dialectical trinity consists of Islam (absolute despotism), the Western world (dominance of the particular over the general), and the Slavonic world (revelation of the divine in the human)[7]; in other places it consists of three levels of social life: economic, political society, and spiritual

---

3. See Solovyov, *Lectures on Divine Humanity*, 164.

4. See Soloviev's Introduction to his *History and Future of Theocracy*, Solov'ev, *Sobraniye sochineniy*, 4:258.

5. Ibid., 4:403.

6. See, for example, a Letter to Prince Dmitriy Tsertelev, July 25, 1875, Solov'ev, *Pis'ma*, 2:227.

7. Soloviev, "Three Forces," 25.

society, that is the church itself;[8] it can also be a positive science, which deals with facts, philosophy, which deals with ideas, and theology, which deals with the absolute being[9]; or, on the contrary, as in *The Critique of Abstract Principles*, theology as a system of religious truths, philosophical and empirical studies of the free human mind, and finally theosophy that absorbs the true knowledge;[10] or finally, as in *Lectures on Divine Humanity*, the East that has kept the truth, the West that has created culture, and God-manhood that needs both.[11] Apparently, in all these examples there is a dominating spirit of Hegel's philosophical method, and if in the later works the "triune Christian idea" is analyzed at various levels, even its biblical characteristics (for example, the three services of Christ) are interpreted by the theological philosopher so that one of them becomes the final synthesis of the others.

Soloviev's first encounter with St. Philaret's ecclesiology takes place in the second, "Khomiakovian," period, in *The History and Future of Theocracy*, where he criticizes St. Philaret's ideas and contrasts them with Khomiakov's "church of Love."[12] A more detailed and consistent criticism of St. Philaret's ecclesiology (of the same point) will be given later, in *Russia and Universal Church*.

In both cases Soloviev chooses as an object of his criticism an early work by St. Philaret, *The Conversations between the One in Search and the One Confident about the Orthodoxy of the Eastern Greek and Russian Church* (1815), where the problem of the boundaries of the church takes an important place.

In his initial message, St. Philaret is based on the testimony of the word of God, "Every spirit who confesses that Jesus Christ came in the flesh is from God" (1 John 4:1–3). "By this feature both the Eastern and Western Churches are from God,"[13] but their differences mean a different "attitude to the Spirit of God."[14] This attitude is a pure or impure doctrine that correctly or not quite correctly "guides to the connection with the spirit of Christ."[15] That is why a church believing that Jesus is the Christ cannot be directly called false. It should be considered as either "purely true" or "not purely true" according to the apostle's distinction, "For we are not as many,

---

8. Solovyov, *The Philosophical Principles of Integral Knowledge*, 27.
9. Ibid., 27–28.
10. Solov'ev, *Sobraniye sochineniy*, 2:348–50.
11. Solovyov, *Lectures on Divine Humanity*, 171–72.
12. Solov'ev, *Sobraniye sochineniy*, 4:251.
13. Filaret, *Tvoreniya*, 402.
14. Ibid., 403.
15. Ibid.

which corrupt the word of God: but as of sincerity, but as of God" (2 Cor 11:17).[16]

Grace once obtained through baptizing, even it is visibly lost, does not leave a man completely. Baptizing gives "something that one does not need to get again."[17] As a result, like part of the body that is its part, if it is not cut off, whenever it is defective or weak, an individual is not completely eliminated from the body of church until the judgment of God condemns him or her to the eternal death.[18] The same is true for the churches that make up the visible body of universal church. The visible body of universal church consists not only of the healthy, but also *weak* members (1 Cor 8:10–11) that *corrupt* the word of God (1 Cor 2:17). In this body, Christ is the heart, the source of life and the head, and only he can fully know the complete composition and structure of church. "We know different parts of it and an external image that is stretched over space and time."[19] The *external* image can be described in the manner given in the book of Daniel:

> in early apostolic church, the image of the head of *fine gold* (Dan 2:32). Then, in strengthening and spreading church, resemblance to breast and arms; then, in abundant church, resemblance to the belly; and, finally, in divided and fragmented church, resemblance to thighs of brass.[20]

In this visible church, there invisibly exists "a glorious church, not having spot or wrinkle, or any such thing" (Eph 5:27), which is all glorious within (Ps 46:14)"[21] that is not visible to us completely, but professed in the Creed.

Of course, St. Philaret's concept is close to St. Augustine's ecclesiology according to which the unity of the church can be considered on two levels, as the unity of sacraments and the unity of love (*caritas*). Heresies and schisms disrupting the unity of love do not harm the sanctity of sacraments that even in the hands of schismatics belong to the church.[22] Thus, the area of sacraments is still the area of the church, and from this point of view there is no fundamental difference between an individual who unrepentantly violates the commandments of God and a schismatic or heretic. All of them fall out of the unity of love, and, consequently, of the church, but at

---

16. Ibid., 408–9.
17. Ibid., 406.
18. Ibid., 406–7.
19. Ibid.
20. Ibid.
21. Ibid.
22. See Augustinus, *De baptismo*, V, 1, 1; V, 2, 2; V, 17, 24.

the same time they can find love and with it find themselves in the church.[23] Consequently, if the unity of the church is ensured by the unity and operation of sacraments so that inside the church there may be those who do not take them to salvation as much as, on the contrary, among the ones, who are apparently separated, there may be those to whom sacraments will be salvific, apparently, St. Philaret's "church-body" with its weak, but not cut-off members, like an individual who has broken the baptismal vows and still remains a weak, but not cut-off member, is described in a similar way. The "external image" taken from the prophecies of Daniel and not contradicting the concept of "purely true church" that cannot be conquered by the gates of hell, points to the inevitable impoverishment of faith together with the last times coming, which is also quite in accordance with the Gospel prophecies (see, e.g., Luke 18:8).

Soloviev most sharply criticizes the following points of this idea. (1) St. Philaret says that the unity and the universality of the church are based on the unity of faith in Incarnation. However, this unity doesn't imply the need for a direct communication between the churches, "it is a unity based on a broad but hollow indifference."[24] This means (2) that the universal church is dead, with only its separate parts being alive. The concept suggested by the saint is "the idea of a dead church." This is confirmed by the fact that (3) St. Philaret attached to the church the image of a great idol, borrowed from the Book of Daniel, whose interpretation describes the church of our times, "in its divided and fragmentary condition," as represented by the idol's feet, where the clay and iron are mixed by human hands. "To accept this ill-omened symbol seriously," Soloviev says with pathos, "would mean the denial of the one, infallible and impregnable church of God founded to last for all generations."[25] He ironically concludes: "It must, however, be confessed that in limiting the application of this symbol to the official Greco-Russian Church the distinguished representative of that institution displayed both acumen and impartiality."[26]

Before we examine and evaluate Soloviev's criticism of this passage from *The Conversations*, we should note that he turns to St. Philaret's idea at least twice and in both cases with an obvious incorrectness.

Soloviev in *The History and Future of Theocracy* writes: "When and why did our church lose capacity for universal action? History gives an indisputable answer (it is accepted by the said Orthodox hierarch [i.e. St. Philaret]).

---

23. Ibid., IV, 3, 4; IV, 5, 6.
24. Solovyov, *Russia and the Universal Church*, 52.
25. Ibid., 53.
26. Ibid.

Since the division any universal or all-church action became impossible for us."²⁷ However, in *The Conversations*, St. Philaret does not talk about this. He says that "since Christianity was divided into two halves, which still remain unconnected, no Ecumenical Councils can take place until the general unification,"²⁸ and thus giving the Western Church to "the judgment of the Universal Church," i.e. to the future Ecumenical Council, and being deeply convinced of the rightness of the Eastern Church, he does not perform this judgment in accordance with the law of love. In other words, "universal action" is now possible neither for the East, nor for the West.

In the other case, Soloviev argues that St. Philaret sees the primacy of Peter as "clear and evident,"²⁹ and again incorrectly. The words quoted by Soloviev are taken from Philaret's *A Word on the Day of the Apostles Peter and Paul* (1825), the ultimate idea of which is the indication that the Apostolic Council was *dominating* over Peter.³⁰

Returning to *The Conversations*, we should first of all stress that Soloviev appears to intentionally ignore the similarity between Philaret's and his own concept of church. Indeed, he writes that the East and the West recognize the power of the hierarchy ascending to the apostles, and the East and the West profess Christ as the Son of God, who became man, the East and the West accept the gracious gifts of the Holy Spirit, therefore, the East and the West have a real mystic connection with the head of the church, Christ, and, consequently, as he put it in *The Great Debate and Christian Politics*, "constitute one indivisible body of Christ."³¹

Why does the unity of the church, professed by the saint and based on the unity of faith in the Savior's God-manhood and sacraments, seem to be "abstract" and appear as "the unity of indifference" to him? Firstly, because it is the Catholic Church rather than the Orthodox Church that he regards as "purely true." Secondly, this happens because the former is much more consistent with his progressive dreams of God-manhood socialization than the latter. Thirdly, this results in an absolute inadmissibility of the prophetic image used by Daniel. Soloviev could not help noticing that it was applied by the saint not to the church as a whole, but only to its "external" historical image, not to the body, but to the organization. However, he stubbornly argues that the saint depicts the *church* as a "dead body." In other words,

---

27. Solov'ev, *Sobraniye sochineniy*, 4:265; a similar place might be found in his *Russia and the Universal Church*, 47.

28. Filaret, *Tvoreniya*, 422.

29. Solovyov, *Russia and the Universal Church*, 112.

30. See Filaret, *Slova i rechi*, 2:216.

31. Solov'ev, *Sobraniye sochineniy*, 4:106.

St. Philaret's concept contradicts Soloviev's ideas in the main point, which remained important for Soloviev regardless of the direction of his research. St. Philaret's concept of the church is eschatological and does not allow an idea of church-and-social progress.

To the credit of Soloviev, it is important to highlight that at the end of his life he revised his views, at least partially. In 1896, in the famous letter to Eugène Tavernier, he points to the following provisions as to the undeniable truth of the word of God:

> 1. The Gospel shall be preached in all over the world, i.e. the Truth shall be proclaimed to the all humankind. 2. The Son of man shall find hardly any faith on the earth, in other words, in the last time true believers shall be in numerically insignificant minority, and the rest of mankind shall follow antichrist. 3. And nevertheless . . . evil shall be overcome and the faithful shall triumph.[32]

As a result, Soloviev continues, "we ought to definitely to give up the idea of the external greatness and power of theocracy as the direct and immediate aim of Christian policy."[33] However, he still believes that the minority of true believers of the last times is to unite around Rome. However, it is clear that this letter contains the program of the last work by Soloviev, *Short Story of the Anti-Christ*.

Without retelling its contents, I will only remind the reader that a change in the course of events occurs when the elder John tells the confession, which, according to St. Philaret, determines one's belonging to church ("For us the dearest thing of all in Christianity is Christ Himself"[34]); and it, in turn, becomes the reason for a separation from the false Christians following the Antichrist and a unification of the Christians retaining a living faith in Christ, and, consequently, a start of "the last genuine Ecumenical Council." Brought into the context of Philaret's *Conversations*, Soloviev's *Three Conversations*, written 85 years later, suddenly appears as a kind of an eschatological epilogue to the former, with their interconnection and similar ideas being even more striking.

We have no evidence to claim that this change in Soloviev's ideas happened under the direct influence of Philaret's concept of church, which apparently irritated Soloviev for such a long time, like a mote in the eye. However, we can see that the philosopher's position finally gets closer to

---

32. Solovyov, Letter to Eugène Tavernier, May, 1896, as quoted by Frank, "Introduction," 25.

33. Ibid., 26.

34. Solovyov, *War, Progress, and the End of History: Three Conversations*, 183–84.

the position of the saint, and a rejection of progress in favor of eschatology becomes for him a return from philosophy to true theology.

Bibliography

Augustinus Aurelius. *De baptismo contra donatistas libri septem*. Online: http://www.augustinus.it/latino/pl_43.htm.

Filaret, mitropolit. *Slova i rechi*. 5 vols. Moscow: Tipografiya A. I. Mamontova, 1873–1885.

———. *Tvoreniya*. Moscow: Otchiy dom, 1994.

Frank, Semen L. "Introduction." In *A Solovyov Anthology*, edited by Semen L. Frank, 9–31. London: SCM, 1950.

Solov'ev, Vladimir S. *Pis'ma*. 4 vols. Saint Petersburg: Obshchestvennaya Pol'za, 1908–1923.

———. *Sobraniye sochineniy*. 10 vols. Saint Petersburg: Tovarishchestvo Prosveshcheniye, 1911–1914.

Solovyev, Vladimir. *Lectures on Divine Humanity*. Translated by F. Jakim. Hudson, NY: Lindisfarne, 1995.

———. *The Philosophical Principles of Integral Knowledge*. Translated by Valeria Z. Nollan. Grand Rapids, MI: Eerdmans, 2008.

———. *Russia and the Universal Church*. Translated by Herbert Rees. London: Geoffrey Bles, The Centenary Press, 1948.

———. "Three Forces." In *Enemies from the East? V. S. Soloviev on Paganism, Asian Civilizations, and Islam*, edited and translated by Vladimir Wozniuk, 24–33. Evanston, Ill: Northwestern University Press, 2007.

———. *War, Progress, and the End of History: Three Conversations, Including a Short Story of the Anti-Christ*. Hudson, NY: Lindisfarne, 1990.

Sukhova, Nataliya "Vselenskaya Tserkov' i Russkoye pravoslaviye v trudakh svyatitelya Filareta (Drozdova) i V. S. Solov'eva." In *Materialy XXII yezhegodney bogoslovskoy konferentsii Pravoslavnogo Svyato-Tikhonovskogo Gumanitarnogo Universiteta*. Vol. 2, 334–41. Moscow: Izdatel'stvo Pravoslavnogo Svyato-Tikhonovskogo Gumanitarnogo Universiteta, 2012.

11

Christianity in the Times of Postmodernism?

A Reconstruction of Answers by Sergey Bulgakov and Nikolai Berdyaev

Katharina Anna Breckner

Postmodernism, as a *terminus technicus*, enhances a random number of individual lifestyles adding up to social life. It hints at a striking liberation of the individual. Individual lifestyle responds to individual self-actualization. Lifestyles differing from each other evolve in parallel and act in various, even contradictory, directions.

European and American postmodern societies are organized by a sort of collective rationality. This rationality defends the idea of usefulness. The rating and appraisal of life's multiple forms and expressions seek and find legitimacy by democracy and human rights, guaranteeing equal spheres of freedom and security for everybody: these spheres represent the condition of self-actualization. Postmodernity raised the ideas of democracy and human rights into absolute value whose valency stage is to some extent comparable with religious virtues. Yet, today's pseudo-belief comes down to a sort of rationalized faith in an arithmetic sum: the sum of individual liberties organizes multifaceted society. Secondly, postmodertnity denotes high speed in many respects: capitalism promoted the general increase of velocity concerning communication and all other means of transport. It permanently stimulates the increase and exchange of products: growth rate easily outnumbers imagination. Thirdly, social heterogeneity has also significantly grown. Social heterogeneity turns into a challenge, for individual self-actualization by individually creating a particular codex of life and estimation of the self—the sense of dignity—as a general rule, needs endorsement by the non-I, be it another person, a (religious) myth, or some sort of community. Rationalized belief in democracy guaranteeing personal liberties does not serve the purpose. There is no merit beyond communication on the horizontal sociological line and/or vertical line of mystical belief in personalized absolute values endorsing one's personal creativity, decisions, and endeavors. Personal and/or communication within the horizons of mystically personalized belief overcomes pure subjectivism and generates a certain objectivism of personal dignity.

Without any doubt (post-) modern societies lack confidence in Christianity's central personalized myth. As a general consciousness, Christian belief is not exactly at a high point either in Europe or the United States. Nevertheless, Christian traditions have functioned as more than just a precursor or catalyst of the (post-)modern normative self-understanding. Especially the ideas of personal dignity, self-estimation, and self-actualization take their origin in Christian values.

This essay then takes a brief look at recent discussions on the future of Christian theology and the question whether Christian belief needs to be modernized in order to amplify its impact anew on people's life at times of postmodernism. Answers on this crucial and extremely difficult question range from denial of axiological dogmatic beliefs (John Milbank, Catherine Pickstock, Graham Ward, Radical Orthodoxy) to more practical solutions in the sense of the aggiornamento (Joseph Ratzinger, Rudolf Bultmann, Karl Rahner et al.): there are proposals that a revival of "social Christianity" and/or the theological demystification of eschatology might significantly add to Christianity's attraction.

Interestingly these questions have been thoroughly debated already by Russian theologians and philosophers (Vladimir Soloviev, Nikolai Berdyaev, Sergey Bulgakov, and others) at the beginning of the twentieth century, a dramatic point in Russia's history which led to immense and sudden civilizational change. The idea of "social Christianity" along with the attempt to introduce new eschatological concepts to (ecumenical) Christianity surely represent the identifying features of Bulgakov's (1877–1944) and Berdyaev's (1874–1948) works completed under the influence of European theology.

After the Bolshevik revolution, both emigrated to Paris, the mecca of revolution, where in 1925, Bulgakov—formerly one of Russian leading Christian socialists—became the founding dean and professor of dogmatic theology at the Orthodox Theological Institute of Saint Sergius. This institute owed its existence to the collaboration of three religious networks: the Western European diocese of the Russian Orthodox Church, secondly, Russian scholars in exile, and protestant ecumenists, especially the American

Methodist clergyman and Young Men's Christian Association leader, John Mott. Initiatives for theological updates and for ecumenism in the twentieths and thirties were initially taken by the Protestant Church seeking to coordinate mission abroad. Simultaneously the social question had arisen and concerned Catholicism, Russian Orthodoxy, and Protestantism alike.

At this time Bulgakov continued to develop his lifelong issue of "Social Christianity" and/or "Christian Humanism." Bulgakov, dismissed by Russian Orthodoxy because of his "heretical" sophiology, maintained that from a metaphysical point of view the church is prior to all creaturely existence: "Creation was raised to its perfection in the Godmanhood, and the realisation of this Godmanhood is the church in the world." The church is both uncreated and created. She is the world's "*entelechia.*" Therefore, she receives "*social, historical*" in addition to "cosmic significance." "Christian life cannot be limited to an individualistic life; it is communal or social, yet not violating the principle of Christian freedom." The church's tasks hence include not only ways of personal salvation but also of the transfiguration of the world, obviously including the history of humanity, which is the "history of the church." She must embrace not only the sacramental, mystical life, but also the prophetic spirit, as a call to new activity, to new tasks, to new achievements. The church must constantly proofread and eventually reformulate its dogmatic corpus that reflects the collective religious experience of a certain time in history.[1] "Social Christianity," or which is the same, "Christian humanism" presumes the "development of all creative capacities of man" and it "may be understood as a new revelation of Christianity."[2]

Bulgakov brings the Eucharist into discussion: bread and wine, as he asserts, give benediction to the natural elements and this sacramental act should find extension to the entire domain of economic production and consumption:[3] life is the "capacity to consume the world" our bodily organs being "like doors and windows into the universe, and all that enters us through these doors and windows becomes the object of our sensual penetration and becomes in a sense part of our body.[4] Nourishment is the most vivid means of "natural communion," because it allows man to partake "in the flesh of the world."[5] It is immanent to our world, whereas the "medicine of immortality," the Eucharist meal, "nourishes immortal life, separated

---

1. Bulgakov, *Social Teaching*, 5–27. For Bulgakov's justification of "Goodmanhood" see Breckner, "A Comparative Study."
2. Bulgakov, *Social Teaching*, 19.
3. Bulgakov, *The Orthodox Church*, 168.
4. Bulgakov, *Philosophy of Economy*, 99–105.
5. Ibid., 103f.

from our life by the threshold of death and resurrection."[6] Production's and consumption's sanctification by the Eucharist would signify the sacramental embedment of human creative economic power transfiguring his economic toil nature.[7] In fact, his theology of the Eucharist postulates that the every single Eucharist act finds doubling in the bosom of the Trinitarian God. And so, man's laborious economic activity in transforming nature and God's creativity working above human power but not outside it, are wholly re-united by the Eucharist that brings benediction into the natural world.

His reinterpretation of the world as a household comprises Bulgakov's particular definition of labour. Labour is meant to elevate Creation and bring it to the promised perfection, viz. re-unite the created and the Uncreated. "Thanks to labour, there can be no subject alone, as subjective idealism would have it, nor any object alone, as materialism holds, but only their living unity, the subject-object, and only when we inspect its one or another aspect by means of methodological abstraction, do a subject and object separate out from it."[8] Economy as a constant modeling of reality, as the objectification of the "I"'s ideas, is a real bridge from the "I" into the "non-I," "from the subject to the object, their living and immediate unity that needs no proof."[9]

Instead of pleasing luxury, production—dependent on labour and sanctified by the Eucharist—would become a serious and responsible way of laborious preservation and reconstruction of life, the *common work* of the whole of humanity.[10] If Christianity is to generate "social Christianity"—whereby the church should play a vanguard role—it should confess this new impact of the Eucharist meal. Yet, "*social Christianity*" is "rather a dogmatic postulate than a completed program of life, more *prophecy* than actuality."[11]

One of most famous Russian modern prophets was Nikolai Berdyaev. He was extremely critical of the historical church and worked out a particular form of Christian existentialism that does not need the church in any respect.

> A new day is dawning for Christianity in the world. Only a form of Socialism, which unites personality and the communal principle, can satisfy Christianity . . . The true and final renaissance will probably begin in the world only after the elementary,

6. Ibid., 104.
7. Bulgakov, *The Orthodox Church*, 69 and footnote 5.
8. Bulgakov, *Philosophy*, 114.
9. Ibid., 111.
10. Bulgakov, *Social Teaching*, 23.
11. Ibid., 20.

everyday problems of human existence are solved for all peoples and nations, after bitter human need and economic slavery of man have been finally conquered.[12]

Yet, Berdyaev's main religico-philosophical concern was not so much Christianity's social perspective, but its *eschatology of salvation*. He agreed with the New-Testament *Kairos* as understood by Paul Tillich, denoting the influx of eternity into time. This is when objectification ends, viz. when

> causal connections of nature are changed into connections of spirit, which are full of meaning and purpose . . . In time everything appears as already determined and necessary . . . But a free creative act is not dominated by time . . . and belongs to a different order of existence . . . The creative act is an escape from time, it is performed in the realm of freedom.[13]

As Will Herberg correctly formulates, "personality is the coming into being of the future, it consists of creative acts. Objectivization is impersonality, the ejection of man into the world of determinism."[14]

Freedom in Berdyaev bears the features of salvation. However, the form of salvation he reasons about finds ways and means of healing during man's lifetime on earth already and not as late as after his death. Freedom in him denotes inner freedom from slavery, the slavery experienced by man because of his dependence on historical time.

Berdyaev discerns "cosmic," "historical," and "existential time." The first is based on "mathematical calculations" depending on objects beyond the range of man's immediate perception; mathematical calculations encompass the cosmic movement, the planet's motions in orbit, the change and succession of years, seasons, months, days, and hours. The symbol that best describes it is the circle. "Historical time" needs the symbol of a "line which stretches out forward into the future," for history did start at a certain point and presumably ends at another. It is embedded into the "cosmic" time[15] and it signifies the realm of what "Heidegger calls *in-der-Welt-sein*," viz. the "rule of the humdrum and commonplace, of *das Man*."[16] By contrast, "existential time" is measureless by definition, it escapes arithmetic calculations. It is as if a point, "telling of movement in depth." It is substantial—even everlasting: it is subjective by definition and thus scarcely finds an adequate externalized

---

12. Berdyaev, *The Fate of Man*, 130–31.
13. Berdyaev, *Slavery and Freedom*, 20–59, and other places.
14. Herberg, *Theologians*, 118.
15. Berdyaev, *The Beginning and the End*, 206.
16. Ibid., 154.

expression.[17] By simple logic, only in existential time man gets a hold of freedom, namely the freedom to create new personal realities, the creation of one's own salvation included. Man's creative vocation is of eschatological import., however, what is eschatology in other philosophers is the *eschaton* in Berdyaev. Eternity is, as we have seen, qualified existentially. His *telos* is supra-temporal as well as temporal. Eternity is decomposed, for while it implies an end to time that end is not limited to future as in a weak temporal teleology, but belongs to eternity-in-time.

Christianity must, therefore, revise its eschatological perspective of salvation. It must face salvation not as something in the unknown future but as something always present in potential terms. Salvation in Berdyaev comes with the Kairos, the end of objective time and the beginning of eternalness bringing forth man's co-creative powers.

His later writing *The Fate of Man in the Modern World* (1934) reflects his deep sorrow that European societies have ended in a totally proletarian status.[18] He refers to Oswald Spengler as having trenchantly distinguished between culture and civilization[19] and discussing the role of the gigantic technical progress that erases culture and melts it down to civilization. He agrees the present was in a cup for technical progress displays "cosmic power" and reduces man to an animal. The "technical epoch" is characterized by life's "dehumanization" and an idolatry to atavistic instincts, to economics, and to technical progress, as well as to many other fetishes ruling the people's life. Impersonal masses socially compose modernity, the "plebs" whose "bourgeois" members lack inner "aristocracy" dominate social life. Egotism sets political paradigms. Parliamentarian democracy comes down to a farce, for it merely serves the welfare of diverse interest groups. Modernity stands for a soulless "organised [*sic*] chaos."[20]

Berdyaev's blueprint for the world was that it should become a "spiritually joined federation," a federation of loosely associated "fraternal units." This is what he called "personalist socialism" in its political order.[21] Considering how this political order could possibly be achieved, it has to be said that in his eyes it was absolutely impossible to reformulate Christianity into a state doctrine. The "crucified truth" would have to be converted into a "doctrine of crucifying."[22] As it were, he believed in a radically new type

17. Ibid., 206.
18. Berdyaev, *The Fate of Man*, 90.
19. Berdyaev, *The Beginning and the End*, 223.
20. Berdyaev, "Man and Machine."
21. Berdyayev, "Problema khristianskogo gosudarstva," 278.
22. Ibid., 280.

of revolution. For him the true basis of life and its organizational forms are of spiritual quality and the acknowledgement of this fact leads to a change of the focus for any revolution: The "personal revolution" was proclaimed a way out of the crisis of modern times. No matter if you looked at the East or the West, it was the same "spiritual crisis." The "personal revolution" would be the consequence of man's efforts to elevate his spiritual values[23] by discovering the *eschaton* as a bearer of salvation, co-creativity, and liberty.

Bibliography

Berdyaev, Nikolai. *The Beginning and the End*. Translated by R. M. French. New York, 1957.

———. *The Fate of Man in the Modern World*. Translated by Donald A. Lowrie. London: Student Christian Movement, 1935.

———. "Man and Machine." Translated by Donald Attwater. In *The Bourgois Mind and Other Essays*, edited by Donald Attwater, 31–67. London: Sheed & Ward, 1934.

———. *Slavery and Freedom*. Translated by R. M. French. London: Maclehose, 1944.

Berdyayev, Nikolay. "Problema khristianskogo gosudarstva." *Sovremennyye Zapiski* 31 (1927) 280–306.

Breckner, Katharina. "A Comparative Study of Godmanhood (Bogochelochestvo) in Russian Philosophy. The Eighth Day in V. Solovëv, S. Bulgakov, N. Berdyaev, and S. Frank." *Rocznik Filozoficzny Ignatianum* 1 (2013) 117–53.

Bulgakov, Sergey. *The Orthodox Church*. Translated by Lydia Kesich. New York: St. Vladimir's Seminary Press, 1988.

———. *Philosophy of Economy. The World as a Household*. Translated by Catherine Evtuchov. New Haven: Yale University Press, 2000.

———. "Social Teaching in Modern Russian Orthodox Theology." In *Orthodoxy and Modern Society*, edited by Robert Bird, 5–27. New Haven, Conn.: The Variable Press, 1995.

Herberg, Will, editor. *Four Existentialist Theologians. A Reader from the Works of Jacques Maritain, Nicolas Berdyaev, Martin Buber and Paul Tillich*. New York: Doubleday, 1957.

---

23. Berdyaev, *The Fate of Man*, 83, and many other places.

12

Towards a New Understanding of Immanence and Transcendence

The Concept of Kairos in the Writings of Nikolai Berdyaev and Paul Tillich

Monika Woźniak

Rethinking the relation between transcendence and immanence could be regarded as one of the most important problems of post-secular thought. This issue was noticed by such researchers as Agata Bielik-Robson, a Polish philosopher and publicist, and Jolyon Agar, who placed emphasis on "the reflection . . . about the decline of simple immediate transcendence"[1] and "some sort of ontological non-duality."[2] The reconfiguration of these two categories should not be perceived as the return of religion in its traditional form, but rather as the enrichment of immanence by transcendent elements; transcendent *traces*. However, the stress is put here on immanence.

This context can give us an extremely significant insight into the works of two religious thinkers of the early twentieth century: Nikolai Berdyaev and Paul Tillich. Each of them introduced a philosophy of history and human activity that joins the immanent order with transcendent elements. Moreover, there is a direct link between these two thinkers—it is the category of *kairos*, which the Russian philosopher adopted from Tillich. In this article, I would like to focus mainly on Berdyaev's late works and exclude from this article his earlier concept of history described in his book *The Meaning*

---

1. Bielik-Robson, "*Deus otiosus*," 8.

2. Agar, *Post Secularism*, 47. For Agar, this ontological non-duality is distinctive not for the post-secular thought at all, but to one of its forms, so called meta-post-secularism.

of History. In this special case, Nikolai Berdyaev plays a very interesting role. Even though he is commonly associated with dualism, he is, in fact, the author of an interesting concept of time and its relation to eternity; the concept which, in my opinion, brings him nearer to post-secular thought that one would think. In Berdyaev's view "the old antithesis between the immanent and the transcendent is out of date."[3] Nevertheless, this association with dualism is not unfounded. As a matter of fact, Berdyaev developed a metaphysical system of two "worlds": *earthly*, *objective* or *natural* (also called by Berdyaev "the realm of Caesar"), and *heavenly* or *personal*—as he called it "the realm" or "kingdom" of spirit.[4] This dualism should not be understood as ontological. Berdyaev explains it in the following fragment:

> First of all, we must eliminate ontological dualism and all use of static concepts of substance. This does not mean the dualism of spirit and body, of spirit and material, which we find in academic spiritualistic tendencies. This is a question of two *conditions* of the world, corresponding to two different structures and ways of knowing, above all the dualism of freedom and necessity; inner unity and disunity and hostility, meaning and the lack of it.[5]

It is rather the opposition of two *modi* of being. Strictly speaking, it does not consist of two worlds, but rather of the reality and the false—rational depiction of it.[6] A similar thought would be found in the book *The Beginning and the End*, where Berdyaev wrote:

> One must not think of the other world, the better world which lies beyond the confines of this life in naturalistic and objectivist terms, though traditional theology has not been free from that. One must think of it above all as a change in the direction taken by the conscious mind and in its structure. One must think of it as the world of spirit, which is not another and different *nature* ... There is a dualism of modes of existence, of qualitative states in a man and in the world.[7]

To expand upon this subject, Berdyaev describes the processes of objectification and transcending. Objectification is the process in which the subject loses itself in the object, in its own product, which becomes

---

3. Berdyaev, *The Divine and the Human*, 172.

4. See Ostrowski, *Bierdiajew*, 152–53.

5. Berdyaev, *The Realm of Spirit and The Realm of Caesar*, 31.

6. See Berdyaev, *Dream and Reality*, 286; Ostrowski, *Bierdiajew*, 153; Matuszczyk, *Mikołaja Bierdiajewa koncepcja obiektywizacji*, 184–86.

7. Berdyaev, *The Beginning and the End*, 87.

something passive and depersonalized. Objectification, therefore, is enslavement and estrangement.[8] The process of transcending, on the contrary, is the way of exceeding itself for the subject, that allows it to remain in the realm of spirit. It is the communication not within the relation *subject-object*, but beyond it; it is the communication with the other subject and also with the unobjectified universe.

According to Berdyaev, this non-absolute understanding of dualism, which could be treated as the modification of Kant's dualism of *noumena* and *phenomena*, serves as the basis for the concept of history. The historical time—linear, infinite and measureable—is the objectified form of time. However, it is possible to transcend it through immersion in existential time, some kind of breakthrough in history—a glimmer of eternity. As Berdyaev points out, the time itself is the product of objectification. Then, the division between presence, past and future is irrelevant in the context of eternity. Therefore, the Kingdom of God and the realm of spirit cannot relate to the future or something expected, something to come. At the same time, the historical process is included in the eternity and absorbed by eternity, since all truly creative acts are in a sense eternal—they belong to existential time and somehow participate in eternity.

The chance to transcend the objectified time is related with creativity, because "the creative power of man as it changes the structure of consciousness, can be not only a consolidation of this world, not only a culture, but also a liberation of this world and the end of history, that is to say, the establishment of the Kingdom of God, not as a symbolic but as a real kingdom."[9] Creativity is understood in this matter as an act of freedom, involving both God and a human being. Jarosław Jakubowski, a Polish historian of philosophy, explains that according to Berdyaev, the metahistorical dimension of creativity is based on the radical novelty of each creative act. This novelty means not only that the creative person gives the world something new, his creation, but also that he creates himself by autotranscending. This is both the novelty of the creation and its author. Moreover, if the creation means something completely new and undetermined, its roots have to be transcendent.[10]

Creativity finds here its metahistorical and eschatological meaning. According to Berdyaev, true eschatology should not be the passive expectation for God to come, but the revolutionary activity of a man. It should be a rebellion against enslavement and objectification with a great sense of

---

8. Calian, *Berdyaev's Philosophy of Hope*, 116–18.
9. Berdyaev, *Slavery and Freedom*, 266.
10. Jakubowski, "Akt twórczy jako akt metahistoryczny," 177–83.

responsibility for the universe, because a man should "take all history into his own infinite subjectivity, in which the world is part of a man."[11] He refers here to Fyodorov's ideas and, although he rejects a scientific and technological understanding of eschatological creativity in Fyodorov, he regards this concept as his biggest achievement and agrees with it. It should be pointed out that Berdyaev consider human activity as *sine qua non* of The Second Coming of Jesus Christ. He is brave enough to write: "The Coming Christ will never appear to him who by his own free effort has not revealed within himself the other, the creative image of man."[12]

As we can see, there is no invincible boundary between eternity and the temporal world. The metahistorical elements, belonging to existential time, shine through historical time and break through the crust of objectification. In the aforementioned quotation, Jakubowski claims that Berdyaev is sure that a man cannot be deprived of his rooting in history, and therefore, he needs to introduce a concept of time with two dimensions: horizontal (linear and historical) and vertical (metahistorical).[13] The points of eternity are not situated beyond history, but in history i.e. within its linear development. At the same time, however, they transcend the history itself, thereby opening the realm of transcendence.

Berdyaev makes it clear that "actively creative events in existential time will have their effects not only in heaven but also on earth; they revolutionize the history."[14] Thus, the Kingdom of God should also become the transfiguration of this world. Berdyaev criticizes the obsession with individual salvation—it is just one side of the Christian truth, which concerns both the fate of an individual and world history.[15] Christians, therefore, are not allowed to escape from history but are obliged to transform it in the name of a spiritual root.

In *Slavery and Freedom*, in order to describe the relationship between time and eternity, Berdyaev uses the term *kairos*, which refers to Paul Tillich's work (who is mentioned in the book). The meaning of this term can

11. Berdyaev, *Slavery and Freedom*, 267.
12. Berdyaev, *The Meaning of the Creative Art*, 107.
13. Jakubowski, "Akt twórczy jako akt metahistoryczny," 165–66.
14. Berdyaev, *Slavery and Freedom*, 266.
15. "The fullness of Christian truth, which can be realized only in a religion of the spirit, involves the union of personal immortality with the messianic solution of the destiny of history, of the mystical idea with the prophetic idea. Both the way of spiritual life which seeks the highest in withdrawal from the destinies of the world and history and is unwilling to share in them, and on the other hand the way which pursues the same end by exclusive attention to the destinies of history, society and the world, and forsakes the personal spiritual path, both these are alike incomplete and mistaken in their exclusiveness." Berdyaev, *The Divine and the Human*, 165.

be explained as the fulfillment of time, the intrusion of existential time into cosmic or historical time,[16] the intrusion of eternity into time, "a breakthrough of one time into the other."[17] It is the moment that enters into the realm of infinity—the moment that allows contact with eternity although *kairos* is not identical with it. Berdyaev claims that *kairos* is a category of messianic and prophetic consciousness that allows to speak about historical time "out of the depth of existential time."[18]

This reference to Paul Tillich's idea came from the time when *kairos* was a central category in Tillich's philosophy, gathering up all the important themes of his religious socialism and giving name to a group of thinkers with the similar views. In his famous essay, called simply *Kairos* (1922, re-written in 1948[19]), Tillich describes the Greek distinction between *kairos* and *chronos*. The concept of *chronos* represents formal and measurable time. The word *kairos* signifies the right time, which is understood as the moment fulfilled with meaning. The general and philosophical meaning of the latter can be paraphrased as "every turning-point in history in which the eternal judges and transforms the temporal."[20] It is, therefore, the moment when the world is ripe to transform—it demands revolution, which is understood as activity towards the theonomy. Theonomy means opening for the unconditional and Tillich notes that theonomy is the time when "the conditioned is open to the unconditional without claiming to be unconditioned itself."[21] It is the saturation of all spheres of life with religious, mythical and spiritual elements.

Tillich distinguishes three *orders*: theonomy, autonomy and heteronomy. Autonomy lies in focusing on the finite, which means that it relies on immanent reason. Autonomy is not an absolute opposition to theonomy, but it appears only after the theonomous unity has been lost. Autonomy exists, deriving from the tradition of the meaning constituted by theonomy, but this tradition became exhausted and formalized with time. This process leads to a new *kairos* opening the possibility for a new theonomy. Thus

---

16. Berdyaev distinguishes between cosmic (natural and cyclic) and historical time.

17. Berdyaev, *Slavery and Freedom*, 260.

18. Ibid.

19. Because the actual influence of Tillich on Berdyaev is not the matter of my text, I have chosen the later, more mature variant of that essay. For more about the evolution of Tillich's thought, see Clayton, *The Concept*, 207–09.

20. Tillich, "*Kairos*," 47. It should be pointed out that for Berdyaev the term *kairos* is connected with every creative act and for Tillich it refers only to holistic transformations of society and cultural order.

21. Ibid.

autonomy might be considered as the principle of historical development. In opposition to both theonomy and autonomy Tillich introduces the category of heteronomy—the dominion of terror and dehumanization.

It is worth pointing out that Tillich apparently attempts to describe *kairos* in such a way that this term, without losing its prophetic dimension, was cut off from the tendency to absolutize any particular historical moment or historical process itself. From this point of view he rejects both the conservative and revolutionary forms of the absolute philosophy of history (trying to notice the soil of truth in each of them). The grounds for this protest against absolutization is the unconditional itself, the unique event of Christ's incarnation. As Tillich explains:

> In each *kairos* the "Kingdom of God is at hand," for it is a world-historical, unrepeatable, unique decision for and against the unconditional. Every *kairos* is, therefore, implicitly the universal *kairos* and an actualization of the unique *kairos*, the appearance of the Christ. But no *kairos* brings the fulfillment in time.[22]

Kairos, as Tillich understands it—as a chance and possibility of theonomy—is the category that allows him to expand philosophy of history in such a way that would not lose the tension between the conditional and unconditional, between the eternal and temporal. History gains here both horizontal and vertical dimensions.

It is clear that what results from such a concept of history is a belief in human activism. It needs to be pointed out that both Tillich and Berdyaev focus on human freedom. It is obvious for Berdyaev (one could recall the beginning of *The Divine and the Human*: "I for my part say that I have based my case upon Freedom"[23]), but for Tillich the role of freedom in historical process is of great importance too. The German thinker rejects the idea of objective laws of historical development—human consciousness plays the main role in the historical moment. *Kairos* is a possibility of a change, but the realization of this chance requires awareness of the exceptionality of this chance and is not and cannot be guaranteed. It is a moment in which the old form of social and cultural order cannot exist any longer, but it is not predetermined that the new form of life will fulfill the theonomous ideal. It is natural for any revolutionary movements to believe in progress, but it is a psychological fact, not a truth about history itself. Tillich concludes:

> A belief in progress is implied in every transforming activity. Progressivism is the philosophy of action . . . But it would be

22. Ibid.
23. Berdyaev, *The Divine and the Human*, v.

a mistake to consider the law of acting as the law of being, for there is no law of universal progress.²⁴

At this time, Tillich was convinced that the bearer of historical consciousness was, above all, the socialist movement. This aspect is covered in *Systematic Theology*, which refers to the historical events of the Second World War. "I do not doubt that the basic conceptions of religious socialism are valid . . . But I am *not* sure that the adoption of the religious-socialist principles is the possibility in any foreseeable future," he wrote.²⁵ He also described the relation between the one "Great *Kairos*" of Jesus Christ's appearance and many particular *kairoi*. Surely, the emphasis on the theme of the criterion for judging the turning point in history could be connected with the great disappointment with political changes in Germany, i.e. the reign of the Nazis.

As mentioned above, both Tillich and Berdyaev focus on human freedom. The meaning of it in the post-secular thought was stressed by Agata Bielik-Robson, who, in her aforementioned book, indicated that post-secular authors are convicted that "the constitution of a free individual, of being a subject, is derived somehow from religious norm that was formulated only on the basis of Judeo-Christianity."²⁶ According to Horkheimer, the religious element can also be treated as an impulse to social change, not as the distraction from it, because religious beliefs contain the belief in perfect justice being inevitably involved in the *praxis* of liberation.²⁷

Of course, the emphasis on emancipation is typical for authors representing the left wing of post-secular thought. In my opinion, however, it is just the right context for Berdyaev and Tillich's thought. In this article I focused on Berdyaev's late works, written at a time when he came back to socialism. The influence of Marx in his late works is important, although his attitude towards Marxism itself is ambiguous. His concept of "personalist socialism" is a concept that joins many of traditionally Marxist ideas combined with Christian and personalist value of an individual. His philosophy of creativity (and we should remember that in his late works Berdyaev also considers social transformation as one of its forms) and eschatological activity also bring him closer to thinkers on the left. This situation is much more obvious for Tillich since after the First World War he was one of the central figures of religious socialism in Germany and, moreover, in 1929 he

---

24. Tillich, "*Kairos*," 48.
25. Tillich, "Beyond Religious Socialism," 732.
26. Bielik-Robson, "*Deus otiosus*," 6.
27. See Stirk, *Max Horkheimer*, 196–98; Ott, "A critique of the ambiguity of bourgeois religion," 107–08.

became a professor at the University of Frankfurt. At the time among his friends and interlocutors were thinkers like Max Horkheimer, Leo Löwenthal and Friedrich Pollock.[28] Nevertheless, Tillich was mainly inspired by Karl Marx. His views at the time can be considered as religious reinterpretation of Marxism charted not in terms of scientific doctrine, but as the theory of the revolutionary *praxis*. He not only accepted Marx' critique of capitalism, but also the dialectics of history, the role of economy, even the idea of class struggle, and at the same time trying to work out the Christian way of understanding these categories.[29] However, after emigration he abandoned his social concerns, and the influence of Marx' philosophy became less explicit and less obvious.

Moreover, both Berdyaev and Tillich criticized the traditional form of religion. Berdyaev points out that the human image of God can be—and indeed was—objectified. Tillich's critique of church is based upon the Protestant principle:

> The Protestant principle . . . contains the divine and human protest against any absolute claim made for a relative reality, even if this claim is made by a Protestant church. The Protestant principle is the judge of every religious and cultural reality, including the religion and culture which calls itself "Protestant."[30]

Both of them reject, in the first place, the monarchical model of God separated from the creation. Both thinkers were also criticized for their anthropocentrism and heterodoxy. David Ray Griffin even wrote that "Berdyaev's position makes the goodness of God problematic."[31] Tillich's project was widely criticized among other theologians. As David H. Kelsey put it, "his non-theist doctrine of God has left him open to the charge of finally being an atheist" and his method of correlation can be suspected of translating religious belief "into the deepest convictions of the secular culture" and depriving itself of truly religious elements.[32] However, both of them did not agree with such accusations.

Halina Rarot, in her article on the Russian prefigurations of postsecular thought, claims that "everything said so far about Berdyaev's attitude to religion seems to lead to the critical conclusion that counting him among the group of philosophers anticipating modern post-secularism is

---

28. See Stenger and Stone, *Dialogues of Paul Tillich*, 174–84.
29. See T. M. O'Keefe, "Paul Tillich's Marxism," 477–86.
30. Tillich, "The Protestant Principle," 163.
31. Griffin, *God and Religion in the Postmodern World*, 38.
32. Kelsey, "Paul Tillich," 74.

somewhat unjustified."[33] In my opinion, this conclusion is closely related to the chosen context of comparison. For the Polish researcher, the main point of comparison is the relationship between science and religion—the context is rather Radical Orthodoxy than the left wing of post-secular thought (in spite of a motive of God's death, understood here in Nietzschean more than Hegelian terms). However, I am convinced that choosing the left wing of post-secular thought and, above all, the tradition of the Frankfurt School is not only more natural because of both thinkers' political views, but also allows to focus on categories which truly join them with the post-secular philosophy. These themes, in my opinion, are history and human freedom. Introducing a concept that allows one to save both vertical and horizontal dimensions of history was the main goal not only for Tillich and Berdyaev, but also for philosophers who are renowned and important for a development of post-secularism, such as Walter Benjamin. Despite all of their obvious differences, Benjamin with his messianic philosophy of history concerned with *Jetztzeit*, can be an extremely interesting background to highlight the concept of *kairos*. The philosophy of *Kairos*, on the other hand, can serve as an interesting context for Benjamin's interpretations. The attempts to show Benjamin's project in the light of Tillich's and Berdyaev's work have already been made, to name the works or Kia Lindroos[34] or Aher Biemann[35] for example.

In this article I have tried to describe the philosophy of history in Berdyaev's and Tillich's works in the light of post-secular thought. The view of the relation between transcendence and immanence in their works corresponds, in my opinion, with the concepts known from the works of post-secular writers. The role of history, freedom and activism is crucial for choosing the thinkers of the left as the context for such comparisons. It should be borne in mind, however, that the symbols of God and theology, typical for left post-secular thought—the puppet, the dwarf, the specter—are completely alien to both authors' way of thinking and this difference in attitude towards religion should not be underestimated in this discussion.

---

33. Rarot, "Russian Prefigurations of Post-Secular Thought," 24.

34. Lindroos, "Benjamin's Moment," 121. The close relation between Tillich and Benjamin was noticed also by James L. Kinneavy, "*Kairos* in Classical and Modern Rhetorical Theory," 64.

35. Biemann, *Inventing New Beginnings*, 54–55.

Bibliography

Agar, Jolyon. *Post Secularism: Transcendence and Immanence from Hegel to Bloch*. New York: Routledge, 2014.
Berdyaev, Nikolai. *The Beginning and the End*. Translated by Reginald M. French. New York: Harper Torchbook, 1957.
———. *The Divine and the Human*. Translated by Reginald M. French. London: Goeffrey Bles, 1949.
———. *Dream and Reality: An Essay in Autobiography*. Translated by Katherine Lampert. New York: Macmillan, 1951.
———. *The Meaning of the Creative Art*. Translated by Donald A. Lowrie. London: Victor Gollancz, 1955.
———. *The Realm of Spirit and the Realm of Caesar*. Translated by Donald A. Lowrie. London: Victor Gollancz, 1952.
———. *Slavery and Freedom*. Translated by Reginald M. French. London: Goeffrey Bles, 1943.
Biemann, Asher. *Inventing New Beginnings: On the Idea of Renaissance in Modern Judaism*. Redwood City: Stanford University Press, 2009.
Bielik-Robson, Agata. "*Deus otiosus*: ślad, widmo, karzeł." In *Deus otiosus. Nowoczesność w perspektywie postsekularnej*, edited by Agata Bielik-Robson and Maciej A. Sosnowski, 5–38. Warsaw: Wydawnictwo Krytyki Politycznej, 2013.
Calian, Carnegie S. *Berdyaev's Philosophy of Hope: A Contribution to Marxist-Christian Dialogue*. Leiden: E. J. Brill, 1968.
Clayton, John P. *The Concept of Correlation: Paul Tillich and the Possibility of a Mediating Theology*. Berlin: Walter de Gruyter, 1980.
Griffin, David R. *God and Religion in the Postmodern World: Essays In Postmodern Theology*. Albany: State University of New York Press, 1988.
Jakubowski, Jarosław. "Akt twórczy jako akt metahistoryczny. Koncepcja Mikołaja Bierdiajewa." *Filo-Sofija* 22/3 (2013), 165–87.
Kelsey, David H. "Paul Tillich." In *The Modern Theologians: An Introduction to Christian Theology Since 1918*, edited by David F. Ford and Rachel Muers. Hoboken: Wiley-Blackwell, 2005.
Kinneavy, James L. "*Kairos* in Classical and Modern Rhetorical Theory." In *Rhetoric and Kairos. Essays In History, Theory and* Praxis, edited by Carolyn R. Miller and Phillip Sipiora, 58–76. Albany: State University of New York Press, 2012.
Lindroos, Kia. "Benjamin's Moment." *Redescriptions. Yearbook of Political Thought and Conceptual History* 10 (2006) 115–33.
Matuszczyk, Ewa. "Mikołaja Bierdiajewa koncepcja obiektywizacji." *Archiwum Historii Filozofii i Myśli Społecznej* 43 (1998) 181–92.
O'Keefe, Terrence M. "Paul Tillich's Marxism." *Social Research* 48/3 (1981) 477–86.
Ostrowski, Andrzej. *Bierdiajew: egzystencja w perspektywie eschatologicznej*. Lublin: Wydawnictwo Uniwersytetu Marii Curie-Skłodowskiej, 1999.
Ott, Michael R. "A Critique of the Ambiguity of Bourgeois Religion: Max Horkheimer's Critical Theory of Religion." In *Religious Innovation in a Global Age: Essays on the Construction of Spirituality*, edited by George N. Lundskow, 97–116. Jefferson: McFarland, 2004.
Rarot, Halina. "Russian Prefigurations of Post-Secular Thought: Nikolai Berdyaev and Ivan Il'in." In *Overcoming the Secular: Russian Religious Philosophy and Post-*

Secularism, edited by Teresa Obolevitch and Paweł Rojek, 11–28. Krakow: The Pontifical University of John Paul II Press, 2015.

Stenger, Mary A., and Ronald H. Stone. *Dialogues of Paul Tillich*. Macon: Mercer University Press, 2002.

Stirk, Peter M. R. *Max Horkheimer: A New Interpretation*. London: Harvester Wheatsheaf, 1992.

Tillich, Paul. "Beyond Religious Socialism." *Christian Century* 66/15(1949) 732–33.

———. "*Kairos*." In *The Protestant Era*, 32–54. Translated by James L. Adam. Chicago: The University of Chicago Press, 1948.

———. "The Protestant Principle and the Proletariat Situation." In *The Protestant Era*, 161–84. Translated by James L. Adam. Chicago: The University of Chicago Press, 1948.

13

Religion in Public Life according to Nikolai Berdyaev

Halina Rarot

In one of my earlier publications I first proposed a perspective in which the philosophical and religious views of Nikolai Berdyaev, along with the countless interpretations they have seen over the last century, would be viewed as a prefiguration of the contemporary western philosophy of post-secularism.[1] One argument to support such an interpretation is the fact that his analysis of religion was conceived in an environment highly reminiscent of the postmodern (post-Enlightenment) context, i.e. one defined by a more or less apparent crisis of social humanism and post-Cartesian philosophy. And the postmodern crisis is now accompanied by the newly emerging post-secular thought or the philosophy of post-secularism.

> These terms refer . . . to the attempts at criticising [sic] or reflecting upon the aftermath of the Enlightenment and the twilight of Western secularism which commonly, albeit not exclusively, stem from the method of postmodernist deconstruction. One of the key premises of post-secularism, as formulated in particular by its most radical "right-wing" advocates, sometimes referred to as the Radical Orthodoxy (John Milbank, Philip Blond, Catherine Pickstock), is the abolition of the modern antagonism between religious and secular processes, between religion as such and the public sphere, between faith and reason.[2]

---

1. Rarot, "Russian Prefigurations of Post-Secular Thought."
2. Ibid., 11.

The second argument to support a post-secular interpretation of Berdyaev's philosophy is found in the fact that the philosopher was demonstrably committed to rethinking the problematic relationship between the religious and the secular, between faith and reason. This goal was reflected in his subsequent works, starting from his early *The New Religious Consciousness and Society* (1907), through *Philosophy of Freedom* (1911), *The Meaning of the Creative Act* (1916), *The Philosophy of Inequality* (1918), and *The Origin of Russian Communism* (1937), and ending with *The Realm of Spirit and the Realm of Caesar* (1949). Notably, Berdyaev perceived science as an alternative to religious spirituality (which might be said to be close to contemporary West-European thinking), while at the same time pioneering the belief in the necessity of unifying said opposites (in which he might have been an inspiration to post-secular thinkers).[3] The innovativeness of his approach lay in his rejection of utopian and retrospective projects, still very much alive in Russian culture, which would abandon science as an inadequate explanation of the abstraction of life, as well as the equally utopian, although in this case prospective dream of freely synthesizing philosophy, theology and empirical science into what Russian philosophy after Vladimir Soloviev refers to as "theosophy."

Berdyaev's Criticism of the Enlightenment

Berdyaev made a holistic attempt at a radical criticism or critical reflection on the consequences of the Enlightenment and the twilight of Western secularism, i.e. sentiments reminiscent of modern post-secular thought, especially in the rightist context. It was, as observed in my book *From Nihilism to Christianity*,[4] a crisis of the ideals of European culture, of everything that had until then been perceived as the very criteria of progress, i.e. the development of cognition, technology and industrialization, urbanization, democratization of social systems, development of greater personal freedoms and social equality, reduction of religiosity, and general social secularization. Humanistic Anthropology, which had laid the foundations of modernity, became more naturalistic and monistic, reducing man in the eighteenth and nineteenth centuries to a product of the society and the natural environment, thus rendering him solely from the outside while inadvertently questioning such notions as individual creativity or freedom. The self-contradictions of humanism only intensified in the nineteenth century when, in the name of progress, man began to transform societies

3. Ibid.
4. Rarot, *Od nihilizmu do chrześcijaństwa*, 227.

by rejecting freedom and individualistic aspirations. The revolt against medieval theocracy (which paved the way for modern culture and humanism), although partially justified in that it sought to secure more freedom, ultimately led to cultural secularization: freedom turned into lawlessness, human self-sufficiency beckoned self-destruction.[5] The autonomous reason of philosophy and modern science was deceived into an illusory conviction of its own power as its general relationship with nature continued to evolve. The classical cultural triad of "God, Man, and Nature" was replaced with another: "Nature, Society, and Man," but in that, the road was being paved for anti-humanism, a new definition of authority, the godless theocracy of socialism. Another factor which was destructive to the humanist concept of European culture was, in Berdyaev's opinion, the technical revolution that gave rise to the deterministic civilization of technology. It would seem to result in human beings relegated to a technologically defined world of their own design, wherein they become simply another type of machine. But technology is but one source of the dehumanization of European culture, another is the prevalence of economic and political systems of an almightily totalitarian character, which are indeed mere side effects of ubiquitous technicality.[6]

The Idea of New Religious Identity

However, the most important source of the crisis was, according to Berdyaev, the weakness of Christian religion, which not only constituted the very foundation of European culture and civilization but also provided permanent protection which shielded our spiritual independence against the designs of science and technology.[7] The said weakness of Christianity was by no means identified with the "death of God," but rather with the process of forgetting about the mystical nature of Christianity, as opposed to its historical and worldly dimensions. The nineteenth century European critics of Christianity, by then already reduced to the personal sphere in the process of secularization, could no longer see its revitalization and generally positive potential: be it revolutionary or just critical. Instead, they saw it only as poison, destructive to the natural life of an individual (Friedrich Nietzsche) or a narcotic capable of detaching people from everyday problems and relegating them to the sphere of psychotic delusions (Karl Marx).

---

5. Berdyaev, "The Problem of Man."

6. Berdyaev, "The Kingdom of God and the Kingdom of Caesar," Rarot, *Od nihilizmu do chrześcijaństwa*, 227.

7. Rarot, *Od nihilizmu do chrześcijaństwa*, 226–27.

Meanwhile, Christianity may still, in fact just as much as it did in the days of its inception, function as a positive social force capable of engaging is followers in the development of the socio-political sphere, it can once again become an existentially "hot" dimension, one that ultimately gives meaning to life. Its failure, as announced by its critics, is in Berdyaev's opinion at best a failure of sacredness or a providential collapse of only a particular civilizational and cultural form of Christianity. However, this particular symptom of crisis, i.e. distortion of a long-term equilibrium, is not synonymous with a disaster. Quite the contrary in fact: it offers a way out. It becomes possible to leave behind one era of Christianity and proceed seamlessly to another, an Era of the Holy Ghost. The very basis of Christianity is in essence suprahistorical, mystical, open to infinity. "The historic church," as observed by Berdyaev in his *Philosophy of the Free Spirit*,

> does not exhaust the fullness of the virtual, mystical, church . . . We must not forget that actualization and incarnation even of the church in history arises from the reactions of human nature, from the limitations of a mobile and dynamic consciousness, and the spiritual orientation of a man. The visible church is only the partial actualization of the invisible church . . . The visible church is the symbolization of the church invisible, the earthly hierarchy of the heavenly. But the symbol necessarily presupposes the infinity which lies beyond it.[8]

Together with other authors contributing to the movement of new religious consciousness, Berdyaev strove to bring forward a new dimension of Christianity capable of replacing the old teachings of law and redemption with the New Revelation of freedom and creation; one that would reveal the other aspect of the Suffering Christ: his Divine Power and Glory:

> The discovery of the life of God-humanity in the church springs from the Christian doctrine of the New Adam and the new spiritual race which has its origin in Christ. But the dominant school of thought in the church only recognizes the existence of the Old Adam, and the natural race of mankind; it seems to be unconscious of the fact that, in and through Christ, man is already a new creature in whom a new freedom and power are revealed.[9]

The notion of discovering a new dimension of Christianity assumed and continues to assume a form that alludes the understanding of many religious

---

8. Berdyaev, *Freedom and the Spirit*, 333–35.
9. Ibid., 342.

philosophers and Orthodox theologians—namely that of neo-Christianity, i.e. Christian modernism rooted in Orthodox tradition.[10]

From the perspective of contemporary post-secular thought, the conclusions reached by Berdyaev can be interpreted as an attempt to introduce Religion into the realm of the Enlightenment by means of a particular compromise—after all, he was forced to admit that the European revolt against medieval theocracy (which paved the way for modern culture and humanism) had been partially justified in that it sought to secure freedom as a basis of humanism. Bearing in mind that the enlightened mind will no longer accept the old, Judean, inhuman "God of punishment and vengeance,"[11] or the Christian "God of mercy, but also justice," Berdyaev proposes a concept of God consistent with the demands of the enlightened mind, a concept to reflect the oldest notion of humanism: "God of freedom and creation." The image and likeness of the thus understood God is, in this theory, a human being: a living act of freedom and creativity. The personalist in Berdyaev claims that "as an individual, a human being is determined by nature and social circumstance in which he or she exists; as a person, he/she is free and active, facing God as his own image and likeness, entering into a deep existential relationship with him."[12]

Even Berdyaev's concept of the development of European ethics stems from this newly discovered dimension of Christianity which renders it acceptable to the enlightened mind. The philosopher distinguishes three eras of moral development in the span of European history: the era of law, era of redemption and era of creation. Notably, the division is hardly chronological, the eras freely permeate and overlap with each other. The Ethics of Law (of prohibition) as provided in the Old Testament relied on the fear of God and unquestioning obedience, and as such attributed no significance to human individuality held in such high esteem modern humanism. The Ethics of Redemption found in the New Testament offered an altogether new set of moral principles. It was the ethics of merciful love: mercy was allowed to transgress particular laws in the name of charity. Its primary focus became an individual and the personal relationship between man, God and fellow human beings. Its exemplar, the personified Christ, the God-man. The third type of morality, so far adopted by only a handful of people, is a system referred to by Berdyaev as the Ethics of Creation. It does not attempt to supplant the previous types of ethics, instead, it seeks to complement and perfect them. Rather than focus on the struggle against evil, as did the

---

10. Rarot, "Modernizm i neomodernizm religijny w Rosji."
11. Bielik-Robson, "Pusty tron," 297.
12. Rarot, "Rosyjski personalizm Mikołaja Bierdiajewa," 92.

earlier patterns of moral thought, it promotes altruistic behavior and active advancement of good. Through these efforts, the freedom and complex divinity of mankind (similarity to God himself) is finally revealed.[13]

The Place of Religion in Secular Culture

This new understanding of Christian religion necessitated a revision of the difficult question of the relationship between religion and science/philosophy. Berdyaev rejected the positivist premise of the cognitive superiority of science over religion, as well as the fideistic belief in the absolute superiority of religion over science, and eventually the Enlightenment secularist concept of a radical dualism of science and faith in which the two are never allowed to coincide. It is worth pointing out that his interest in the relationship between science and religion was limited to the context of Christianity. As his personal thinking continued to evolve, Berdyaev eventually contributed to this long standing European debate by accepting a synthesis of autonomous constituents into a single, consistent entity. On the one hand, he emphasized that religious faith and scientific knowledge, i.e. the two ways in which human spirit relates to the world, are indeed focused on two opposite spectra of reality: the former aiming to reveal its invisible aspects, the latter preoccupied with the visible; faith is the freedom of accepting that which has been revealed, while scientific knowledge is the compulsion to do so.[14]

On the other hand, however, he noticed that the two approaches are perfectly complementary, together giving way to the varied conditions and needs of the irreducible human spirit. It was a departure from the typical, immature, binary view of the world that predominates in European disputes on the significance of religion and science, in favor of the more mature, dialectic perspective on the same. In this unity of opposites, he often perceived the superiority of cognition through faith over scientific knowledge. He justified said superiority by observing that: in cognition through faith one may resign one's individual, small reason preoccupied with the wisdom of the world in favor of gaining access to the great, universal Reason of Christian mystics and saints (the sole champions of the complete experience, unaffected by the demands of pragmatism). This Reason may finally encompass the entire order and sense of the world, a feat far beyond the capacity of the little reason.[15] The thinker objectively observed that autonomous philosophers were at times able to transcend the wisdom of the world, to tap

13. Volkogonova, *Berdyayev*.
14. Rarot, "Russian Prefigurations of Post-Secular Thought," 22.
15. Berdyayev, "Filosofiya svobody," Chapter 2.

into the Logos-Reason, but in his opinion they still voiced visions of realty marked with particularity. Only religious philosophers, in this case Christian thinkers, by freeing themselves from sin and vice, i.e. the sources of cognitive errors, are able to fully transcend the exclusively worldly wisdom, which is but "folly in the eyes of God."[16] But despite its evident superiority, religious faith should remain respectful of scientific knowledge which, at the present stage of development of both the world and the human spirit, must be considered the necessary good (a view he would extend to the existence of the earthly state which he deemed necessary until mankind is mature enough to finally establish the Kingdom of God).[17]

The Place of Religion in Politics

Having considered the important social dilemma of the place of religion in the realm of science/philosophy, Berdyaev proceeded to analyze another, rather painful (for secularist political philosophers) issue: the presence of religion in socio-political life. His vision of the relationship between religion and state is in principle analogous to the above mentioned concept of merging religion and science. It is the acceptance of the unity of opposites, which contemporary, post-secular language would describe in terms of reconciling Revelation and Enlightenment.[18] It is the ultimate version of his philosophy of politics, the final result of his evolutionary considerations concerning the place of religion in public life. The analyses were able to accommodate his personal aversion towards the state as an institution which is impersonal, harsh, less significant than a community or an individual human being; an institution perceived as only a singular manifestation of individual existence. His somewhat poorly developed theory of state and law required a rather lengthy justification of the existence of state. He approached it in several ways: (i) it may be a pagan, pre-Christian organization, a creation of the fallen man,[19] but it also sustains the cosmic order in a chaotic, sinful world;[20] (ii) its existence is reminiscent of the natural law; (iii) both state and power originate from religious and mystical sources and the primary function of said state is negative: it is the prevention or reduction of evil's presence in the world through the use of force, fear and Machiavellian lies.[21]

16. Rarot, "Russian Prefigurations of Post-Secular Thought," 23.
17. Ibid.
18. Bielik-Robson, "Pusty tron," 303.
19. Berdyaev, *The Destiny of Man*, 207.
20. Berdyaev, "The Kingdom of God and the Kingdom of Caesar."
21. Alyayev, "Nikolay Berdyayev i teoriya gosudarstva," 263.

Negative though it may be, this function is a necessary one as it allows the existence of religious communities that oppose it by protecting the same from the "dictate of good."

As perceived by Berdyaev, the state as such—even despite its religious genesis—is an institution devoid of spirit (it lacks God), and the diagnosis is not limited exclusively to modern times which saw the separation of the secular from the personal and religious, but extends also to pre-Christian times. By its nature, it is therefore unable to interfere with matters of the spirit: "the state can only affect the 'human shell,' it is religion that lays claim to human soul."[22] The spiritual needs of a citizen ought to be satisfied in a sphere free of politics, within a personalist community: a community of free individuals which is neither a monarchy nor democracy, neither theocracy nor oligarchy. Only in such an environment is it possible to pursue social good, as it is a community of human beings and the God-Person, with whom people collaborate in the creation of the good they seek.

This unity of the state and personalist communities is by no means a closed binary opposition, as Kant would have it. Such was the premise of the Enlightenment ideology of secularism in Europe, which ultimately led to the modern derailment of social life, often referred to as the "unwanted corollaries of modernity": the French, American and Russian revolutions as well as the Holocaust.[23] Instead, it is the unity of compromise, wherein religion (and its institutions) may at times stand in opposition to the state and its dealings, hamper the ideology of progress (particularly in modern times). In turn, the state ensures relative peace in a world inhabited by people of incompatible intensions: those loving God and those preoccupied exclusively with material goods. It also allows the performance of tasks which could not otherwise be realistically achievable. It does so by protecting personal freedom and spiritual independence within one's autonomous spiritual sphere. In other words, it is entitled to step into it in order to protect a person[24] "entirely dependent upon moral traits, whether from the love or hatred of some other man,"[25] which can also occur within a personalist community (and which necessitates the use of law and coercion).

Religion, Christianity in Berdyaev's considerations, thus becomes an element critical of the hegemony of the Enlightenment's instrumental mind. Christians are able to oppose the degeneration of the state, regardless of the actual political system, and even strive for social revolution.[26] When work-

22. Fiktus, "Religia i Kościół a komunizm," 162.
23. Bielik-Robson, "Pusty tron," 286.
24. Rarot, *Od nihilizmu do chrześcijaństwa*, 252.
25. Berdyaev, "The Philosophy of Inequality," 81.
26. Berdyayev, *Novoye religioznoye soznaniye*, 103.

ing hand in hand with the state, a religious community may offer perfection without coercion, through simple criticism. In general terms, the influence of a spiritual and mystical community (also referred to as a *sobornost'*) on the state is, in Berdyaev's opinion, "equally unpredictable and real as the impact any great mystic will have upon history. Absolute moral clarity of a community facilitating personal strength, inspiring spiritual self-discipline and protecting God's image and likeness in particular individuals, would allow it to unerringly distinguish good from evil (particularly evil masquerading as good) and would render resistance to the forces of evil in social life a viable option."[27]

In concluding so, Berdyaev heralded and anticipated the ideas Jürgen Habermas voiced in his essay *Glauben und Wissen* of 2001, which has since become fundamental for contemporary post-secular thought. Indeed, what the German philosopher is currently trying to accomplish in his post-secular considerations is to introduce European religions into the realm of the Enlightenment by treating them as elements critical of the state and its Enlightenment ideologies, he perceives their apparent irrationality as a form of deep rationality. As observed by Agata Bielik-Robson, Habermas sees in this a manifestation of the Hegelian cunning of reason, which takes advantage of oblivious religious people who seek to block their instrumental mind striving for technological advancement despite not even knowing its purpose.[28] As a Christian philosopher, Berdyaev, "despite being critical towards the ideology of the Enlightenment, accepted the fact that modern states as such could have entirely rid themselves of the transcendental religious sanction. At the same time, he could not help but consider their future in this light, concluding that they were likely to decay as progressing secularization deprives them of their inherent foundations. The same will come to pass once the western culture becomes completely bereft of its faith and belief that divine laws are imprinted onto human hearts. In other words: when the natural rights of human beings are completely replaced by statutory law dependent on something as random as parliamentary consensus."[29]

Berdyaev's vision of a secular state is one of *open secularity*, wherein religion does not interfere but rather interacts with the processes of secularization, which in turn interacts with religion. As a result, a fluid line is formed between the secular and the religious, with a significant presence of religion in the public sphere (religion constituting the creative opposition towards the state). Said concept of open secularity is consistent with its

27. Rarot, *Od nihilizmu do chrześcijaństwa*, 253.
28. Bielik-Robson, "Pusty tron," 296.
29. Rarot, *Od nihilizmu do chrześcijaństwa*, 253.

understanding of the ultimate meaning of history: the return of creation to the Creator, a universal free union of everyone and everything with God. The path towards this goal requires the social and creative involvement of Christians, who must lay the foundation for the future Kingdom of God here on Earth: "if we fail to practically implement Christian truth, we will be progressively enslaved by anti-Christian and anti-Christ values."[30] However, the critical role of Religion towards the state must be accompanied by self-awareness and maturity of Christians themselves, with the humble acceptance of their own sinfulness and imperfection. This conclusion stemmed directly from the philosopher's observations of his contemporary Christian criticism of the communist state in Russia, which was defined by hatred and entirely oblivious to Christians' own mistakes. Berdyaev would proceed to ask of them certain rather difficult questions: had they done enough to realize the Christian truth of social life? Had they made any effort to promote the brotherhood of men without the hatred and violence they now saw in the communists? Had they not accepted the role of the Orthodox Church as a tool legitimizing the dominance of the propertied classes and in doing so driving so many away from the thus distorted Christianity?[31]

The Place of Religion in Economics

An important part of social life is the question of the economic system. This particular problem, however, was unfortunately approached by Berdyaev in a somewhat fragmentary manner and barely sketched in his criticism of other solutions. This was largely due to the fact that the philosopher's interests focused predominantly on the shape of the spiritual community of Christians, sometimes referred to as communitarianism or *sobornost'*. He understood the same as a collaboration of spiritual aristocracy, equals among equals in the eyes of God, varying only in terms of individual talents and skills. Any other type of equality, including economic parity, was in his eyes little more than an empty concept or disrelish. He rarely spoke about Christians holding worldly possessions, which were in his opinion of entirely secondary importance *vis-à-vis* spiritual development: he saw them as mere tools that could either facilitate or hinder the same. His considerations were a search for a way to strike a balance between "social life, which necessitates an element of coercion, and the brotherhood of men, a genuine community, with its premise of personal freedom and the effect of

---

30. Berdyaev, "The Kingdom of God and the Kingdom of Caesar."
31. Berdyaev, *The Origin of Russian Communism*, 171.

Grace."[32] In a truly personalist community, one can no longer be a citizen, manufacturer or owner.

However, where the philosopher did comment on economic matters, his view of private ownership was generally favorable, although as a religious thinker he postulated the necessity of limiting it[33] to "functional property" for the sake of allowing asceticism and reducing carnal desires. Individual ownership of the means and tools of one's trade might help overcome the heartless attitude to work. More so, if the workers were to establish economic alliances and corporations and the principle of competition was to be replaced by the paradigm of cooperation.

The religious postulate of restraint and asceticism in terms of the possession and consumption of material goods is the most evident in his *The New Middle Ages* (1924), published in English as *The End of Our Time*, where he proceeds, among other considerations, to criticize the capitalist system:

> is there in fact so much reality, in the sense of being, ontological reality, in their stock-exchanges, banks, paper-money, monstrous manufactories, of useless things or of weapons for the destruction of life, in the ostentation of their luxury, the oratory of their politicians and men-of-law, their newspaper-journalism? Is there so much reality in the progressive increase of our insatiable wants? We see malignant endlessness everywhere, an endlessness that has a horror of solutions. The whole economic system of Capitalism is an offshoot of a devouring and overwhelming lust, of a kind that can hold sway only in a society that has deliberately renounced the Christian asceticism ... Capitalism is ... the result of a secularization of economic life, and by it the hierarchical subordination of the material to the spiritual is inverted.[34]

It is therefore hardly surprising that he perceived the communist definition of economy, wherein an individual is to serve others, the society, the state, while at the same time being provided with everything needed to survive, as closer to Christianity than the free-market economy, in which individuals are preoccupied solely with the advancement of their own economic goals, which is allegedly expected to eventually contribute to the common good, the good of the state.[35]

---

32. Ibid., 169.
33. Volkogonova, *Berdyayev*.
34. Berdyaev, *The End of Our Time*, 91–92.
35. Berdyaev, *The Origin of Russian Communism*, 187.

Conclusions

Nikolai Berdyaev's idea of new Christianity, Christianity of the Holy Ghost in which theologians, be it Orthodox or Catholic, would have rather little to say, misunderstood though it was a century ago, nowadays seems to be falling on much more receptive ears. The ultimate fate of any idea—philosophical or otherwise—is always dependent on the composition of social forces which, as demonstrated in Max Scheler's sociology of knowledge, may eventually allow it to come to pass. Modern Christianity, not just in Latin America and Africa but increasingly also in Europe, is now leaning further and further towards pentecostalism, i.e. the charismatic movement of Christianity of the Holy Spirit. Only this form of Christianity seems capable of approaching the actual economic and existential problems of the postmodern man. Moreover, advocates of rightist and centrist post-secularism alike claim that the postmodern mind is now ready to revise its assumptions concerning strict separation between Religion and Reason, and to become involved in socio-political cooperation with the so-understood Christianity and its God, presented in Enlightenment terms as the God of freedom and creation, as the Holy Ghost. As noted by Berdyaev, it will be

> the opening of a new epoch of the Spirit, which will include higher achievements of spirituality, presupposes a radical change and a new orientation in human consciousness. This will be a revolution of consciousness which hitherto has been considered as something static. The religion of the Spirit will be the religion of man's maturity, leaving behind him his childhood and adolescence.[36]

Bibliography

Alyayev, Gennadiy E. "Nikolay Berdyayev i teoriya gosudarstva." In *Metamorfozi svobodi: spadshchina Berdyaeva v suchasnomu diskursi*, 262–69. Kyiv: Parapan, 2003.

Berdyaev, Nicholas. *The Destiny of Man*. Translated by Natalie Duddington. New York: Harper and Brothers, 1960.

———. *The Divine and the Human*. Translated by Reginald Michael French. London: Geoffrey Bles, 1949.

———. *The End of Our Time*. Translated by Donald Attwater. London: Sheed & Ward, 1933.

———. *Freedom and the Spirit*. Translated by Oliver Fielding Clark. New York: Charles Scribner's Sons, 1935.

---

36. Berdyaev, *The Divine and the Human*, 222.

———. "The Kingdom of God and the Kingdom of Caesar." Online: http://www.berdyaev.com/berdiaev/berd_lib/1925_303.html.

———. *The Origin of Russian Communism*. Translated by Reginald Michael French. London: Geoffrey Bles, 1948.

———. "The Philosophy of Inequality." In N. Berdyaev. *The Philosophy of Inequality. Spirit of Russian Revolution*, 1–291. Translated by Fr. Stephen Janos. Mohrsville, PA: FRSJ Publications, 2015.

———. "The Problem of Man: Towards the Construction of a Christian Anthropology." Translated by Fr. Stephen Janos. Online: http://www.berdyaev.com/berdiaev/berd_lib/1936_408.html.

Berdyayev, Nikolay A. "Filosofiya svobody." In *Filosofiya svobody. Smysl tvorchestva*, 11–250. Moscow: Pravda, 1989.

———. *Novoye religioznoye soznaniye i obshchestvennost'*. Moscow: Kanon.

Bielik-Robson, Agata. "Pusty tron miłosierdzia. *Zemsta Boga* Gilles'a Kepela w perspektywie postsekularnej." In Gilles Kepel, *Zemsta Boga*, 279–307. Warsaw: Wydawnictwo Krytyki Politycznej, 2010.

Fiktus, Paweł. "Religia i Kościół a komunizm w myśli politycznej Mikołaja Bierdiajewa." *Studia Erasmiana Wratislaviensia* 5 (2011) 157–74.

Rarot, Halina. "Modernizm i neomodernizm religijny w Rosji." *Kultura i Wartości* 14 (2015) 145–65.

———. *Od nihilizmu do chrześcijaństwa. Historia i współczesność idei filozoficzno-religijnego przezwyciężania nihilizmu*. Lublin: Wydawnictwo UMCS, 2011.

———. "Rosyjski personalizm Mikołaja Bierdiajewa." *Kultura i Wartości* 7 (2013) 87–101.

———. "Russian Prefigurations of Post-Secular Thought: Nikolai Berdyaev and Ivan Il'in." In *Overcoming the Secular: Russian Religious Philosophy and Post-Secularism*, edited by Teresa Obolevitch and Paweł Rojek, 11–28. Krakow: The Pontifical University of John Paul II Press, 2015.

Volkogonova, Ol'ga D. *Berdyayev. Intellektual'naya biografiya*. Online: http://philosophy2.ru/library/volk/berd.html.

14

Religious Revival and Post-Secular Society according to Pavel Florensky

Nikolai Pavliuchenkov

In the history of both Western and Eastern Europe, several periods can be highlighted as falling under the concept of "religious revival." In the West this in particular includes the activities of religious orders seeking to clear church life of elements that are alien to the spirit of Christianity; in the East, among other things, the revival of this kind may include the activities of St. Sergius of Radonezh and several generations of his disciples, who have reestablished Christian life in Russia after the decline caused by the Mongol invasion. Thereafter, when it comes to Russia, we should certainly point out the middle of the nineteenth century, when first of all thanks to the works of St. Paisius Velichkovsky and the publishing activities of Optina Hermitage, lots of people rediscovered for themselves the Christian asceticism which, along with worship, in fact constitutes the very heart of religious tradition kept by the church.

But at the same time if we talk about Russia, in the beginning of the twentieth century here was a fundamentally new situation in a certain sense. Older trends associated with the search for a "mystical" church[1] now combined with the belief in an unprecedented flowering of intellectual and creative abilities. Furthermore, the more doubtless that the further progressive development of humanity was perceived, the more legitimate the question of the "old," "outdated" forms of Christianity could seem. The term

---

1. See, for example, the contraposition of "internal" and "historical" Church in the writings of Ivan Lopukhin (1756–1816). In his opinion, "external religion" and thereby the "historical" Church, "has rejected from its source, and the governance of light, which had founded it, has hidden from it," see Lopukhin, *Nekotorye cherty*, 18–19.

"new religious consciousness" introduced at the time obviously implied a certain fairly radical degree of renovation, as a result of which the vector of the religious quest itself could and should be changed. The "external" or "historical" church in Russia turned out to be in a situation where a new "religious revival" was conceived without its participation, as shown for example in the works by Dmitry Merezhkovsky and Zinaida Gippius about the organization of a "new church," or the trips of Andrei Bely to Rudolf Steiner for attending lectures and for the construction of the anthroposophic "temple." The sublime words about the christian church as the eternal cosmic "mystery of redemption" in writings of Nikolai Berdyaev could be found side by side with the naming of the "official" Orthodoxy as a "pernicious anti-Christian heresy."[2] "The church of Christ is the eternal divine-human movement,"[3] and in ordinary church life, as it is known, it was often common to severely restrict the religious aspirations of a human by a set of standard commandments: "go to church, pray to God, fulfill the commandments, do good—here is the goal of a Christian life as is."[4]

> For theologians and church dignitaries the higher spirituality was often more suspect than the sins of the body and the soul. Here, indeed, we are confronted by a very difficult problem. The church forgave the sins of the flesh, and was infinitely indulgent towards the weaknesses of the soul, but it manifested the most implacable rigor towards the temptations and pretentions of the spirit.[5]

Essentially, Vladimir Soloviev, who in this case can be rightfully considered to be the mastermind behind the religious and philosophical revival in Russia in the early twentieth century, was speaking of the same things. Never rejecting the christian church as such and, moreover, considering it as the only way of finding the full implementation of the "God-Man" process, Soloviev, however, preferred to distinguish the reality of the Universal Church and the reality of the church which exists in Russia in a specific historical form of Greek-Russian Orthodoxy. It is easy to observe that in the end it was exactly this historic church in Russia which was the addressee of the reproach actually contained in the following remarkable words of the philosopher:

---

2. Berdyayev, "Tipy religioznoy mysli," 630–32.
3. Ibid., 631.
4. Nilus, "Dukh Bozhiy," 179.
5. Berdyaev, *Freedom and the Spirit*, 29–30.

> No, there will never be and should not be a pacification for our spirit in this world. There is no, there cannot be, and there should not be such an authority which would replace our reason and conscience and which would make free research needless. The church, just like motherland, just like biblical "wife of his youth" should be our inner power of relentless movement toward eternal goal, but not spiritual pacification.[6]

The general situation of Russian society was no less remarkably expressed by Lev Lopatin, who said after the Soloviev's death in 1900:

> In the epoch when the mind of the greater majority of educated people, harassed by the contradictions in life and thought, helplessly rushed after every will-of-the-wisp, incessantly embracing new ideals as soon as the old ones ceased to satisfy it, Soloviev alone with the unbridled energy of his vigorous mind called all and sundry to the true light.[7]

Only a few years later, especially after 1905, did it become clear that in fact Soloviev in one way or another was followed by many people. In 1900 one of those people was Pavel Florensky. In the years of study at Moscow State University (1900–1904) he met with close friends and followers of the great philosopher and at the same time entered the circle of seekers of "new religious consciousness," and was also in close friendly relations with Bely.

Then something happened to Florensky and this seemed contrary to all expectations and the natural logic course of events and still surprises and attracts special attention of a number of researchers. Being brought up in a very secular, "worldly" environment, he has seen (to be more precise, he has deeply felt[8]) the futility of secular thinking and lifestyle. But at the same time, devoting himself to work for the future of religious revival, he proceeded from the revealed organic connection of the church "mystical" and the church "historical." Through the outer, not always attractive, shell of official Orthodoxy he discovered for himself a sanctity, the experience of which he shared with Bely in 1905:

> I have entered into the inner space of all shells and found myself on the other side of all drawbacks. I have discovered a life, perhaps hardly pulsating, but a life, I have certainly revealed the

---

6. Solov'yev, "Pamyati Mitskevicha," 257.

7. Lopatin, "The Philosophy of Vladimir Soloviev," 460. This article has been published first in the journal *Voprosy filosofii i psikhologii* in 1901.

8. Florenskiy, *Detyam moim*, 243–44.

holy core. And then I realized that I will never quit from where I saw it.[9]

In the correspondence of 1904–1905, Florensky and Bely, as it is known, among other things discussed the topic of a symbol, and already here one can see elements of the future symbolic ontology of Florensky. The symbol means a reality in which different levels of being are not integrally but not separately connected, are harmonically "merged" together;[10] in the most general case this means the "lower" world and the "higher" world, the visible world and the invisible world, "earth" and "heaven." In other words, it is the unity of the two worlds which one way or another are present in any religion. The highest level in relation to the lower level forms noumenal-phenomenal couple that is the essence and its effects so that the essence can be really perceived and reported to the perceiving subject through these effects. To split this couple, to "tear off" phenomenon from noumenon, is to violate the very foundations of being, to destroy its "symbolic" structure. In the philosophical system of Florensky it seems to be an unnatural act having disastrous consequences.

On a personal level, to experience this split means to touch the absolute nothingness, the pitch darkness, or the pangs of hell as described by Florensky in *The Pillar and Ground of the Truth*.[11] Ultimate evil on the Day of Judgment becomes the phenomenon without the noumenon, or an exfoliated "shell,"[12] however even before the final destination of world history "shell" can be formed and live its own illusory life.[13]

In 1905 Florensky wrote to Bely about "thousands of deficiencies" and even "exhausted" symbols that can be found in the external life of the church, but all of this, he felt that, is only the outer shell, a thick (or even "thickest") crust of dirt that covered real life, which is continuing in the holy "grain."[14] In other words, the fundamental symbol is not broken and moreover it is here that the seeds of the future spiritual revival mature.

In later works of Florensky this idea is concretized and derives its justification in a polemical term "ontologism," which in this case refers to the

---

9. Letter to Andrei Bely, July 15, 1905, Ivanova, *Pavel Florenskiy i simvolisty*, 470.

10. See "The symbol is such a substance, the energy of which being merged or, more precisely, co-melted with the energy of another more valuable in this respect substance contains the latter," Florenskiy, "U vodorazdelov mysli," 287.

11. Florensky, *The Pillar and Ground of the Truth*, 151–52.

12. Ibid., 160–62, 171, 175–76.

13. Florensky, *Iconostasis*, 55.

14. Letter to Andrei Bely, July 15, 1905, Ivanova, *Pavel Florenskiy i simvolisty*, 470.

adoption of such a reality as it is given to a human by God.[15] This is the way God created the world; this is the spiritual reality given by the Creator, which a human may clothe into the "shell" of secularization but cannot destroy or alter at will. Secularization stunned the world, but in the case of the church, from Florensky's standpoint, we are talking about the "crust" which does not (and cannot) reach the noumenal foundations. From these foundations the world continues to receive the sanctifying energy, without which the world would lose its ontological stability. Searching for sources of sanctification and the future religious revival somewhere on the side, or tearing apart within the uniform church its mystical and historical realities means the rejection of this dispensation of the world and the striving to alter it according to our own tastes. This can result in attempts to create our own spiritual reality which cannot lead to anything but a mirage, misleading the Truth seeker. Spiritual reality in this case is psychologized, and apparently for this reason religion escapes the latest researchers sui generis. Religion is reduced to psychology, and the latter rejects to find in a human even a soul as a substance and only studies the streams of mental states which a person experiences.[16]

In fact, Florensky brings to a common denominator of subjectivism not only a number of religious experiences deliberately carried out outside the historical the church (for example, secret prayer meetings in the house of Merezhkovsky,[17] spiritualism, theosophy, and others), but also some movements of thought in the Russian church that took place in the recent past (Alexei Khomiakov[18]) and in the early twentieth century (*imyaborchestvo*, Onomatoclasm). Soloviev also did not avoid the reproach of subjectivism, already from young Florensky, as can be seen, in particular, from his correspondence with Vladimir Ern.[19] It is for this reason in Sophia "meetings" and the experiences of Florensky that Soloviev did not find anything later that, in his view, could be taken as a genuine religious experience.[20]

15. "Ontologism" is "the acceptance of the reality of given by God as is, but not as created by humans," which means first of all "humility and thanksgiving." This is opposed to "immanentism" recognized by Protestantism as "an idea of humanity from itself, beyond of God, and aside from God, to recreate from nothing any reality, especially the reality of holiness—to recreate it in every sense, from the construction of concepts and ending with spiritual reality." Florenskiy, "Okolo Khomyakova," 294–95.

16. Florensky, *The Pillar and Ground of the Truth*, 129–31.

17. Letter to Dmitry Merezhkovsky, Ivanova, *Pavel Florenskiy i simvolisty*, 514–15. On creation by Merezhovsky of the "secret Church" with own service and rituals, see in particular Hippius, *Between Paris and Saint Petersburg*, 101–69.

18. Florenskiy, "Okolo Khomyakova," 305.

19. Pavlyuchenkov, "Perepiska," 219.

20. Letter to Sergey Bulgakov, Andronik, *Perepiska*, 54.

Of course, on the other hand, Florensky was not prepared to severely restrict the church by any purely external feature (e.g., formal communication with the hierarchy or the only participation in church services). If, in his opinion, even natural elements are involved "in the life of the church,"[21] the more justified is a sufficiently broad search of evidence of genuine spiritual experiences across the entire space of ascetic and mystical literature, "polite literature," fine arts and music.[22]

Florensky has not left only Soloviev, Andrei Bely[23] or other contemporary "searchers," outside of that search but also a variety of mysticism, including that of an explicitly non-Christian nature. Crucially, Florensky was sure that any search for truth which is carried out only for the sake of Truth itself inevitably leads to the christian church. In his student essay in 1906 he said:

> Only at those times there will be truly faithful sons of the church, when they will not be tied to the church and will be every minute free to mentally come down to the beginnings motives of faith, and after having so come down they will be able to go back, because *the Truth so requires*.[24]

The "Truth" we are talking about is obviously the reality of super-psychological order; it is based on the very depth of the human being, as it has been discovered by Florensky in *The Pillar and Ground of the Truth* and in his later lectures in 1918–1922. The things he said about the image of God in a human and the tasks of "theurgy" ("god-making"),[25] may be summarized in the form of the original concept of embeddedness of every person in the church. Early sophiology and later the "specific metaphysics" of Florensky only expressed this concept in different ways, leaving unchanged the very idea of symbolic (noumenal-phenomenal) connection of the mystical and external both in the church and in a human himself. At the same time, on the mystical (ideal) level, a human belongs to the church already upon its establishment as the "image of God."[26]

The whole drama of the breaking away of a human from the church, or what is the same, from the noumenal foundations of its existence, takes

---

21. Florenskiy, "Iz bogoslovskogo naslediya," 200.
22. Florenskiy, "Dogmatizm," 459–60.
23. Florenskiy, "Spiritizm," 130.
24. Florenskiy, "Dogmatizm," 460.
25. "Those who reject theurgy reject from themselves," Florenskiy, "Iz bogoslovskogo naslediya," 107.
26. For an attempt of theological examination of this concept see Pavlyuchenkov, *Religiozno-filosofskoye naslediye*, 190–213.

place in the empirical world where both the sanctity of the church and the sanctity of a human are hidden behind the "shell."[27] Images essential for understanding of the thought of Florensky give us a sensual, empirical world as the "most forward" plane or sphere of universe, which must abandon its self-affirmation and give itself to another, deeper, being. Then it will become a genuine symbol, "bearer of another world," and, having become transparent to the higher being, will acquire properties of the fury and effulgence.[28] On the contrary, affirmation of empirical being as such converts its transparent shell into light-tight "crust." And this is true at the level of each individual, which, from the point of view of Florensky, has a self-conscious and intuitive personality in the empiricism.

"De-consecration" and secularization in this view are only special cases of a more profound phenomenon, namely the attempt of a human self to assert itself in the sensual world. This is the way in which the "shell" is formed and hence the only basis on which all the processes of religious revival should be built, becomes apparent. This is, first and foremost, a self-abnegation, a sacrificing of time, "planar" interests in the sensual world for the sake of deepening of reality, in which the sensual world will "return" to the giver in its full-valued, transfigured form. The ideal, which correlates with sacrifice, has always been one and the same for both the early and late Florensky.

> By different paths and from different slopes we climbed, but came together on the same top in a higher principle—Christ. Now do not we care about our paths, perhaps not direct and uncomfortable. Now the essence of our worldview is Christology; of Christ we can deduce, on Christ we can build on, in Him confide, by Him unite and live in Him.[29]

After nearly twenty years in Soviet Russia Florensky stressed that in an environment where "various phases of human activity are dropped from the religious system,"[30] all Christians must be united around a common value, which is Christ, and make this value the main value of their lives. "No sphere of life, art, philosophy, science, politics, economics, etc., can be considered a self-sufficient substance."[31]

---

27. Florenskiy, *Radost' naveki*, 4–6.

28. Florenskiy, "Empireya i empiriya," 401–02.

29. Unsent letter to Valery Bryusov, end of 1904, Ivanova, *Pavel Florenskiy i simvolisty*, 527.

30. Florensky, "Christianity and Culture," 422.

31. Ibid., 425.

> Belief in God does not permit any belief in a self-contained world and does not conceive of the world as a "noumenon" but as a "phenomenon". If we have at least a spark of faith in Christ we cannot but admit that "the fashion of this world passeth away" and that it changes through the power of Christ into the image of Christ.[32]

At the start of the twenties, Florensky believed that the epoch of so called "New time" with all its secular, humanist and atheist features, had entered its final stage. But Christianity faces these changes in a decomposed form, and the main reason for this is the loss of Christ as the supreme value of their lives by Christians. Exactly this thing in the ontology of Florensky ultimately means a threat of breaking ties within the symbol and the closure of the phenomenon to itself, which, in turn, forms a "crust" and a "shell." Thinking of the "historical" Orthodox Church as the most adequate and complete expression of the essence of religion as such, Florensky, has first of all acknowledged here the symptoms of spiritual disease common to all Christians. In 1907 he wrote:

> Now the situation is too bad. We are talking not about the political situation, which can always be corrected, but about the more important religious situation, which may appear to be irreparable... Already in the next storm we risk to sink. And the storm is already coming to us.[33]

According to Florensky, the rectification of the situation, "inventorying our fleet and careful inspecting our ships" in particular was meant to show, through the collecting evidences of the experiences of believers gained from church sacraments, that "Christianity is not archeology, but real life, ever evolving within the whole body of mankind."[34]

In 1909 Florensky wrote about the over-reliance of Russian Orthodoxy on empirical conditions for the existence of the church. As a consequence of this dependence the state of Orthodoxy in Russia follows the state of centuries-old "orthodox way of life." Florensky wrote:

> Having ruined Orthodox way of life, reform of Peter the Great dealt a severe blow to Orthodoxy... The results of the second historical strike on Orthodoxy, the revolution, still cannot be assessed. Anyway, the revolution has reinforced the decline and decay of the Orthodox way of life, and therefore the Orthodoxy,

---

32. Ibid.
33. Florenskiy, "Voprosy religioznogo samopoznaniya," 424.
34. Ibid., 423.

which have been for a long time committed by capitalism, cities and factories. No matter how slowly cultural (not political) history moves—orthodoxy is now in the proximity of some limit, where it should either completely decay, or to reborn, having first changed.[35]

From other works of Florensky it becomes clear that the "decay," in his opinion, may and will affect only everything superficial, everything that hides the sanctity of the church. In his lecture on November 4, 1921, in response to private questions, Florensky expressed his confidence that "the Russian church will withstand in a certain minority, will be released onto a right road, but through even greater suffering and shocks." But before that, "there shall to be the greatest collapse of church life, decay into many individual flows, all of which can be heretical and not canonical."[36] Having stated the immutability of "absolutely valuable layer" of church life, comprised in dogmas, sacraments and canons, Florensky, however, pointed out the absolutely unsatisfactory state of affairs in respect of those things in which "spirituality is embodied" within church life. For example: "Six days we live aside, and on the seventh day we come to a church for two-three hours and leave it again. We don't live for church, but only sometimes visit it"; "Everything belongs to non-church culture. In essence everyone, even religious people, are positivists"; "We are like the owners of a coffer with valuables, the key from which is lost," etc.[37]

In view of the foregoing point of view of this Russian thinker, who dedicated his entire life to the service of the church, the true meaning of prediction which remained recorded in his work written in 1933 in Butyrskaya prison becomes clear.

> The Orthodox Church in its modern form cannot exist and will ultimately inevitably decay; both the support of the church and the fight against it will result in the strengthening of the foundations, for which time has come to go into the past, and at the same time will delay the growth of young shoots that will grow where they are less expected . . . When religion is gone, then yearning will come. This will not be an old religion, but a cry of hungry spirit . . . This will happen 10–15 years later, and until then there shall be a pause, emptiness and silence.[38]

---

35. Florenskiy, "Pravoslaviye," 188.
36. Florenskiy, "U vodorazdelov mysli," 275.
37. Ibid., 275–77.
38. Florenskiy, "Predpolagayemoye gosudarstvennoye ustroystvo," 19–20.

Essentially, this is one of the most striking pieces of evidence of Florensky's foresight of the trends in public opinion which today is called "post-secular revolution." Based on his philosophical and theological-anthropological concepts, the Russian thinker was convinced that society cannot exist without religion, the highest expression of which is Christianity. Florensky considered the existing gap between religion and the main areas of human activity and human knowledge as violence against human nature and talked about it in the environment of progressive militant atheism in Russia. He expected the inevitable actualization of the ontological needs of humanity in religion and a religious cult, and was convinced that the post-secular society would declare Christ as the main aim. Thereby society would secure genuine progress in all areas of its activities, gradually approaching the realization of the ideal of "integral knowledge." Florensky dedicated his life to the movement toward this ideal.

Bibliography

Andronik (Trubachev), igumen, editor. *Perepiska svyashchennika P. A. Florenskogo so svyashchennikom S. N. Bulgakovym*. Tomsk: Vodoley, 2001.

Berdyaev, Nicholas. *Freedom and the Spirit*. Translated by Oliver Fielding Clark. New York: Charles Scribner's Sons, 1935.

Berdyayev, Nikolai A. "Tipy religioznoy mysli v Rossii." In *Sobraniye Sochineniy*. Vol. 3, 620–51. Paris: YMCA, 1989.

Florenskiy Pavel. *Detyam moim. Vospominaniya proshlykh dney*. Moscow: Moskovskiy rabochiy, 1992.

———."Dogmatizm i dogmatika." In *Khristianstvo i kul'tura*, 443–64. Moscow: Folio, 2001.

———. "Empireya i empiriya." In *Khristianstvo i kul'tura*, 369–420. Moscow: Folio, 2001.

———."Iz bogoslovskogo naslediya." *Bogoslovskiye trudy* 17 (1977) 88–242.

———."Okolo Khomyakova." In *Sochineniya v chetyrekh tomakh*. Vol. 2, 278–336. Moscow: Mysl', 1996.

———."Pravoslaviye." In *Istoriya religii*, edited by Aleksandr V. El'chaninov et al., 161–87. Moscow: Pol'za, 1909.

———. *Predpolagayemoye gosudarstvennoye ustroystvo v budushchem*. Moscow: Gorodets, 2009.

———. *Radost' naveki*. Sergiyev Posad: Izdatel'stvo Sv. Troitse-Sergiyevoy Lavry, 1907.

———."Spiritizm kak antikhristianstvo." In *Sochineniya chetyrekh tomakh*. Vol. 1, 129–45. Moscow: Mysl', 1994.

———."U vodorazdelov mysli." In *Sochineniya chetyrekh tomakh*. Vol. 2, 17–446. Moscow: Mysl', 1990.

———. "Voprosy religioznogo samopoznaniya." In *Khristianstvo i kul'tura*, 421–42. Moscow: Folio, 2001.

Florensky, Pavel. "Christianity and Culture." *The Pilgrim. A Review of Christians Politics and Religion* 4 (1924) 421–37.

———. *Iconostasis*. Translated by Donald Sheenan and Olga Andrejev. Crestwood, NY: St. Vladimir's Seminary Press, 1996.

———. *The Pillar and Ground of the Truth: An Essay in Orthodox Theodicy in Twelve Letters*. Translated by Boris Jakim. Princeton: Princeton University Press, 2004.

Hippius, Zinaida. *Between Paris and Saint Petersburg: Selected Diaries*. Translated by Temira Pachmuss. Urbana: University of Illinois Press, 1975.

Ivanova, Evgeniya V., editor. *Pavel Florenskiy i simvolisty*. Moscow: Yazyki Slavyanskoy Kul'tury, 2004.

Lopatin, Lev M. "The Philosophy of Vladimir Soloviev." *Mind* 25/100 (1916) 425–60.

Lopukhin, Ivan V. *Nekotorye cherty o vnutrenney Tserkvi*. Saint Petersburg, 1798.

Nilus, Sergey. "Dukh Bozhiy, yavno pochivshiy na prep. Serafime Sarovskom v besede ego o tseli khristianskoy zhizni." In *Velikoye v malom*, 171–212. Sergiyev Posad: Izdatel'stvo Sv. Troitse-Sergiyevoy Lavry, 1992.

Pavlyuchenkov, Nikolay N. "Perepiska P. A. Florenskogo i V. F. Erna." In *Russkoye bogosloviye: issledovaniya i materialy*, 199–231. Moscow: Izdatel'stvo Pravoslavnogo Svyato-Tikhonovskogo Gumanitarnogo Universiteta, 2014.

———. *Religiozno-filosofskoye naslediye svyashchennika Pavla Florenskogo. Antropologicheskiy aspekt*. Moscow: Izdatel'stvo Pravoslavnogo Svyato-Tikhonovskogo Gumanitarnogo Universiteta, 2012.

Solov'yev, Vladimir S. "Pamyati Mitskevicha." In *Sobraniye sochineniy*. Vol. 9, 251–63. Saint Petersburg: Tovarishchestvo Prosveshcheniye, 1911–1914.

15

The Philosophy of Culture of Semen Frank and its Significance for the Post-Secular World[1]

Teresa Obolevitch

To begin with, let us put the expressive observation, according to which

> The idea of crisis of religion stems from the classical sociological division between pre-modern religious traditional societies and modern secular ones . . . Secularization becomes a stand-in category for modernization, more generally, thus, forging a synonymous relation between the two terms . . . However, this assumption of a "great divide" between the religious and secular ages has been viewed as controversial or even false on both theoretical and empirical grounds.[2]

Nowadays the suggestion that a border between "the religious" and "the secular" realms or epochs is not so clear and distinct as it was believed has grown into a well-established fact. The notion of "post-secular" includes many meanings, such as a renewed interest in the spiritual life, a relaxation of the secular suspicion towards spiritual questions, etc.[3] In this context "post-secularism" does not mean just a return to "pre-secularism," but an awareness that "that all thought is in some way theological"[4] or religious.

---

1. This publication is a result of research generously supported by a grant from the National Science Center, Poland, No. 2014/15/B/HS1/01620.

2. Rundell, "Multiple Modernities, Sacredness, and the Democratic Imaginary," 25–26.

3. See Dalferth, "Post-Secular Society," 320–21.

4. Mrówczyński-Van Allen and Montiel, "Aspects of the Russian Tradition," 15.

The debate on post-secularism has brought together many famous contemporary philosophers and theologians from all over the world. Russian religious thinkers of the first half of the twentieth century delivered the great example of discourse with a secular oriented society, revealing the hidden spiritual character of human life.

In the present article I will consider the concept of religious culture (which can be considered as a "post-secular" in the aforementioned sense) of Semen Frank (1877–1950) and analyze its significance for contemporary reflection on post-secularism. As long as the challenge of aggressive secularization concerns all Christians of different denominations,[5] the heritage of the outstanding Orthodox philosopher of the twentieth century can deliver fresh inspiration in facing this process and in the dialogue between churches.

The Spiritual Foundation of Human Life

Semen Frank was deservedly called "the most outstanding among Russian philosophers generally."[6] Born into a Jewish family and having confessed nihilism and Marxism in his youth, he took a long way through philosophical and spiritual soul-searching which was to be crowned with his conversion to Christianity at the age of thirty-five.

Since his first publications after conversion Frank maintained a keen interest in the problems of culture and the religious foundations of human life. These questions were of a particular importance at a time which saw the Russian Revolution, various civil wars and World War II. Frank himself experienced the totalitarian regime[7] and the progressing secularization of post-revolutionary and post-war society. Some Russian thinkers believed that situation can partially be traced back to the modernist tendency of the first decades of the twentieth century and which—according to Fr. Georges Florovsky—"has never been solved, or even visualized, *theologically*, and it still with us."[8]

In that context Frank reflected on the decline of Christian culture both in Russia and on the West and it was described by him as follows:

---

5. See Pabst and Schneider, "Transfiguring the World through the Word," 2.

6. Zenkovsky, *A History of Russian Philosophy*, 853, cf. Zenkovsky, "S. L. Frank," 562.

7. See Luks, "Semen Lyudvigovich Frank o totalitarnykh soblaznakh XX veka."

8. Florovsky, Letter to Theodore Hesburgh, 2.

> That Christian Europe, the site of the highest spiritual culture yet known to man, became the arena an unspeakably cruel mutual mass destruction—to call it bestiality would be an affront to the animal world—of this the whole of Christian Europe is guilty beyond any doubt . . . Christendom has had a terrible lesson. In its secularised [sic] state it had lost its conscience and had begun to think that politics and life on earth in general can be put right satisfactorily by means of "enlightened egotism" and that Christian morality is at its best a kind of extra accessory for human souls in their intimate individual existence.[9]

Faith in God was replaced with exclusive faith in man and his dignity. Subsequently, "secular humanism became more and more a pseudo-religious faith" which "lacks religious or metaphysical ground."[10] At the same time, Frank maintained that this sorrowful state of affairs had not destroyed the deepest foundation of man created in the image and likeness of God. As the Russian thinker put it, "holiness turns out to be weak and powerless in the world, *but it does not therefore stop being holiness.*"[11] As a consequence, not only does an individual human entity, retain their sacral dimension despite the numerous attempts to suppress any manifestations of the inner religious component (that is, concerning the relationship between the Creator and creation), but so also does the whole of society and culture. To put it differently, "*every* society, even the most secularized, has a 'theocratic' basis."[12]

Was Frank too optimistic? The answer is clear: no. We cannot describe the Russian philosopher as utopian or naïve. Moreover, it was Frank who warned about the heresy of utopianism and "the idolatry of culture,"[13] that is its crisis. Considering the imperishable endurance of the spiritual foundation of human life, Frank apparently referred to the Christian tradition and determined his own stand as "Christian realism" which is *via media* between utopianism and the cynic, materialistic "real politics."[14] In the book entitled *The Light Shineth in Darkness* written during World War II and published in 1949, Frank noted the following words:

9. Frank, "Christian Conscience and Politics," 582.
10. Frank, *The Light Shineth in Darkness*, 23, 30; cf. ibid., 187.
11. Ibid., 32.
12. Svoboda, "Semën Frank's Expressivist Humanism," 220.
13. Frank, "Krusheniye kumirov," 174–91, cf. Porus, "S. L. Frank: antinomii dukha," 129–30.
14. See Frank, *The Light Shineth in Darkness*, 219, 235, cf. Nevleva, *Filosofiya kul'tury S. L. Franka*, 91; Aliaiev, "A Discussion on Christian Socialism," 137–38; Boobbyer, "A Russian Version of Christian Realism."

> The makeup of religious experience, i.e., the perception of the reality of Holiness, also includes the *immediate experience* that this Holiness is an invincible, all-conquering force, i.e., that its *supremacy* signifies its inner, *immanent* all-powerfulness. This experience is so immediate, so self-evident to our "heart" that, insofar as we really have this experience, it cannot be shaken by any "facts," by any empirical truths. Let the problem of theodicy remain involved, let it be the case that we are unable to understand how the metaphysical all-powerfulness of holiness is compatible with the empirical lordship of evil—this contradiction shakes the certainty of religious experience as little as the certainty of any empirical fact is shaken by our intellectual inability to harmonize it with other known facts.[15]

The same can be said about the observable presence of secularizing forces in the world. Furthermore, all the claims of modern humanism stem from the divine origin of man, even though this fact is currently neglected or ignored. In Frank's opinion, the fault for this negligence is partly on the side of Christianity itself which over the course of history emphasized the insignificance and sinfulness of man. Secular humanism was just a reaction to this approach, hence, the post-war collapse of modernist idea of man appeared as a challenge to restoring the primordial, metaphysical and religious foundation of anthropology and society as a whole. In his early work entitled *The Man's Soul* (1917) Frank wrote:

> For whatever may concretely constitute the way out from the difficult crisis we are experiencing, there is no question that the only way to this "way out" is a raising of the spiritual level of our culture, a deepening of the plane of discussion of all vital questions, and the overcoming of all ignorance and barbarism.[16]

The attempts to increase the spiritual and moral maturity of mankind should be accompanied by the awareness of "the presence of something *mystical* in even the most prosaic, secularized, 'worldly' social phenomenon."[17] Insofar as the concealed existence of the transcendental dimension of reality, Frank stressed that it is impossible to delineate a clear border between "the religious" and "the secular" spheres of human life and activity, i.e., between

---

15. Frank, *The Light Shineth in Darkness*, 43. According to Frank the fact of the existence of evil is a mystery which cannot be solved: "to 'explain' evil would be 'ground' it and therefore to 'justify' it." Frank, *The Unknowable*, 279.

16. Frank, *Man's Soul*, xxxiii. See Akulich, "Metodologicheskie osnovaniya filosofii kul'tury S. L. Franka."

17. Frank, *The Spiritual Foundations*, 80.

"the domain of prayer, contemplation, participation in the liturgy" and "the domain of economic, social, and state activity, and scientific, artistic, and cultural creativity," between "the church" and "the 'worldly' part."[18] Such a distinction, typical also for contemporary society,[19] was termed by Frank "double-bookkeeping."[20] In his opinion, this attitude was in opposition to the appropriate content of the Gospel and caused secularism on the one hand and clericalism on the other. A true Christian "cannot be a 'layman' in the strict and precise sense, for he belongs not to the world, but to Christ and God."[21] Therefore, the so-called religious life of man cannot be treated simply as his private affair, just one among many other spheres of human person. On the contrary, it consists of "his very being,"[22] since

> the light of Christ's truth shines or ought to shine through the whole of human life and culture . . . In all secular departments of his life man is a member of the mystical church in so far as he participates in Christ's truth.[23]

Hence, also the church cannot be considered as the peculiar entity or power of social life. As reported by Frank, the church

> appears to be such only from outside, i.e., when it is perceived by a consciousness that is directed at the objective world and is not inwardly rooted in the reality of the church. In its inner essence, the church is the potency in this world of the kingdom of God, in which God is "all in all."[24]

These statements should raise the question of whether the Russian thinker, accentuating the indestructible saturation of sacral and lay matters, was a sort of a "religious fundamentalist." In order to prevent such a possible

---

18. See Frank, *The Light Shineth in Darkness*, 141.

19. See Ziebertz and Riegel, "Europe: A Post-Secular Society?," 298, 303; Calhoun, "Time, World, and Secularism?," 351.

20. See Frank, *The Light Shineth in Darkness*, 148; Frank, "Religiya i nauka v sovremennom soznanii," 146.

21. Frank, *The Light Shineth in Darkness*, 142. Frank wrote: "It is characteristic of Russian philosophy and of all of Russian thought that its outstanding representatives did not regard man's spiritual life simply as a special sphere of the world of phenomena, the domain of the subjective, or as an appendage or epiphenomenon of the external world. On the contrary, they always saw it as a special world of its own, as a unique reality, which in its depths is intermeshed with cosmic and divine being." Frank, "Essence and Leading Themes," 42–43.

22. Frank, *The Light Shineth in Darkness*, 144.

23. Frank, *God with Us*, 250.

24. Frank, *The Light Shineth in Darkness*, 144.

misunderstanding, one has to specify that Frank conducted his considerations about the spiritual dimension of man and society on the basis of his metaphysical view, which was a common element of the whole of Russian philosophy of the Silver Age, namely, the concept of all-unity (*resp.* total-unity). It is impossible to comprehend the philosophy of culture of Frank without taking into account his ontological investigations and thus in the next part I will present some of the most crucial points of all-unity.

All-Unity as a Justification of the Spiritual Nature of Reality

In a nutshell, all-unity implies the inward bond of all beings, both visible and invisible, the empirical and the transcendental, the creation and the Creator. Using the words of Sergey Khoruzhy, "All-unity is a category of ontology, designating the principle of the internal form of the perfect unity of the many, in accordance with which all elements of the many are identical with one another and identical with the whole but at the same time do not merge into an indifferentiable and total unity but rather form a special polyphonic structure."[25]

All-unity, which is described in the social context as *Sobornost'* or "togetherness," "the unity of we" (which consists of the inner essence or "soul" of society[26]) supposing the unity between each individual being and God who is its genuine "motherland." For this reason Frank determined his own position and the whole of Christianity as panentheism, i.e., "the recognition of *the rootedness of man and the world* (in their primordial deep essence) *in God*, the immanent presence of Divine powers, of the energy of the Divine essence, in creation itself."[27] In his letter to the prominent Swiss psychiatrist, Ludwig Binswanger, Frank expressed his opinion according to which every empirical being belongs to the kingdom of Spirit (*Geisterreich*).[28] He regretted that all German philosophy after Hegel, Schelling and Baader had suffered from an anti-religious complex. The only remedy for it was the rebuilding of the metaphysical foundations of anthropological and social reflection, since "the human in man is the Divino-human" and "anthropology in its essence is theo-anthropology." Holiness (*das Heilige*) is the root of

---

25. Khoruzhy, "The Idea of Total-Unity," 33.

26. See Slesinski, "The Spiritual Foundations of Society," 172; Ehlen, "Chto svyazyvayet obshchestvo v samoy glubine?"

27. Frank, *The Light Shineth in Darkness*, 188. Cf. Frank, *Reality and Man*, 112–13; Frank, "Contemporary Russian Philosophy," 8.

28. Frank, Letter to Ludwig Binswanger, 337.

the individual existence (*Dasein*).²⁹ During World War II Frank, who was forced to hide from the Nazis in the French forests, wrote in his philosophical diary:

> What can philosophy teach religion? It can show that man has reason to *trust* the primordial ground of being, to be aware of his *consanguinity* with it.³⁰

Man is related with God, and this is the ultimate foundation of religion. In other words, religion is not just a temporary, purely human investigation, but the ontological fact of the whole of reality including culture.

The Task of Christian Politics

In view of the inner connection between God and man, the latter is obliged to manifest his divine origin in the empirical world. It concerns, first and foremost, the duty of personal moral self-education and perfecting. At the same time, individual perfection is equivalent to caring for the other members of society. As stated in Frank, "From the general moral principle according to which every man (owing to the total unity of spiritual-moral being) is responsible for the fate of all people" stems

> the obligation, as one of its secondary, derivative tasks, to *creatively christianize* the general conditions of life, to reform these conditions in the direction of their maximal agreement with the Christian truth. In brief, Christianity must implement *Christian politics*.³¹

Yet again, one should pose a question: is the notion of a "Christian politics" correct or not? Is Christian politics possible in a secular society? In his *The Light Shineth in Darkness* Frank explained that Christian politics is nothing but politics of love, that is Christian life; to be more precise, the process of the Christianization of life. Christian politics is not something external towards the individual entity or society, but the inner mode of existence. Consequently, "in Christian activity commands and prohibitions are merely an *ultima ratio* or, so to speak, emergency measures, justifiable only when freedom is an insufficient protection against evil."³²

---

29. Ibid., 340.
30. Frank, "Mysli v strashnyye dni," 354. Cf. "Razmyshleniya S. L. Franka, zapisannyye T. S. Frank," 234.
31. Frank, *The Light Shineth in Darkness*, 220.
32. Frank, *God with Us*, 274.

Various domains of human life are permeated by the immanent presence of God as all-unity. So-called "Christian family," "Christian economic and social order," "a Christian attitude towards property," etc. are just temporary, earthly appearance of the Kingdom of God. In Frank's opinion, the whole of reality, including social being, is "mystical" in essence:

> The political state is mystical . . . The "law" is mystical: we obey it and it commands us coldly and pitilessly . . . The family and marriage are mystical: in these unions persons appears to be subordinate to higher forces that emanate from the profound depths of their inner being and unite them. Even "public opinion," customs and fashions are mystical, despite the fact that we clearly see their "human, all-too-human" origin and often feel it our duty to despise them.[33]

This mystical character of different spheres of culture does not mean that all of them always remain a divine nature, since in reality there also exist the forces of evil, nevertheless, it is impossible to deny the transcendental, supratemporal dimension of society and reduce the latter to human or merely secular factors. Therefore, one should develop and express the ontologico-religious ground in ordinary, everyday life, especially for the sake of the destructive powers. It means that Christians have to care not so much about the external order, but rather about their struggle with sinful tendencies and temptations. In Frank's words,

> The task of externally and deliberately protecting life from evil by compulsory organization is so urgent and imperative that in pursuing it man is apt to forget his other and more fundamental task of truly overcoming the actual source of the trouble—sin . . . The only thing that the law and the state can and may do is to create the most favourable [sic] external . . . conditions for man's free striving after moral improvement and the development of the divine aspect of his being.[34]

To be Christian means to be aware of one's own transcendental provenance in spite of the observable suppression of the role of religion.

The aforementioned statement of Frank, according to which culture is not just "Christian," but "mystical" leads us to the assumption that the Russian thinker considered Christianity as an outward historical (although very privileged!) manifestation of the primordial bond between God and man, or religion as such. Indeed, Frank was extremely open towards other,

---

33. Frank, *The Spiritual Foundations*, 80–81.
34. Frank, *Reality and Man*, 186–87.

non-Christian religious traditions. He taught about "visible" and "invisible," or ontological church that is wider than the empirical fact of Christianity. The invisible church contains, "first of all, the Old Testament church, the divinely chosen nation of Israel," but also "Islam and Buddhism, and even pagan faiths, possesses, in the final analysis, the nucleus of the true faith."[35] Hence, any external ecumenical or interfaith dialogue is possible due to metaphysical foundations of the church.[36] As Frank explained, this "profound, mystical concept of the church" draws not on the human agreement, but the divino-human unity—"a unity arising from the rootedness of human life in Holiness, in God."[37] Also in his early works Frank defended the position of "religious humanism" which combines religiosity with spiritual latitude and freedom.[38] Every man and the whole of society are necessarily grounded in the invisible church,[39] or *Sobornost'* (spiritual community) which is the ultimate foundation of objectively existing solidarity, dignity, tolerance, freedom, and other values.

This observation has important consequences for the reflection about the contemporary multicultural world. Frank was convinced that each religion has to be in dialogue with others. In this way the secularized (or, more precisely, visually secularized) society can return to its deepest spiritual foundations. Whereas nowadays in Russia the so-called post-secular movement emphasizes the leading role of Orthodoxy,[40] often excluding other confessions, Frank accentuated the universal significance of Christianity as such which also involves tolerance towards other religions. Once more, Frank was in any respect a religious fundamentalist or extremist. As he claimed:

> Religiously-moral radicalism, guided by the motto "all or nothing" regards the whole history of the Christian nations as one continual deviation from the Christian truth and dismisses all the traditional foundations of European culture and the prevailing forms of social life as simply "non-Christian." But such radicalism is both theoretically false and practically harmful. Its adherents unconsciously play into the hands of the undisguisedly anti-Christian forces. Necessary as it is to insist upon the fullest possible realization of goodness and righteousness, it

---

35. Frank, *The Spiritual Foundations*, 107. See Ehlen, *Russische Religionsphilosophie*, 270–73.

36. See Aliaiev, "The Universalism of Catholicity."

37. Frank, *The Spiritual Foundations*, 108.

38. See Frank, "Kul'tura i religiya," 160–61.

39. See Breckner, "Semyon Frank: An Apotheosis of Democracy," 241.

40. See Knorre, "Rossiyskoye pravoslaviye," 43–45.

behoves us to detect and appreciate even the feeble and imperfect manifestations of them.[41]

In the same spirit, Frank wrote against any form of nationalism, especially Russian "Slavophilism."[42] Generally speaking, "the work of Christian renaissance must overcome all temptations of sectarian exclusiveness and self-conceit."[43]

Faith and Reason

In Soviet Russia the favorite argument against the existence of God consisted in claiming that He could not be an object of empirical experience. Religious faith supposedly contradicts reason, especially scientific data. In this connection Frank tried to overcome this misunderstanding. In many of his texts he stressed that faith and reason, theology and science are not separate but complementary spheres. What is more, science itself deals with the objects which are rooted in all-unity and also have divine origin. In short, the object of religion is all-present. Only stubbornness enables us to notice the "traces of God" in the world. Although in Frank's reflection on the nature of science and religion one can notice the tendency to concordism,[44] it is noteworthy that the Russian thinker showed unassailable place of faith in the secularized world. As he maintained, "the difference between faith and unbelief is not that between two judgments, the contents of which are mutually contradictory, but is merely the difference between a wider and a narrower outlook."[45] In such a way Frank protested against the use of the naturalistic assumption of science as conflicting with religion and attempted to bridge the gap between religious and non-religious claims.

In the context of the relationship between faith and reason one should also mention the role and limit of religious language. In contemporary Russian post-secular society religious terminology is often abused,[46] being extensively (although unsuccessfully) applied in different contexts (political, economical, etc.). Frank, on the contrary, stressed the inadequate character of any religious notions, postulating that the Absolute is unspeakable and

---

41. Frank, *God with Us*, 217.
42. Frank, Letter to Georgiy Fedotov, 16.
43. Frank, *God with Us*, 285.
44. See Obolevitch, *Problematyczny konkordyzm*, 269, 289.
45. Frank, *God with Us*, 51.
46. See Knorre, "Rossiyskoye pravoslaviye," 58–60.

unknowable.⁴⁷ The religious nature of the whole of reality is the primordial ontological datum, and not a consequence of the users (or abusers) of religious language.

Concluding Remarks

As far as one can see, the reflection of Frank on the permanent existence of the spiritual aspect of different spheres of human life is in agreement with the contemporary post-secular thought on the inseparable connection between "religious" and "non-religious" forces which together compose the actual shape of culture. The Russian thinker wanted to overcome the split between religion and culture, faith and reason, *sacrum* and *profanum*. He "did not believe in 'secularized' culture"⁴⁸ and considered its various branches (anthropology, social philosophy, economics, etc.) from the profound ontologico-religious perspective. According to Frank, every man (even those who openly deny God) keep faith deep down in the absolute values containing culture as such,⁴⁹ and it is the premise for the renewal of religious convictions. Religion is still an inviolable foundation of culture, even though this dimension is not always expressed outwardly. Some scholars contest such a concept claiming that the divine justification of culture generates the relativization of human rights.⁵⁰ It is difficult to agree with this critique: Frank did not by any means refuse civil liberties to any extent. It is true, the philosopher wrote that

> the individualistic idea that the individual has the right to a definite, strictly fixed, an idea which is based on the false notion of the "innate" rights of man, must be rejected as incompatible with the supreme principle of *service*, which alone can justify the idea of individual freedom.⁵¹

Nevertheless, in this statement he only highlighted the significance of solidarity and mutual help which limit anarchic wilfulness and are present in the whole, not only Christian world.⁵²

---

47. See Frank, *The Unknowable*, 81; Frank, *God with Us*, 70–71; Frank, "Sovremennaya dukhovnaya situatsiya," 124–27.
48. Porus, "S. L. Frank: antinomii dukha," 140.
49. See Frank and Struve, "Ocherki filosofii kul'tury," 42, 47, 49.
50. Cf. Kusse, "Dialogicheskaya model' kul'tury," 509.
51. Frank, *The Spiritual Foundations*, 139.
52. See Frank, "Iz zapisnoy knizhki 1944 goda," 99.

In conclusion, it is worth considering whether the post-secular paradigm is correct. Certainly, we observe the appreciation of the role of religion, yet, on the other hand, there exist aggressively atheist societies persecuting each manifestation of religious life (i.e., North Korea). The possible answer of Frank could be as follows: any forces of evil ruling in the atheistic state would not be able to destroy the invisible church, embracing all people of all time and overpassing all borders. Referring to the title one of the most important books by Frank, one should say that God still remains with us.[53]

Frank was a witness to the strong effort of secularization of culture—both in Soviet Russia and in the West. In this regard he opposed the privatization of the religious sphere, claiming that the latter is primordial toward other human activities and permeates all domains of both individual and social life. In Frank's opinion, the age of religion has not declined. Together with Peter Berger, he could say that the world is "as furiously religious as it ever was."[54] But whereas Berger teaches about *de-secularization* (or return to religion), the Russian thinker claimed that *religion is an inalienable element of culture*. From Frank's point of view this can be confirmed by the permanent religious need inborn to all people. Answering the question posed by post-secular turn: "how do we know where religions and religiosities are located, observed, reproduced?"[55] in other words, where is the place of religion, Frank would say: everywhere. Every man, even an atheist, is latently religious in terms of their participation in the mystical church. The empirical world is not just immanent, but is opened to the transcendence. The so-called *deus absconditus* of secularism[56]—the "idol" of postmodern culture—keeps revealing itself in all aspects of reality, although it is beyond the possibility of its own accurate expression in religious language.

Bibliography

Akulich, Natal'ya. "Metodologicheskie osnovaniya filosofii kul'tury S. L. Franka." *Vestnik Baltiyskogo federal'nogo universiteta im. I. Kanta* 12 (2011) 108–13.

Aliaiev, Gennadii. "A Discussion on Christian Socialism: Semen Frank's Forgotten Paper." In *Overcoming the Secular. Russian Religious Philosophy and Post-Secularism*, edited by Teresa Obolevitch and Paweł Rojek, 132–43. Krakow: The Pontifical University of John Paul II Press, 2015.

———. "The Universalism of Catholicity (*Sobornost'*): Metaphysical and Existential Foundations for Interdenominational Dialogue in the Philosophy of Semen

---

53. See Frank, *God with Us*.
54. Berger, "The Desecularizaton of the World: A Global Overview," 2.
55. Bender, "Things in Their Entanglements," 46.
56. Kyrlezhev, "A Post-Secular Conceptualization of Religion," 19.

Frank." In *Apology of Culture. Religion and Culture in Russian Thought*, edited by Artur Mrówczyński-Van Allen, Teresa Obolevitch, and Paweł Rojek, 218–26. Eugene, OR: Pickwick Publications, 2015.

Bender, Courtney. "Things in Their Entanglements." In *The Post-Secular in Question. Religion in Contemporary Society*, edited by Philip S. Gorski, David Kyuman Kim, John Torpey and Jonathan Van Antwerpen, 43–76. New York: New York University Press, 2012.

Berger, Peter L. "The Desecularizaton of the World: A Global Overview." In *The Desecularization of the World: Resurgent Religion and World Politics*, edited by Peter L. Berger, 1–18. Grand Rapids, MI: Eerdmans, 1999.

Boobbyer, Philip. "A Russian Version of Christian Realism: Spiritual Wisdom and Politics in the Thought of S. L. Frank (1877–1950)." *The International History Review* 1 (2015) 1–21.

Breckner, Katharina. "Semyon Frank: An Apotheosis of Democracy in the Name of Personal Service." *Forum Philosophicum* 18/2 (2013) 231–49.

Calhoun, Craig. "Time, World, and Secularism?" In *The Post-Secular in Question. Religion in Contemporary Society*, edited by Philip S. Gorski, David Kyuman Kim, John Torpey and Jonathan Van Antwerpen, 335–64. New York: New York University Press, 2012.

Dalferth, Ingolf U. "Post-Secular Society: Christianity and the Dialectics of the Secular." *Journal of the American Academy of Religion* 2 (2010) 317–45.

Ehlen, Peter. "Chto svyazyvayet obshchestvo v samoy glubine? K osnovnomu voprosu sotsial'noy filosofii S. L. Franka." In *Samyy vydayushchiysya russkiy filosof: Filosofiya religii i politiki S. L. Franka*, edited by Konstantin Antonov, 168–94. Moscow: Izdatel'stvo Pravoslavnogo Svyato-Tikhonovskogo Gumanitarnogo Universiteta, 2015.

———. *Russische Religionsphilosophie im 20. Jahruhundert: Simon L. Frank*. Freiburg and Munchen: Verlag Karl Alberg, 2009.

Florovsky, Georges. Letter to the Rev. Theodore M. Hesburgh, July 5, 1966, 1–3. The Archive of Fritz Lieb, The University of Basel. Nl 353: O. Cullmann A V c 2 46.

Frank, Semen. "Christian Conscience and Politics." In *Issledovaniya po istorii russkoy mysli. Ezhegodnik za 2001/02 god*, edited by Modest A. Kolerov, 571–82. Saint Petersburg: Aleteyya, 2002.

———. "Contemporary Russian Philosophy." *The Monist* 1/37 (1927) 1–23.

———. "The Essence and Leading Themes of Russian Philosophy." *Russian Studies in Philosophy* 30/4 (1992) 28–47.

———. "Fragmenty iz zapisnykh knizhek 1941–1944 gg." *Solovievskiye Issledovaniya* 48 (2015) 93–101.

———. *God with Us: Three Meditations*. Translated by Natalie Duddington. London: Jonathan Cape, 1946.

———. "Krusheniye kumirov." In Semen Frank. *Sochineniya*, 147–244. Moscow: AST, 2000.

———. "Kul'tura i religiya (Po povodu stat'i o "Vekhakh" S. V. Lur'ye)." *Russkaya mysl'* 7 (1909) 147–61.

———. Letter to Georgiy Fedotov, April 27, 1949, 15–18. Online: http://www.rusliberal.ru/books/Frank_to_Fedotov.pdf.

———. Letter to Ludwig Binswanger, July 12, 1942. In Semen Frank, *Neprochitannoye. Stat'i, pis'ma, vospominaniya*, 336–41. Moscow: Moskovskaya shkola politicheskikh issledovaniy, 2001.
———. *The Light Shineth in Darknes*. Translated by Boris Jakim. Athens, OH: Ohio University Press, 1989.
———. *Man's Soul. An Introductory Essay in Philosophical Psychology*. Translated by Boris Jakim. Athens, OH: Ohio University Press, 1993.
———. "Mysli v strashnyye dni." In Semen Frank, *Neprochitannoye. Stat'i, pis'ma, vospominaniya*, 347–93. Moscow: Moskovskaya shkola politicheskikh issledovaniy, 2001.
———. "Razmyshleniya S. L. Franka, zapisannyye T. S. Frank." In *Samyy vydayushchiysya russkiy filosof: Filosofiya religii i politiki S. L. Franka*, edited by Konstantin Antonov, 206–40. Moscow: Izdatel'stvo Pravoslavnogo Svyato-Tikhonovskogo Gumanitarnogo Universiteta, 2015.
———. *Reality and Man. An Essay on the Metaphysics of Human Nature*. Translated by Natalie Duddington. New York: Taplinger, 1950.
———. "Religiya i nauka v sovremennom soznanii." *Put'* 4 (1926) 145–56.
———. "Sovremennaya dukhovnaya situatsiya i ideya otritsatel'nogo bogosloviya," *Filosofskiye nauki* 4 (2008), 122–127.
———. *The Spiritual Foundations of Society. An Introduction to Social Philosophy*. Translated by Boris Jakim. Athens, OH: Ohio University Press, 1987.
———. *The Unknowable. An Ontological Introduction to the Philosophy of Religion*. Translated by Boris Jakim. Athens, OH: Ohio University Press, 1983.
Frank, Semen, and Petr Struve. "Ocherki filosofii kul'tury." In Semen Frank, *Neprochitannoye. Stat'i, pis'ma, vospominaniya*, 37–62. Moscow: Moskovskaya shkola politicheskikh issledovaniy, 2001.
Khoruzhy, Sergey. "The Idea of Total-Unity from Heraclitus to Losev." *Russian Studies in Philosophy* 1 (1996) 32–69.
Knorre, Boris. "Rossiyskoye pravoslaviye. Postsekulyarnaya institutsionalizatsiya v prostranstve vlasti, politiki i prava." In *Montazh i demontazh sekulyarnogo mira*, edited by Aleksey Malashenko and Sergey Filatov, 42–102. Moscow: ROSSPEN, 2014.
Kusse, Holger. "Dialogicheskaya model' kul'tury F. Stepuna i S. Franka." In *Antichnost' i kul'tura Serebryanogo veka*, edited by Elena A. Takho-Godi, 502–12. Moscow: Nauka, 2010.
Kyrlezhev, Alexander. "A Post-Secular Conceptualization of Religion: Defining the Question." *State, Religion and Church* 1 (2014) 7–22.
Luks, Leonid. "Semen Lyudvigovich Frank o totalitarnykh soblaznakh XX veka." In *Samyy vydayushchiysya russkiy filosof: Filosofiya religii i politiki S. L. Franka*, edited by Konstantin Antonov, 50–75. Moscow: Izdatel'stvo Pravoslavnogo Svyato-Tikhonovskogo Gumanitarnogo Universiteta, 2015.
Mrówczyński-Van Allen, Artur, and Sebastián Montiel Gómez. "Aspects of the Russian Tradition of Philosophical-Theological Synthesis in the Post-Secular Context. Georges Florovsky, Sergey Bulgakov, Alain Badiou, and the Theology Dwarf." In *Beyond Modernity: Russian Religious Philosophy and Post-Secularism*, edited by Artur Mrówczyński-Van Allen, Teresa Obolevitch, and Paweł Rojek, 13–24. Eugene, OR: Pickwick Publications, 2017.
Nevleva, Inna. *Filosofiya kul'tury S. L. Franka*. Saint Petersburg: Aleteyya, 2007.

Obolevitch, Teresa. *Problematyczny konkordyzm. Wiara i wiedza w myśli Włodzimierza S. Sołowjowa i Siemiona L. Franka*. Tarnów: Biblos, 2006.

Pabst, Adrian and Schneider, Christoph. "Transfiguring the World through the Word." In *Encounter Between Eastern Orthodoxy and Radical Orthodoxy: Transfiguring the World Through the Word*, edited by Adrian Pabst and Christoph Schneider, 1–25. Burlington, VT: Ashgate, 2009.

Porus, Vladimir. "S. L. Frank: antinomii dukha kak osnovaniya kul'tury." In *Ideynoye naslediye S. L. Franka v kontekste sovremennoy evropeyskoy kul'tury*, edited by Vladimir Porus, 123–40. Moscow: BBI, 2009.

Rundell, John. "Multiple Modernities, Sacredness, and the Democratic Imaginary: Religion as a Stand in Category." In *Discoursing the Post-Secular. Essays on the Habermas Post-Secular Turn*, edited by Péter Losonczi and Aakash Singh, 1–39. Berlin: LIT Verlag, 2010.

Slesinski, Robert. "The Spiritual Foundations of Society according to V. S. Solovyov and S. L. Frank." *St. Vladimir's Theological Quarterly* 2/39 (1995) 157–84.

Svoboda, Philip J. "Semën Frank's Expressivist Humanism." In *A History of Russian Philosophy. Faith, Reason and* the Defense of Human Dignity, edited by Gary M. Hamburg and Randall A. Poole, 205–23. Cambridge: Cambridge University Press, 2010.

Zenkovsky, Vasily. *A History of Russian Philosophy*. Vol. 2. Translated by George L. Kline. London: Routledge, 2006.

———. "S. L. Frank. 1977–1950." *The Slavonic Review* 29 (1951) 562–67.

Ziebertz, Hans-Georg and Riegel, Ulrich. "Europe: A Post-Secular Society?" *International Journal of Practical Theology* 13 (2009) 293–308.

16

The Way Journal (1925–1941) and the Question of Freedom in the Context of European Post-Secular Culture

Olga Tabatadze

"Then you will know the truth, and the truth will set you free"

(JOHN 8:32)

"Where the Spirit of the Lord is, there is liberty"

(2 COR 3:17)

Since the beginning of European philosophical thought, the question of freedom has always been present. Today, in the "post-secular era," the culture of freedom understood mainly in its juridical and legal framework, its alienated concept of "human rights" as criterion, and objective truth replaced by the idea of plurality of opinions along with the concepts of good and evil, of truth and lie being identified or relativized, the idea of true freedom, inseparably linked to the idea of God-man and Godmanhood developed by Russian Christian thinkers, enlightens the mind on this question and shows the right direction towards man's authentic freedom.

The *The Way* (*Put'*) journal, published in Paris from 1925 to 1941, described by its editor-in-chief Nikolai Berdyaev as the "journal of spiritual culture,"¹ whose aim was to struggle for "the freedom of the religious, of the philosophic, of social thought, for freedom of creativity"² and, according to the thinker's words, "was successful somehow in this regard."³ In our opinion, it is a prominent and interesting publication that was the source for the expression of Russian culture (becoming, also, an integral part of it), heir of the free Russian religious and philosophical thought of the nineteeth and twentieth centuries, and of its specific anthropology.

It must be said that, unlike its Muscovite predecessor, created by the same authors and published from 1909 to 1919,⁴ the Parisian *The Way* journal was a place of free expression of thought to both the thinkers in exile and those who remained in the Soviet Union,⁵ and offered its pages for the free communication and collaboration of followers of different creeds.⁶

In the conscience crisis and new quests going on in that period, *The Way* journal helped the presence of Christian truth and the increase in the religious conscience in public life, contributing thus to the elaboration of answers to the complex universal questions, including the question about true freedom.

The problem of freedom, which was discussed in the pages of *The Way*, was faced by Nikolai Lossky, Fr. Vasily Zenkovsky, the, at that time, hieromonk Ioann Shakhovskoy, Boris Vysheslavtsev, Mother Maria Skobtsova, Fr. Sergey Chetverikov and, of course, the editor, Nikolai Berdyaev. These thinkers analyzed the problem of freedom from the point of view of metaphysics, Christian anthropology and culture. In their articles they dealt with the problem of the freedom of God and man's free will, freedom of conscience, of thought and the creation; the relationship between freedom and salvation, love, responsibility, vocation, authority, equality, choice, eternity, etc. In this article we will approach the most important thoughts; however, we want to emphasize that almost all the above mentioned thinkers

1. Berdyaev, "The Russian Spiritual Renaissance."
2. Ibid.
3. Ibid.
4. Arjakovsky, *The Way*, 18.
5. Antoine Arjakovsky points out that among the 127 authors that wrote for the journal there were some that lived in Latvia, Poland, Yugoslavia, Czechoslovakia, Germany, Sweden, France, Belgium, Italy, England, the USA, China, Japan, the USSR, etc., ibid., 18–20.
6. Though the main part of the authors were Orthodox, *The Way* published also articles of Catholic thinkers (Cardinal Andrieu, P. Archambault, E. Belenson-Elson, R. de Becker, S. Fumet, L. Kozlovsky, J. Maritain, J. Sazonova, Fr. G. Bennigsen, Fr. Augustyn Jakubisiak, Pope Pius XI), Protestants (Pastor Blumhardt, H. Erenburg, G. Kuhlmann, S. Kavert, F. Lieb, P. Tillich) and Anglicans (P. Anderson, S. Ollard, F. Gavin, K. Kirk), ibid., 19.

considered themselves heirs to Vladimir Soloviev[7] and saw true freedom in an inseparable relationship with God-man, revealed in the divine-human body, that is, the church.

Nikolai Lossky, in his article "On the Creation of the Universe by God," reflects on the free creation of the universe by God as an absolute creation, as the creation of the universe from "nothingness."[8] "The Creator of the universe does not need any datum to create it; the first form and the first content of the universe are created by Him as something new, inexistent if compared with Him."[9] Establishing what exactly was created by God, he ranks the universe in events, that is, in actions in time, and actors that carry out these actions, whom he characterizes as creators in possession of freedom:

> God creates the creators and offers them to carry out by themselves their lives in time, even to elaborate more or less autonomously the ways of life. All the actions carried out by the substantial actors are free centripetal acts. In each one of his actions the actor, freely (at least, regarding the formal freedom) tries to carry out or to use some values.[10]

The thinker points out that the freedom of a created being is necessarily linked with the possibility of choosing the path of evil, which may never be a reality because, even if the actor uses his freedom incorrectly, the "Divine Providence, disturbing no being whatsoever's freedom, finds the way of placing the fallen actor in some circumstances in which, after a long, difficult and devious developing process, the actor condemns the path of evil and starts ascending towards the threshold of the Kingdom of God."[11]

In his article "The Image of God in the Being of Man," Boris Vysheslavtsev still deals with the subject of freedom and creation, and considers the question of man as a Divine-human problem. Talking about the likeness of the person to the Absolute, the thinker points out: "The person is

---

7. For more details on the legacy of Soloviev, see Losskiy, "V. Solov'yev i yego preyemniki" (the English version: Lossky, "The Philosophy of Vladimir Solovyev," and "Preyemniki Solov'yeva" (the English version: Lossky, "The Successors of Vladimir Solovyev").

8. In his article "The Metaphysical Problem of Freedom," Berdyaev turns also to the Christian theology teaching that states that God created the universe from nothingness, that is, out of freedom; God created the universe freely and created it free. The idea that the source of freedom is to be found in nonexistence also appears in Berdyaev "The Problem of Man."

9. Losskiy, "O tvorenii mira Bogom," 5.

10. Ibid., 7.

11. Ibid., 13.

the primary freedom of creation and its own aim. The same can be said about the Absolute: all exists from him and for him"[12] and further on he says: "God is the Creator, the Poet of existence; but man is the creator too, the poet of culture, as he cultivates and does not destroy the Eden created for him."[13] For Vysheslavtsev, the divine-likeness of man, which constitutes the basic premise for the comprehension of his essence, consists on the one hand, of man's rational soul (*anima rationalis*), his intelligence, logos, spirit and, on the other, of his freedom. The author bases the godlike essence of freedom in man on the statements of Macarius the Great ("no natural being is free: neither the sun, the moon, the earth, the animals; but God is free and man is free")[14] and Gregory of Nyssa (freedom "consists of the lack of bondage by natural force, of one's own capacity to decide and choose, out of one's own essence. Outside freedom there is no intelligence, since there is no gift of judgement or reason").[15] He insists on John Damascene's determination that the image of God in man is his intelligence and freedom[16] and, besides, he relies on the words of Gregory Palamas, who considers that the peculiarity of the human soul, which is having not only the subordinate and obedient part, like that of the angels, but also the ruling and domineering one, transforms human freedom into creative freedom.[17] Thus, the thinker concludes that man, that is, a person of spirit, is the light of conscience and the power of freedom, not alienated spirit, intelligence and freedom, but incarnated spirit, intelligence and freedom, that is, the freedom of the incarnation of his ideas.[18]

Vysheslavtsev also emphasizes the interaction between freedom and love, underlying the primacy of love over freedom:

> The heart is more central than intelligence and . . . is more central than freedom and action, since all actions are born in the heart. My freedom belongs to me and it is not me that belongs to an impersonal freedom . . . It is free that which arises from my being's deepest foundation and absolutely out of "nothingness." I am really free only when I know, create and contemplate what

---

12. Vysheslavtsev, "Obraz Bozhiy v sushchestve cheloveka," 50.
13. Ibid., 52.
14. Ibid., 56.
15. Ibid., 57.
16. Ibid.
17. Ibid., 58.
18. Ibid., 57.

I love most and not when "I do what I detest," since love is the fullest expression of myself.[19]

In "Work, Creation and Freedom," D. Semenov-Tian-Shansky also examines to what extent the problem of freedom is closely related both to the problem of creativity and vocation, and to the problem of time and eternity.[20] The author considers that being a means to an end means being a prisoner and, this is why liberation is overcoming the means. Experiencing what is valuable brings freedom, because in what is truly valuable the element "means" is already absent or it has been transformed. Time, at least in some aspects, is precisely a pure means, an empty form, full of nothing, that can be overcome only through a creative act, becoming a receptacle of values. Creative activity is "the conception, or contemplation, and affirmation of value."[21] The thinker insists:

> Only creation, as involving appreciation of purpose, can open the door to eternity and freedom. Eternity is the reigne of purpose, time is the reigne [sic] of nonsense. All non-creative work, particularly mechanical labour and the work of machines themselves, is like the meaningless flickering of disconnected moments.[22]

And, the other way round, the author considers that the highest creation, the one that in its fullest expression goes beyond the power of time and truly liberates is religious creativity, or the spiritual life.[23]

Semenov-Tian-Shansky insists that "creativeness is the path to freedom," and "vocation, that is, true creativity is freedom,"[24] by pointing out two ways of valuing cultural creativity and saying that the first one, creativity itself is the more valuable the higher the value that can be achieved is, and that the second, a particular man's creativity, is considered the more authentic, the more authentic is his vocation (understood as love to labour, through which man becomes an instrument of God alive).

---

19. Ibid., 63.

20. On the senselessness of time flow itself, the enslavement of man by time and the discovery of the sense of life only in relation to eternity see also Berdyaev's article "The Spiritual Condition of Contemporary World" (in Russian "Dukhovnoye sostoyaniye sovremennogo mira").

21. Semyenov-Tyan-Shan'skiy, "Trud, tvorchestvo i svoboda," 25 (the English translation: Semenoff-Tian-Shansky, "Work, Creativity and Freedom," 4).

22. Ibid., 26 (the English version: "Work, Creativity and Freedom," 5).

23. See ibid., 27 (the English version: "Work, Creativity and Freedom," 6).

24. Cf. ibid., 30 (the English version: "Work, Creativity and Freedom," 7).

In his article "Freedom and the Sobornost'" the priest Vasily Zenkovsky points out the existence of two freedoms: the "natural" one and the freedom in Christ.[25] The author remarks that both experiences of freedom do not replace each other, nor do they merge in one: they are just the expression of man's inner splitting. "The paths of Christian development are determined, precisely, by the task of overcoming this splitting, and the profound sense of asceticism consists, exactly, of tending towards the correct organization of the soul,"[26] towards inner integrity. "The life of grace that the Lord grants us as a gift opens authentic freedom to us, precisely because in it all is saved, transfigured, liberated from the 'slavery to corruption' (Rom 8:21)" and is situated in eternity.[27] According to Zenkovsky, the call to freedom in Christ, which at first creates an inner splitting between the natural and grace, later on opens in the soul as an anticipation of resurrection and sanctity, as the possibility of salvation, that is to say, the reestablishment of all the natural in grace.

> Freedom in Christ is given to us only by grace, it can be reached neither in the order of "natural" evolution, nor in the order of self-improvement, there isn't here any need or conformity with a law. The freedom of Christ comes to us only as an inspiration of the Holy Spirit grace and its previous condition is usually humbleness and surrender to God's will. With this, the attitude of the freedom in Christ towards the natural freedom is immediately determined: the former does not rest in the elimination of the latter, nor in its improvement or development; it is simply another order, an order of grace that tends only to transfigure

---

25. Nikolai Berdyaev and Mikhail Artemiev also emphasize these two freedoms in man, though they call them differently. Artemiev in the article "On the Freedom of Will" talks about quasi-freedom and true freedom or, in other words, the freedom of choice (in the sense of keeping something, after having previously refused the rest) and the freedom of choosing (in the sense of directly preferring this thing rather than the others). He warns against the risk of pseudo-freedom becoming quasi-freedom if man is gobbled by his environment. See Artem'yev, "O svobode voli." Berdyaev in the article "The Metaphysical Problem of Freedom" talks about the freedom of infinite power and the freedom of Divine Grace's infinitude, that is, about irrational potential freedom (the freedom to choose good or evil; freedom as the way; the freedom that conquers and not the freedom that is conquered; the freedom with which Truth and God are accepted and not the one that is received from Truth and God) and about rational, actual freedom (freedom in truth and good; freedom as the object and the major achievement; freedom in God, which is received from God). See Berdyayev, "Metafizicheskaya problema svobody," 42, 50 (the English translation: "The Metaphysical Problem of Freedom").

26. Zen'kovskiy, "Svoboda i sobornost'," 4.

27. Ibid.

natural freedom, "justifying it," letting it flourish in all its fullness and truth.[28]

Natural freedom, showed in our aspiration of getting rid of external determination and constraint, wants to transform our activity in the activity of our own self, making it arise from our inner world. But our inner world gathers in our heart and man becomes himself only if determining himself in his heart. However, the plea to the heart, taken from the law of the Old Testament by Christianity, hides the exceptional difficulties which, without the Lord, are impossible for us to overcome. If we follow the imperative of the heart, we soon discover that our inner world, while taken in its lack of light and naturalness, appears chaotic and dark. We start to understand that just the way towards the inner man, towards his heart, still does not introduce us in the mystery of freedom, although it does take us out to its vast extension. The shift of the center of gravity to the inner man and the overcoming of the external law, which coincides with it, the path towards the heart taken in its natural movements are correct only as the first step in the path of the enlightenment of man by Christ's light. Christ widens our natural freedom immeasurably, but with the aim to make us arrive at Him freely, to make us enlighten the "natural" darkness of our heart in Him.[29]

The author points out that the liberation from the law can truly be overcome only in the church and with the church, which is a divine-human organism:

> Only in the church does personality flourish; outside it, it is impotent and cannot dominate its freedom . . . By overcoming the fantasy of one's self-sufficiency and fulfilling oneself in the church one can for the first time give free rein to everything that is original and unique in us, trying to introduce it in the life of the church; not the external and formal one, but the inner one, through the purification of the heart and through the inner enlightenment of the soul by grace.[30]

The author insists on the fact that the path towards freedom in Christ is to be found in the church and through humbleness[31] growing from the love to God:

---

28. Ibid., 8.
29. Ibid., 9.
30. Ibid., 13.
31. Humbleness, as the path of spiritual liberation of man, which presupposes freedom and is in itself already an action of freedom that awakens love, contemplation, knowledge, creativity in man, preventing him from slavery, egoism and cowardice, can be found in Berdyaev's article. See Berdyaev, "Spaseniye i tvorchestvo" (the English

> Man achieves his freedom only by giving himself to God, in humble bow before Him, and the Lord acts in us, not outside our freedom but only through it. Thus, the mystery of freedom is only a special aspect of God's Incarnation, such as this one remains in the church and, through the church, in us.[32]

Zenkovsky concludes: "Everything can, everything must be transfigured in order to be free in Christ: through the church we walk towards freedom and through our incorporation in the life of the church and of our life and the world, we achieve our freedom."[33]

Berdyaev dealt with many aspects of freedom in his writings, but out of all of them we would like to point out, first and foremost, the problem of freedom of conscience and, closely linked to it, the questions concerning responsibility[34] and the choice of good and evil, tackled in the articles "Discord in the Church and Freedom of Conscience," "The Metaphysical Problem of Freedom," "The Problem of Man (Towards the Construction of a Christian Anthropology) and On Authority," "Freedom and Humanity," and, secondly, the problem of freedom of thought and its inseparable issues on truth and authority,[35] analyzed in the collected letters between Berdyaev, Lossky and Fr. Chetverikov, published in the philosopher's articles "The Spirit of the Grand Inquisitor" and "Concerning Authority, Freedom and Humanness," and the open letters to Berdyaev by Lossky and Chetverikov.

As far as freedom of conscience is concerned, Berdyaev refers to true freedom, the freedom that God asks from man, and defends the unity of freedom and truth, of freedom and love in the life of the church and in the world, declaring himself against obscurantism, clericalism and blind subordination to authority. The thinker defends that the sense of the creation of the world lies in the fact that "God needs man's free conscience, man's

---

translation: "Salvation and Creativity"). The author also warns us to understand correctly what true humbleness is, and to tell it from false humbleness or slavery.

32. Berdyayev, "Svoboda i sobornost," 21.

33. Ibid., 22.

34. Freedom understood as responsibility and, even, as a heavy burden that man cannot and must not get rid of, transferring it to others, is also found in Fr. Zenkovsky's articles "Autonomy and Theonomy" and "Freedom and the Sobornost," Semenov-Tian-Shansky's "Work, Creativity and Freedom" and Mother Maria Skobtsova's "Justification of Pharisaism" and "On the Imitation of the Mother of God." See Zen'kovskiy, "Avtonomiya i teonomiya," Semyenov-Tyan-Shan'skiy, "Trud, tvorchestvo i svoboda," Skobtsova, "Opravdaniye fariseystva," "O podrazhanii Bogomateri."

35. On Berdyaev's defense of freedom of thought in the political field, read his article "Does there Exist Freedom of Thought and Conscience in Orthodoxy?" (in Russian Berdyayev, "Suschestvuyet li v Pravoslavii svoboda mysli i sovesti?")

free resoluteness, man's unfettered love."[36] The author warned against the violation of freedom of conscience, which implies its interaction with the Spirit of God;[37] against the formal incorporation of man's life into the life of the church, that is to say, the subordination of all the aspects of his life to the hierocratic principle, because the true incorporation into the life of the church is "an ontologically real Christianization of life, the introduction of Christ's light, Christ's Truth, Christ's love and freedom in all spheres of life and creativity," his enlightenment and transfiguration[38] and, also, against the distortion of the idea of freedom because "freedom is not the isolation of the soul, opposing it to all other souls and to the whole world," but the mysterious union of that which is individual and unique with what is universal and common to all.[39]

Berdyaev speaks about the responsibility of freedom, about the temptation to renounce to it to lead an easier life, of transferring freedom to others, to authority: "we are living in a time of fear and timidity in the face of the freedom of conscience, refusing to take upon ourselves the burden of freedom, the burden of responsibility."[40]

> Man himself . . . very readily tends to refuse freedom and is afraid of freedom, he prefers slavery, reckons it easier a thing. Freedom is not easy, it is terribly difficult, it is a burden, it is severe . . . Freedom reflects the maturity of man, and life of the mature however is more difficult, more severe, more answerably responsible, than the life of children. The refusal of freedom is a fear of responsibility, is a wish to pass it off from oneself onto others. Only slaves possess such an understanding of freedom, as a self-indulging, as a giving in to their own lower nature, as the temptation to do whatever one desires. People, consciously aware of the dignity and responsibility of man . . . In the modern world with extraordinary force have awakened herd instincts, and the herd however does not know freedom. The Christian revelation is not oriented towards the herd, but to rather the human person, conscious of God-like a dignity. The sin is also in a renouncing of the dignity of freedom, a submitting to slavery.[41]

36. Berdyayev, "Tserkovnaya smuta i svoboda sovesti," 53 (the English translation "Discord in the Church and Freedom of Conscience").

37. Ibid., 45.

38. Ibid., 52–53.

39. Ibid., 44–45.

40. Ibid., 44.

41. Berdyayev, "Ob avtoritete, svobode i chelovechnosti," 40–41 (the English translation "Concerning Authority, Freedom and Humanness").

The author is also concerned about freedom in the choice of good and evil, linked with the path of man's freedom of conscience:

> Freedom lies at the basis of God's design concerning the world and man. Freedom begets evil, but without freedom there is also no good. Compulsory goodness would not be good. In this is the fundamental contradiction on freedom. The freedom for evil is, evidently, a condition for the freedom for good. Forcefully abolish evil without a trace and there remains nothing of a freedom for good. Here is why God tolerates the existence of evil. Freedom begets the tragedy of life and the suffering of life.[42]

And remembering the thoughts of Fyodor Dostoevsky on freedom, he writes that "man readily abdicates freedom in the name of mitigating the suffering of life through a compulsory organising [sic] of the good."[43]

Berdyaev concludes that in the political sense freedom is usually understood as a right and a claim of man,[44] but freedom, considered in its metaphysical depth, is an obligation, a weight that man has to carry until the end,

> since in freedom is included God's idea about him, his God-likeness. God demands, that man be free, he expects of man the act of freedom. God has need of the freedom of man moreso, than does man himself. Man readily renounces freedom in the name of the easing of life, but God does not renounce the freedom of man, since with this is bound up his design for the world-creation.[45]

As for the issue of freedom of thought, of truth and authority, Berdyaev declares that

> Truth, however, is discovered only through freedom, and not through authority smothering thought ... No one except a slave can accept by binding authority a doctrine, if his conscience does not agree, if the freedom in it is not consentual [sic]. Without my freedom nothing for me has meaning ... Religious life

---

42. Berdyayev, "Metafizicheskaya problema svobody," 51 (the English translation "The Metaphysical Problem of Freedom").

43. Ibid.

44. On political freedom, understood as equality, see Reymers, "Svoboda i ravenstvo."

45. Berdyayev, "Metafizicheskaya problema svobody," 52 (the English translation "The Metaphysical Problem of Freedom").

relates to the spiritual plane of being and this means that nothing in it has meaning without freedom.⁴⁶

In full agreement with Lossky's and Chetverikov's statements that the supreme value of life is not freedom but truth, given to the Church by the Holy Spirit, and that only truth guarantees the authentic freedom that man has to accept freely, since he is not free from sin and is limited as creature, Berdyaev answers:

> I likewise think, that highest of all stands truth, and it is truth namely that I desire to strive for. But there exists a Christian Truth concerning freedom. Knowledge of the Truth gives us freedom, and such is one side of the question, but there is also another side—knowledge of truth demands freedom, without freedom truth is not given us nor has value. To God, to God namely, and not for man, nothing is of interest or needful without freedom. Truth and freedom are inseparable and it is impossible to deny freedom in the name of truth.⁴⁷

Thus, we see how Russian thinkers understood man's true freedom not only as the freedom granted by God, but also as the freedom that God expects from man, the true and creative freedom that transfigures man, that saves him from the "slavery to corruption" and brings him to the inner integrity. This freedom of preference is the basis of the love for God and for the neighbor, the basis of the knowledge of Truth, of doing good and of contemplating God, which lies in eternity. True freedom is not lived in isolation or individually, but in the church, in this divine-human body, in which the person, who, among other things, is also the power of freedom remaining in the communion, in the community, flourishes with its true color. Being a gift of God granted to man only by Grace, true freedom is not achieved through self-improvement or by means of some evolution, but it grows in humbleness, asceticism and the surrender to God's will. True freedom means man's freedom of conscience and thought. He is responsible and this is a difficult and heavy burden for man, which he cannot or should not transfer to others or free himself from it in order to make his life easier.

To finish our article with Berdyaev's words, we would like to keep in mind, most especially now, in our post-secular time, that the authentic philosophy of freedom is Christian philosophy and that

---

46. Berdyayev, "Dukh Velikogo Inkvizitora," 78–79 (the English translation "The Spirit of the Grand Inquisitor").

47. Berdyayev, "Ob avtoritete, svobode i chelovechnosti," 48 (the English translation "Concerning Authority, Freedom and Humanness").

the authentic solution to the problem of freedom is to be found only by departing from the idea of the Godmanhood. Nobody understands better the issue of freedom, as well as those of indeterminism and infinitude, than the Russian Religious Philosophy.[48]

Bibliography

Arjakovskiy, Antoine. *The Way. Religious Thinkers of the Russian Emigration in Paris and Their Journal (1925–1940)*. Translated by J. Ryan. Notre Dame, IN: University of Notre Dame Press, 2013.

Artem'yev, Mikhail. "O svobode voli." *Put'* 32 (1928) 43–72.

Berdyaev, Nikolai. "Concerning Authority, Freedom and Humanness." Translated by Fr. Stephen Janos. Online: http://www.berdyaev.com/berdiaev/berd_lib/1936_409.html.

———. "Does there Exist Freedom of Thought and Conscience in Orthodoxy?" Translated by Fr. Stephen Janos. Online: http://krotov.info/library/02_b/berdyaev/1939_441_eng.html.

———. "The Metaphysical Problem of Freedom." Translated by Fr. Stephen Janos. Online: http://www.berdyaev.com/berdiaev/berd_lib/1928_329.html.

———. "The Problem of Man (Towards the Construction of a Christian Anthropology)." Translated by Fr. Stephen Janos. Online: http://www.berdyaev.com/berdiaev/berd_lib/1936_408.html.

———. "The Russian Spiritual Renaissance of Beginning XX Century and the Journal Put'." Translated by Fr. Stephen Janos. Online: http://krotov.info/library/02_b/berdyaev/1935_403_eng.html.

———. "Salvation and Creativity." Translated by Fr. Stephen Janos. Online: http://krotov.info/library/02_b/berdyaev/1926_308_eng.html.

———. "The Spirit of the Grand Inquisitor." Translated by Fr. Stephen Janos. Online: http://www.berdyaev.com/berdiaev/berd_lib/1935_404.html.

———. "The Spiritual Condition of the Contemporary World." Translated by Fr. Stephen Janos. Online: http://www.berdyaev.com/berdiaev/berd_lib/1932_377.html.

Berdyayev, Nikolay. "Dukh Velikogo Inkvizitora." *Put'* 49 (1935) 72–82.

———. "Dukhovnoye sostoyaniye sovremennogo mira." *Put'* 35 (1932) 56–68.

———. "Metafizicheskaya problema svobody." *Put'* 9 (1928) 41–53.

———. "Ob avtoritete, svobode i chelovechnosti." *Put'* 50 (1936) 37–49.

———. "Spaseniye i tvorchestvo." *Put'* 2 (1926) 26–46.

———. "Suschestvuyet li v Pravoslavii svoboda mysli i sovesti?" *Put'* 59 (1939) 46–54.

———. "Tserkovnaya smuta i svoboda sovesti." *Put'* 5 (1926) 42–54.

Losskiy, Nikolay. "O tvorenii mira Bogom." *Put'* 54 (1937) 3–22.

———. "Preyemniki Solovy'eva." *Put'* 3 (1926) 14–28.

---

48. Berdyayev, "Metafizicheskaya problema svobody," 53 (the English translation "The Metaphysical Problem of Freedom").

———. "Vl. Solovyev i yego preyemniki v russkoy religioznoy filosofii." *Put'* 2 (1926) 13–25.
Lossky, Nikolai. "The Philosophy of Vladimir Solovyev." Translated by Nathalie A. Duddington. *The Slavonic Review* 5 (1923) 346–58.
———. "The Successors of Vladimir Solovyev." Translated by Nathalie A. Duddington. *The Slavonic Review* 7 (1924) 92–109.
Skobtsova, Maria, mat'. "O podrazhanii Bogomateri." *Put'* 59 (1939) 19–30.
———. "Opravdaniye fariseystva." *Put'* 56 (1938) 37–46.
Reymers, Nikolay. "Svoboda i ravenstvo." *Put'* 41 (1933) 25–60.
Semenoff-Tian-Shansky, A. D. "Work, Creativity and Freedom I." Translated by K. R. *Sobornost: New Series* 17 (1939) 4–10; *Sobornost: New Series* 18 (1939) 23–27.
Semyenov-Tyan-Shan'skiy, A. D. "Trud, tvorchestvo i svoboda." *Put'* 52 (1936–37) 24–44.
Vysheslavtsev, Boris. "Obraz Bozhiy v syschestve cheloveka." *Put'* 49 (1935) 48–71.
Zen'kovskiy, Vasiliy. "Avtonomiya i teonomiya." *Put'* 3 (1926) 46–64.
———. "Svoboda i sobornost'." *Put'* 7 (1927) 3–22.

17

Overcoming the Secular

Viktor Nesmelov's Teaching on Personhood as the Justification of the Radical Theological Commitment in the Dialogue between Faith and Reason

Alexei Nesteruk

When the adherents of the Radical Orthodoxy movement criticize secularism, they defend the inerasable presence of the Divine in human existence and its activities, and advocate such a theological perspective that must encompass every form of knowledge, for otherwise this knowledge defines realms apart from God, "grounded literally in nothing." It is not difficult to grasp that this perspective has an anthropological basis, for it refers to the human capacity to have experience of God. This means that before mediating politics, ethics, philosophy and science, that is, that which Radical Orthodoxy advocates as a *gift* to humanity at large, there must be an explication of the possibility of accepting this *gift* in the human condition. In a way, Radical Orthodoxy as a Christian theological commitment in all aspects of life must be subjected to the *radical justification* of its own possibility. One of the dimensions of such a justification is the notion of *personhood*, that is the hypostatic existence of humanity which makes it possible to establish a point of contact, namely communion with God. Thinking of personhood was typical for the Russian religious philosophers, according to whom persons contemplate themselves as free causes and goals of their actions, so that they affirm themselves through the principle of the reasonable foundation manifesting not the world, but the true nature of the infinite and unconditional person. Persons are defined as carriers of moral consciousness whose content expresses the natural self-determination of humanity independently of the conditions, interests and goals of their physical existence. Morality is thus related to the *need to attain immortality*, that can only be achieved within the ecclesial setting. The radical quest for the possibility of Radical Orthodoxy can be responded trough the activation of the inherent desire for eternal communion with the source of life, society, knowledge and politics.

The need for justification and legitimacy of the radical theological commitment arises from the necessity to respond to some trends of the "radical secularization" in societies in the West, as well in the East. One can characterize the essence of the present state of that part of the world which is associated with the symbol of the "West" with the help of three words: secularism, atheism and nihilism. This implies that all aspects of the traditional Christian life become non-observable and are hidden under the cover of the politically correct ideologies. Any talk about belonging to Christianity is encouraged only at the level of private life and no Christian values are taught in schools and universities. There is also a characteristic hostility and suspicion with respect to anything religious in academic circles (both in the West and the East). Whereas the militant scientific atheism is no more viable as being discredited in the recent past, it becomes replaced by its transformed and socially adjusted remnant which can be labelled as secularism, that is, a kind of trans-ideological *laïcité* and servility to the alleged ideal of humanity understood only empirically. Here atheism acquires the features of secularism under the disguise of the authority of scientific and technological culture. Indeed, for example, in order to define the sense of humanity in categories overcoming racial, national, class and religious differences, one needs a universal language, and it is science and technology that pretend to be such a language so that the phenomenon of humanity is reduced to the physical and biological. Thus modern atheism turns out to be no more than an already known scientific atheism that is more aggressive,[1] sinister and advanced philosophically and anti-theologically,[2] than was the case, for example, in Soviet Russia. The reason for this is that modern atheism is motivated by the logic of material production and human resources, that is by the needs of the developing economies and not abstract ideologies. The fact that a scientific outlook represents the most obvious trend for secularism is not so disturbing for the natural and exact sciences, which deal

---

1. See Dawkins, *The God Delusion*.
2. See Comte-Sponville, *L'esprit de l'athéisme*.

with the phenomena most remote from the inner life of humanity. However, it becomes more serious for the humanities and social sciences.³

Secularism as an Encroachment on Personhood

Science and technology make human life dependent on its own advance while having no power of foreseeing its outcomes. It is sometimes claimed that technology is getting out of control so that the vision of the future is often depicted as being grey and sorrowful. But this intuition reflects not so much the problems of technology but rather the problems of moral self involved in in its advance. Whereas the abandonment of technology is inconceivable and utopian, technology is capable of making its adherents "transcendent-vision-blind" by diminishing their ability to be attentive to those experiences which cannot be explained or imitated through scientific methods and technology. It is because of the dominance of the scientific in collective consciousness that the secularism affects societies through the lack of the spiritually tantalizing identity leading to the fallacy of liberalism as a movement against everything that is traditional and historically immutable, potentially capable of undermining the cohesion and stability of society at least for a limited period of time.

However, as recognized by the Orthodox thinkers, the problem of secularism has its material causes in the search for indefinite wealth and consumption. This aspiration for greed and illusion for the ultimate value of life in *this age* has a strong political connotation with the ideology of "historical materialism," whose essence is to subdue all material and human resources to the strategy of survival and dominance of political forces aiming to control life and nature over the planet. Christos Yannaras gives a concise formulation of the consequences of such an ideology as it relates to diminution of human persons:

> On a global scale, capitalism thoroughly imposes upon peoples and nations the most vulgar practical application of historical materialism: consumerism made absolute . . . Metaphysics, art, love, morality, are pushed to the margin of human life, as mere complements of "entertainment" or of psychological preferences, as an inactive "superstructure" on economic priorities that have been rendered absolute . . . Our everyday experience is an intoxication with the ephemeral and the passing.⁴

---

3. Woodhead, "Restoring Religion to the Public Square," 6.
4. Yannaras, *The Church in Post-Communist Europe*, 2–4.

The logic of this diminution of persons receives further reifications in socio-cultural realities. Capitalism imposes the demand for "Globalisation" and hence "Multiculturalism" as a disguised form of international economic slavery. This naturally leads to the question of the possibility of traditionally orientated ethnic and religious communities. Within the logic of capitalism, all such formations must become obsolete since they hinder the growth of the oligarchic economy. Thus there is a question: "Where is the place of tradition, religion, religious communities and ultimately of the church as asserting personal creativity of the human existence?" One can further ask about the place of a critical function of theological and ecclesial thinking. Are all of them irrelevant? For the advocates of moral capitalism, the answer is probably "Yes!" Here is a quote from the Nobel-Prize winner in literature Mario Vargas Llosa:

> The notion of "cultural identity" is dangerous. From a social point of view, it represents merely a doubtful, artificial concept, but from a political perspective it threatens humanity's most precious achievement: freedom . . . The notion of "collective identity" is an ideological fiction and the foundation of nationalism.[5]

According to this view all "religious traditions" fall under rubrics of collective identities and thus are fictional and prone to nationalism. However, what is forgotten here is the historical meaning of religious identity related to the civilizational delimiters of the European civilization which modern generation takes for granted. It is also forgotten that the very technological advance and scientific appropriation of the world became possible because of the once initiated support of education and research in Europe by the christian church. In addition, one must raise a purely philosophical argument that any supposed all-unity of people such as the unity of mankind remains no more than an eschatological ideal, unachievable in the present age.[6] Thus the appeal to a non-collective, non-cultural and non-religious identity remains an abstract idea devoid of any existential meaning and represents the encroachment on the person.

The apology for the impersonal collective identity as belonging to the global mechanism of economic self-perpetuation naturally leads to another, most grave fallacy of the secular mind, to *nihilism* as that *state* of consciousness which questions not only particular arrangements of the human social life, but even life itself. Nihilism doubts the basics: what is the point of the humanity of humans, the naturalness of nature, the justice of the polis, and

---

5. Llosa, "The Culture of Liberty," 117.
6. Gutner, "Edinstvo cheloveka v eskhatologicheskoy perspektive," 230–36.

the truth of knowledge? Why not rather their opposites, the dehumanization of humans to improve humanity, the systematic "raping" of nature to develop the economy, injustice to render society more efficient, the absolute empire of distraction by irrelevant information to escape the constraints of the true? Nihilism manifests itself as much of an advanced and sinister attack on humanity as personhood. Here the very sense of the truth of scientific progress, being a most efficacious form of a political and collective argument, is distorted. Science is being effected in the name of human persons, but these same persons turn out to be outside of scientific description. The same is true with respect to society that needs not persons but masses of individuals which are easier adapted to the norms of materialistic thinking and criteria of consumption. Nihilism, as a natural consequence of modern atheism exploits modern science by insisting on effective non-existence of personhood. The oblivion of the person is treated by Christian philosophy and theology as an *encroachment* on the absolute priority of the human world and those communal links in societies which have formed the spirit of the Christian civilization and integrity of its historical path through communion with God. The oblivion of the person is the *encroachment* on the significance of its history impressed in the architectural image of European cities, masterpieces of art and literature, in the very way of European thinking and its values.

Thus here is the fundamental question that Christians should address: "What is the church and its theology?" And their response is possible only this way: *Church and its experience represent humanity's deepest need to attain personal immortality*, that is to achieve the state of unlimited love and freedom from necessities of this world. Immortality must not be understood in a biological sense, for even physics makes it clear that the present state of the universe will not last forever and our physical survival is doomed. To attain immortality means to have an awareness of death as an ontological delimiter of absolute life. We are lucky of living at that cosmological era which supports biological life (anthropic principle), but, at the same time, we are contingent upon the billion of years of not well understood evolution of the universe. Living without God we remain no more than the *freaks* of the universe (Erich Fromm) existing in the conditions of *non-attunement* to it (Jean-François Lyotard) and inherent incommensurability with it. This universe, being also devoid of the Divine presence, is "enframed" through scientific modeling and computational synthesis thus accelerating our "*planetary homelessness*" (Martin Heidegger). Whereas fear of death chains human beings to solitude and despair, the awareness of death frees humanity for the restoration of its God-given, hypostatic centrality in the universe.

Personhood as a Primary Theological Mystery

In spite of the fact that modern social psychology doubts the very relevance of the notion of personhood, the question of its definition and its persistence in any discourse on the sense of existence indicates that this is a relevant problem. The history of the philosophy of the twentieth century shows that the systematic diminution of personhood within the frame of scientific thought caused a philosophical and theological resistance to that which Gabriel Marcel called the "disappearance" of human personality: "People would not bother to appeal to the idea of 'the person' so constantly if human personality were not on the way towards its disappearance."[7] The fact that scientific approach to the world makes the whole phenomenon of humanity part of the cosmic determinism thus, in words of Sergey Bulgakov, mortifying life,[8] made an illusion that personality, personhood, or simply the person, is a psychological epiphenomenon which does not have any relevance for the objective scheme of things. In this case, since it was believed that the origins of human life could be found within cosmic determinism, the question about existence of persons can be dismissed on the same grounds as the question about God.

It is exactly in a situation like this that the Russian philosopher and theologian Viktor Nesmelov argues in the opposite but positive direction that the question of personhood and God cannot be separated:

> If anyone, who does not trust the reality of intuitive knowledge would ask me to prove to him the reality of God's being by means of scientific method, then I would ask this prudent follower of the positive science to produce me a scientific proof of his own existence. Then, I think, that one would have grasped that to produce such a proof is impossible in a scientific sense."[9]

"All living religion, in fact, originates only from man's consciousness that man himself, as well as the whole world together with him, are entirely immersed in the power of death and evil, and that it is this state of the world and man that constitute an ancestral guilt of every man and the whole humanity before God. And finally that true and complete salvation from this state could come only from God."[10] "The living presence of God constitutes the immediate datum of the intellectual contemplation and,

---

7. Marcel, *Men Against Humanity*, 127.
8. Bulgakov, *Philosophy of Economy*, 183.
9. Nesmelov, *Vera i znanie*, 82.
10. Ibid., 88–89.

hence, immediate and by no means removable main content of religious thinking."[11] Nesmelov implicitly follows the theology of the Divine image by referring the sense of the Divine presence in human persons to the Incarnation as the ultimate archetype of the human condition: "in the actual world of sin and death, there is certainly no unity between God and the world; but this unity must exist because the Son of God became man in order to reconcile the world and God and transform the world into such a Kingdom of God for which God would be . . . the real beginning of all living activities."[12] In this sense the presence of the Divine Image in man in his present condition may be interpreted as the unfaded light of the Kingdom, that light which forms the essence of personhood and justifies the radical theological commitment in all spheres of human affairs.

Russian religious philosophers made this last stance explicitly present by approaching personhood on the grounds of that which cannot be conditioned by rubrics of the cosmic order. Russian philosophers understood well that no accomplished definition of personhood is possible, and that the problems and contradictions in any definition would be characteristic of that which personhood is. According to Nesmelov, the main ambiguity of personal existence originates from the limited being of man on the one hand, and the presence of the image of the unconditional being on the other hand: "all particular contradictions of thought and life arise from man's aspiration to fulfil the ideal image of the unconditional in the necessary boundaries of the external conditions."[13] However, since this aspiration cannot be accomplished, the main ambiguity of man's being is revealed to him as eternally irremovable. The image of the unconditional being thus constitutes the image of man as an unconditional essence in spite of the fact that man remains a simple thing in the physical world. The assertion of personhood thus becomes a strange procedure from an epistemological and spiritual point of view, because in its affirmation of the affinity to the absolute and unconditional humans understand that they can never achieve the state of existence of this unconditional being. Then the unconditional character of personhood, being placed in the constant contradiction with the conditional being in the world, evokes thinking of the Divine as the other pole of the unconditional in man.[14] Man as a person can only be an unconditional being: this is the "fact" which man knows through knowing himself. The person asserts itself as a free agent of its own volitions and

---

11. Ibid., 89.
12. Ibid., 90.
13. Nesmelov, *Nauka o cheloveke*, 246.
14. Ibid., 261.

this mode of being is called by Nesmelov absolute and unconditional: "only an unconditional being can be person; every man is directly aware of this and truly knows this through knowing of himself."[15] Correspondingly, the human person represents that link, or pole of being, where the unconditional and conditional meet. Here Nesmelov again points to the vanity of all scientific attempts to "explain" personhood in its incarnate condition. In its displayed givenness it can be studied, but the fact of its existence, as a *real fact*, can only be interpreted through the help of the Bible, in which the existence of man is posed as a fact of the relationship between God and the world. It is the mystery of the facticity of personal beings that leads all philosophy and science to the idea of the free *creation* of persons by God. According to Nesmelov:

> existing as a person and, at the same time, as an ordinary thing of the physical world . . . man is not an unconditional being, but only expresses in itself the real link between conditional and unconditional being . . . If scientific thought had not denied this mysterious fact through its pseudo-scientific explanations . . . [it] would have come to the Biblical vision of humanity as made in the image of God. This could be possible because the existence of man as an image of Absolute Being can be established strictly scientifically and independently of the Bible just from the psychological analysis of the nature and content of human person, so that one can appeal to the Bible . . . only in order to find in it the explanation of the *real fact*. Both, the objective being of God, as well as true knowledge of his nature are directly given to man through the real being and natural content of its own personhood. But why and how is human person as the real image of God is possible within conditional being, this we do not know and cannot know, so that the Bible tells us about creation of man by the will of God.[16]

Let us accentuate the important aspect of Nesmelov's thought, namely, that the very assertion of personhood as a sheer *fact* that takes place from within human life reflects upon and finds in itself the irreducible presence of some absoluteness and freedom not determined by the external conditions. The presence of the absolute in human consciousness is a *fact*. The usage of the language of *fact* (in contradistinction with the language of objects) positions the existence of persons in the category of *events*, whose phenomenality can never be exhausted through the representation of objects and

---

15. Ibid., 264.
16. Ibid., 264–65.

represents such a puzzle for human consciousness that this consciousness is constituted by this puzzle. Said bluntly, "personhood" is given to men as such a phenomenon which can never be presented in the phenomenality of objects because it entails the image of the infinite absolute being that can neither be objectified. Nesmelov insists that the fact of existence of man, the reality of its very being, *de facto*, justifies the idea of God, and that the two-fold hypostatic constitution of man justifies knowledge of God.[17] In a way, the inherent sense of the Divine which justifies religious experience, faith, theology, as well as all other modes of the human activity proceeds from the fact of life, that is existence of human persons. But the fact of existence of persons is inferred by man exactly because personhood cannot be realized under the form of representation. Person, as a free cause and goal of its actions, affirms itself not through the physical law of mechanical necessity, but through the trans-sensible principle of the reasonable foundation. Correspondingly the trans-sensible being is known to man through the immediate consciousness of being and the content of his own personhood: "In knowledge of ourselves we know truly, that although our own person exists only in the necessary conditions of the physical world, by its nature it manifests not the world, but the true essence of the very Infinite and Unconditional, because the infinite and unconditional is free being for itself, but this free being for itself is and can only be the being of the self-existing Person."[18]

The question then is how the meaning of personhood can be explicated in, so to speak, "practical" terms. In other words, what can be an existential objective of human beings in order to realize their personhood, that is the image of the unconditional and absolute, in the conditions of necessities of nature. Nesmelov points towards moral consciousness as that characteristic of spiritual and personal existence which leads man not to the idea and knowledge of life as *the good*, but also as *truth*. Nesmelov writes:

> What is expressed through the content of moral consciousness is exactly a natural self-determination of a human person in the conditions of its physical existence. It is that is *moral* for man which must be fulfilled by him; but man *must fulfill* that which is *truly human*, then it is that truly human *which expresses by itself true nature of human person independently of the conditions, interests and goals of its physical existence*.[19]

---

17. Ibid., 266.
18. Ibid., 269.
19. Ibid., 287.

Moral consciousness is that which seeks the determination of the sense of personal existence independent of the natural conditions of existence. However, it is exactly this real living in the world in accordance with moral consciousness that becomes impossible; it remains no more than a representation of the moral consciousness: "the point is exactly that, that true life whose existence man grasps through moral consciousness, in fact, cannot be realized because man exists not only as a free agent in the world, but as a simple thing of the world, a thing which is subordinated to the general laws of the physical existence."[20]

This negative assertion of man's incapacity to fulfill his humanness according to the ideal of moral consciousness has, so to speak, a positive dimension, for it is through this incapacity that human person asserts itself through his will as an image of the absolute personal being. On a level of practical existence, however, the gap between the ideal on the one hand, and the impossibility of achieving freedom from the necessities of the world on the other hand, creates a feeling of ontological solitude that remains an inerasable sign of the human existence. The presence of this sign and the possibility of its articulation point towards the image of the absolute and unconditional in human person. Nesmelov concludes that "the ultimate result of the science of man is the irresolvable mystery of his existence; how could man appear in the world whereas by the *essence of his personhood* he denies the world, and as such he is in turn denied by the world?"[21] In a different passage Nesmelov reasserts this point: "all man's deliberate virtue, in fact, rests only in his disdain of the world and its denial, and not at all in his desire to unfold in it and by its means the truth of the moral order, and through this unfolding to reflect in the world the life of the Absolute Person."[22]

Correspondingly, if such a denial of the world is effected, man cannot have any meaning in this world and thus mentally displaces himself into a different unknown world, still with no hope to reach that world existentially. The search for the hope of finding the sense of existence is then transferred to the realm of that absolute and unconditional. But even if God comes to mind as a savior and guarantor of the sense of existence, in its physical life man does not reach its destined place, so that his faith in that he occupies a very selected and special place in creation remains only a matter of his eschatological conviction with no possible justification on the grounds of reason. Reason becomes redundant as a practical tool of solving the mystery

20. Ibid., 287–88.
21. Ibid., 372 (emphasis added).
22. Ibid., 391.

of the human existence so that faith has to replace it but not as an epistemological sentiment, but as a *way of existence*.

The denial of the world on the grounds of asserting personhood effectively means that when man talks about person he intuits and contemplates his own existence as something which cannot be formalized and expressed in the phenomenality of objects. In this sense, the very assertion of personhood as an exclusively human feature positions humanity beyond the world of objects. But, remaining a thing among other things, man is disturbed by this strange contradiction that not everything in man can be known and understood on the grounds of personal reason. There is something in the human condition which escapes understanding at all thus leaving man to be unknowable for himself. In fact, the very denial of the world means no less than the impossibility to know the meaning of the world in the conditions of not being able to know what is man. The mystery of human existence and its ambiguous standing in the world as it was explicated by the Russian philosophers ultimately means that man is brought into existence subject to the condition, that he cannot be known to himself. In a contemporary parlance it is exactly this paradox that constitutes man's phenomenality consisting in that man can be shown to himself in such a way that he cannot be known to himself.

Russian religious philosophers were not the first ones who had to reaffirm the unknowability of man to himself. If one refers to the Biblical account of the creation of man in Genesis, one finds Adam was given the privilege of naming, understanding and dominating the world of all non-living and living things. However, the first man-Adam exercises this privilege only upon the animals, never upon God, and, what is even more interesting, not upon himself. The fact that any attempt to define God always fails can easily be conceived by remembering that God is the Creator of all, so that he cannot be comprehended by man, that is by a creature, who is, ontologically distant from God and, for whom the mystery of his own creation is existentially and epistemologically inaccessible. The question is why does not man exercise the privilege of naming and hence comprehending himself? The answer comes from the Biblical account of what is man and how he was created: among all living creatures man alone was created *not according to various kinds of living creatures (including man himself)* but "in *the* image" and "after *the* likeness" of God (Gen 1:24, 26). Man remains unnamable, that is not being able to be defined in terms of other things and species because he is *created*, that is formed and constituted in the image of God who admits no creaturely image. Man as the image of the Personal God, being a hypostatic creature, is infinitely distant from anything which he names. Thus man resembles nothing in creation, because he resembles

God. God, being incomprehensible and beyond any measure with the created, transfers this quality to man. This means that manhood exceeds any definition, be it anthropological or psychological, or any classification among other beings. Man appears to himself and to the other immediately within the image of the Absolute and Unconditioned God who surpasses all manifestations of his light to man. The incomprehensibility of man toward the incapacity of his own understanding makes him invisible not because of the lack of light of the Divine in him, but because of its insurmountable excess originating from God himself. Man is thus radically separated from every other being in the world by a definitive difference that is not any longer only ontological,[23] but iconic.[24]

To know man thus requires referring him to the incomprehensible God and thus by grounding man's incomprehensibility in the Incomprehensible, by virtue of man's being its image and likeness. St. Augustine, makes such an observation that man can be known only by God: "there is something of the human person which is unknown even to the 'spirit of man which is in him.' But you, Lord, know everything about the human person; for you made humanity." If man realizes this fact of its own incomprehensibility, its own ignorance of himself is to be transformed through confession towards God's knowledge of himself: "what I know of myself I know because you grant me light, and what I do not know of myself, I do not know until such time as my darkness becomes 'like noonday' before your face."[25] Man as a thing of the world is infinitely distant from man as a hypostasis of the universe. It is this intrinsic split in his consciousness as an infinite difference of man from himself, that difference which he cannot comprehend and, probably, should not comprehend at all.

His own incomprehensibility tells man that he passes beyond and above his own physical means. He has to conclude that only the infinite and incomprehensible can comprehend man, and this tells him *of* and shows him *to* himself; only God can reveal man to man, because man only reveals himself by revealing, without knowing it, the one whose image he bears. If this image is obscured or abandoned, man can no longer appear in the proper context of his predestined humanity, but disfigures himself by attempting to refer his "image" to something other than himself, that is by allowing himself to resemble something other than God. It is this dissimilarity with the image that devalues man making him devoid of God so that

---

23. One means here the contrast between humanity as consubstantial to the rest of creation and humanity as hypostatic creatures.

24. Gregory of Nyssa, "On the Making of Man," 396–97.

25. Augustine, *Confessions*, 182–83.

man loses the human face as an icon of God: man's soul "is not sufficient to itself, nor is anything al all sufficient to him, who departs from Him, who is alone sufficient."[26]

Now one can conjecture that man's solitude in the world is *de facto* his existence in the conditions of the inherent incapacity to know himself and then to know the sense of his life. While attempting to verbalize this unknowability man discovers the paradox and contradiction of his condition, that contradiction which constitutes ultimately the content of the only mystery in the world. According to Nesmelov, this mystery is not reduced to our present ignorance, or inability to know about existence of God as the archetype of man as person. Even if this knowledge could be acquired on the ways of spiritual life and communion with God, the question would remain as to why, by having such a knowledge, man cannot live in accordance with it. Even if every man realized himself as an image of God, this sense of being *from* God entirely contradicts to the actual existence of man as a simple thing *in* this world. Then the question of how to alleviate this contradiction and to avoid existential incertitude of being born into this world without knowing why and for what purpose, can be addressed through an appeal to Christianity which recognizes this mystery and proposes to solve it.[27] This is the reason why, according to Nesmelov,

> man aspires not only to the explanation of his situation in the world, but also to knowledge of that way *through which he could indeed overcome this situation* . . . To reach knowledge of the eternal mystery of being means the same as to, *de facto, remove* this mystery in being, that is to produce the *true way* for accomplishment by man of his destiny in the world and to give him *true possibility* for the accomplishment of this destiny. It is about this way and this possibility that Christian teaching tells man. It communicates to man that knowledge without which man cannot manage, but which he, unfortunately, cannot create.[28]

Personhood as Radical Theological Commitment

If humanity's sense of existence is approached from the perspective without God, that is being "grounded literally in nothing," it can be described in three equivalent ways: as existence in solitude, as existence with no sense, as

---

26. Augustine, *On the Trinity*, 50.
27. Nesmelov, *Nauka o cheloveke*, 418.
28. Ibid., 409–10.

existence whose meaning can never be known (understood). On the level of the human psychology this leads to fear of both life and death which enslaves man and chains him to his earthly fate. According to Russian philosophers, the slavery to the fear of death cascading towards society, politics and economics, perpetuates death to an ever greater extent.[29] Berdyaev links this post-lapserian deficit of personhood, with its under-development and overall impotence of man to reach its fullness. He identifies this insufficiency of man with his finitude which emerges when the manifestation of the Unconditional Absolute in him is dimmed because of slavery to death. Berdyaev advocates for the rediscovery of infinity and eternity in the hidden propensity of the Fallen humanity (still archetypically present through the impetus of restoration of the Divine Image).[30] The impetus of restoration of the image finds its fulfillment in creativity as manifestation of freedom: "Victory over death cannot be evolution, cannot be a result of necessity. Victory over death is creativeness, the united creativeness of man and God, it is a result of freedom.[31] Creativity as freedom brings man to the ecstatic exit from time towards the instantaneous synthesis of being where all modalities of space (generating the sense of solitude) and time (perpetuating despair) are suspended and human spirit achieves the climax in its practical imitation of its Creator. Creativity as freedom, as the overcoming of solitude and incomprehensibility of existence, makes a breakthrough from this world to a new and transfigured world. And the very possibility of this break into the other world is inherent in the God-given symphonic and creative economy in this world. The fulfillment of person is a constant transcendence of the mundane and self-evident, the overcoming of the constraints and slavery to the incarnate physical existence. It is in this movement that the sense of solitude and despair disappears because the whole of the human history, as well as the whole universe, are brought inside the infinite and incomprehensible

---

29. "From fear of death man sows death, as a result of feeling a slave, he desires to dominate. Domination is always constrained to kill. The state is always subject to fear and therefor it is constrained to kill. It has no desire to wrestle against death." Berdyaev, *Slavery and Freedom*, 251. A manifesting discrepancy between the desire to find the sense of life on the one hand, and the collective state-like life of man where human dignity is dismissed was described by Evgeniy Trubetskoy in following words: "On the one hand there is a powerful appeal of love to every man, on the other hand all peoples are armed from top to toe for the mutual extermination. On the one hand there is an attempt of man to break the closed loop of the struggle for survival, to rise from the Earth in a joyous enthusiasm of love and, on the other hand, there is another illustration of the impotence of any of such an attempt, namely the state with its periodically repetitive and triumphant slogan *all is for war.*" Trubetskoy, *Smysl zhizni*, 38.

30. Nesmelov, *Nauka o cheloveke*, 251.

31. Ibid., 252.

subjectivity of man in the image of the Divine. Thus freedom and creativity imply such a transformation in the vision of the world where human personhood regains its central place in the universe: this is an ideal of God-manhood so heartedly fostered by all Russian religious philosophers. All of the Russian philosophers quoted in this paper expressed a deep thought and care for man, the world and God. It was their radical theological commitment to look for the consolation of the soul of all humanity from within a limited historical period in the twentieth century, a period of history full of apostasy and demonic inhumanity. Their hymnology to man is the perennial attempt to affirm this world as still imbued with faith, hope and love.

Bibliography

Augustine of Hippo. *Confessions*. Translated by Henry Chadwick. Oxford: Oxford University Press, 1991.

———. *On the Trinity*. Translated by Stephen McKenna. Cambridge: Cambridge University Press, 2002.

Berdyaev, Nikolai. *Slavery and Freedom*. Translated by R. M. French. London: Geoffrey Bles, 1943.

Bulgakov, Sergey. *Philosophy of Economy. The World as Household*. Translated by Catherine Evtuhov. New Haven: Yale University Press, 2000.

Comte-Sponville, André. *L'esprit de l'athéisme*. Paris: Albin Michel, 2006.

Dawkins, Richard. *The God Delusion*. London: Black Swan, 2007.

Gutner, Grigoriy. "Edinstvo cheloveka v eskhatologicheskoy perspektive." In *Bogoslovie tvoreniya*, edited by Aleksey Bodrov and Mikhail Tolstoluzhenko, 230–36. Moscow: Izdatel'stvo BBI, 2013.

Gregory of Nyssa, St. "On the Making of Man." Translated by William Moore and Henry Austin Wilson. In *The Nicene and Post-Nicene Fathers*. Vol. 5, edited by Philip Schaff and Henry Wace, 387–427. Grand Rapids, MI: Eerdmans, 1996.

Llosa, Mario V. "The Culture of Liberty." In *The Morality of Capitalism*, edited by Tom G. Palmer, 114–22. Ottawa: Jameson, 2011.

Marcel, Gabriel. *Men Against Humanity*. Translated by G. S. Fraser. London: Harvill, 1952.

Nesmelov, Viktor. *Nauka o cheloveke*. Kazan': Tsentral'naya Tipografiya, 1905.

———. *Vera i znanie s tochki zreniya gnoseologii*. Kazan': Tsentral'naya tipografiya, 1913.

Trubetskoy, Evgeniy. *Smysl zhizni*. Berlin: Slovo, 1922.

Woodhead, Linda. "Restoring Religion to the Public Square." *The Tablet*. 28 January 2012, 6.

Yannaras, Christos. *The Church in Post-Communist Europe*. Berkley: InterOrthodox, 1998.

18

The Crisis of the Classical Anthropological Model

The Anthropological Mission of Post-Secularism according to Sergey Horujy

Roman Turowski

Sergey Horujy bases his philosophical research of the human being on the general postulate of human crisis, which manifests itself today on a practical as well as on theoretical level. In the first case, we are dealing with the rapidly growing dynamic changes of modern man, in the second with the lack of adequate theoretical tools, that would help us to understand the reasons and the logic of such dynamics. Horujy believes that the theoretical tools that exist today, first of all philosophical anthropology, based on classical metaphysics with three fundamental concepts of the subject, the essence and the substance, have little effect. The model developed within such frames Horujy defines as "the classical model of European man," or "the classical anthropological model" and criticizes it for a lack of a holistic understanding of a person.

An adequate description of the anthropological situation cannot, according to Horujy, offer today even those philosophical trends that have developed as a discourse of opposition towards metaphysics.[1] On this basis we have not yet developed such theoretical tools that would enable us to fully replace the anthropology built in the paradigm of European metaphysics. In these discourses, a holistic view of human rights is also missing. As a result,

---

1. Here we are talking about "two-way and countervailing impulses: standing under the banner of Systems or Structures and the banner of the History or Life," see Khoruzhiy, "Novaya antropologiya," 4.

today we are talking not only about the death of the subject, but also the death of a person as such. In addition, due to the refusal from metaphysics, the entire field of the humanities has lost, according Horujy, an integrating episteme, understood as their common ground.² Under the absence of such methodological foundation, "heuristic disorientation is being created in scientific knowledge, a fragmentation and disunity among the different disciplinary discourses in particular."³ Therefore, as Horujy says, one of the main tasks of the modern humanities is a search for a new episteme, emerging from a certain holistic understanding of the anthropological reality.

The core of such an episteme should be, according to Horujy, some new anthropology "understood as a common basic methodology for the whole ensemble of humanitarian discourses,"⁴ and it "should not take the form of a theory or a system of syllogisms construction and essentialist abstract concepts."⁵ In the spirit of Husserl *zu den Sachen selbst*, Horujy seeks the grounds for such anthropology at some form of holistic anthropological experience. Such experience should "correspond to the two conditions or principles of epistemological transparency and anthropological depth."⁶

According to Horujy, the anthropological experience of Christian ascetics ordered in the form of hesychastic spiritual practice (ἡσυχασμός) meets the conditions. Firstly, it developed its own organon (οργανον), its own holistic method of providing this spiritual practice with epistemological transparency. Secondly, the subject of hesychastic spiritual practice is "the ontological and religious experience, in which person seeks to overcome his own existential modus."⁷ Thus, the experience in which human relationship with the being is actualized, is constitutive for the structures of human personality and identity. As a certain methodological mirror, looking in which Horujy builds his own anthropology, philosopher uses the classical anthropological model referred to at the beginning of this article. The latter is a kind of a meta-discourse built by Horujy of anthropological content implicite present in European philosophy. He analyzes, in terms of such contents, the philosophy of Aristotle, Boethius, Descartes and Kant. Anthropology appears in these authors as sections of metaphysics, but not the central ones.

2. Horujy uses the notion Episteme in the interpretation by Michel Foucault, "where the culturally-historical dimensions are on the foreground; so that the episteme becomes the leading characteristic of cultural formations" (ibid., 4–5).

3. Ibid.

4. Ibid., 5.

5. Khoruzhiy, "Proyekt sinergiynoy antropologii," 1.

6. Ibid., 2.

7. Ibid., 3.

Metaphysics has been charged with defining the status and place of man in the world for centuries. Wherein, as Horujy points out rightly, "a person, as such, his dramatic situation, has never been its main subject."[8] As a part of metaphysics, a person was present, firstly, as a being made up of parts and described using the refined structure of categories. Secondly, the justification for such a structure is the concept of "essentially unchanged" sub specie aeternitatis regarded as "true regardless of the time, [true] that has no historical aspect."[9] And with all this, the intuition of incompleteness of metaphysical description of the person has always been present in the philosophy. Its main source, according to Horujy, was a direct anthropological experience, which could conflict with the harmonic image built in metaphysics. The point here is, for example, the mystical or aesthetic experience, the sphere of human emotion etc. As we know, for a long time metaphysics was a synonym for philosophy in general. However, in the twentieth century increased awareness of the fact, that the metaphysical discourse was unable to explain many of the phenomena of a new era such as, for example, the growing dynamics of changes to the anthropological reality. According to Horujy, "in the twentieth century life outside of metaphysics gets its own language."[10] Today, as he points out, in the field of modern culture attempts are made to form a new integrating episteme that could fully replace the classic anthropological model.

According to Horujy, there are two fundamental concepts at the base of the classical anthropological model: "nature" and "subject," the emergence of which is associated with the names of Aristotle (οὐσία) and Descartes (*cogito*), respectively. In addition, he notes the role of Boethius, who introduced the concept of individual substance (*individua substantia*). The latter concept was an intermediate stage in the evolution of the European anthropological models from Aristotle through Descartes, and to its final form in transcendental philosophy of Kant. Horujy identifies five key predicates of this model: (i) individuality (*individuirovannost'*), (ii) duality (*dualistichnost'*), (iii) substantiality (*substantsional'nost'*), (iv) gnosiologicality (*gnoziologirovannost'*), (v) secularity (*sekulyarizirovannost'*).

The Man of Aristotle and the Man of Boethius

Aristotle describes the person, firstly, with the help of the concept of nature (οὐσία). A specific feature of the man, according to Stagirite, is the

8. Ibid.
9. Khoruzhiy, *Lektsii*, part 3.
10. Ibid.

subordination to reason, understood as the ability to obtain objective knowledge about the basic being constants. In building its all-encompassing metaphysics, Aristotle faced however "the impossibility of conceptualizing the person as a volatile, elusive and multidimensional reality."[11] Summarizing, the anthropological model contained *implicite* in the metaphysics of Aristotle, Horujy highlights its two features. First, the substantiality (the man as an autonomous substance). Second, the gnoseologicality (selfless knowledge as a central strategy of human life).

The next stage, after Aristotle, in the formation of the classical anthropological model was the idea of Boethius, who creatively developed anthropological thought, contained in the Christian discourse *implicite*.[12] Boethius, defining personality as *naturae rationabilis individua substantia*, transforms it from a theological category to anthropological one. Wherein, Boethius was oriented not only on the patristic discourse, but also on the Roman law, which widely used the concept of a persona. According to Horujy, "a person here is an anthropological concept, and its development in Boethius may be considered as the beginning of a personalistic paradigm, not a theological but anthropological one."[13]

The Man of Descartes

The Man of Descartes is the formal unity of the two radically different from each other realms: *res cogitans* and *res extensa*, that "has an anthropological sense of setting the fundamental cutting of man."[14] According to Horujy, Descartes replaces anthropological problems with the issue of the subject, body-machine and mixed phenomena. According to Horujy, "the Anthropology of Descartes is basically anti-antropology: as its source and the main thesis of the person is the thesis of his absence as an integral unity."[15] In the philosophy of Descartes "there is neither love nor death (only writing

---

11. Khoruzhiy, *Fonar' Diogena*, 24.

12. In Christian experience a meeting with God was expressed primarily as the essence of personal character with a name. Based on this experience a new personalist theological paradigm was built. That is why the development of the Trinitarian and Christological dogma occupies an important place in the problem of personality, developed primarily by Cappadocian Fathers. The concept of personality appears here as a theological notion sui generis, as the Divine hypostasis, as a special kind of ontological horizon different from any empirical existence.

13. Khoruzhiy, *Fonar' Diogena*, 26.

14. Ibid., 40.

15. Ibid.

off your old car), there is no God of Abraham, Isaac and Jacob."[16] The Man of Descartes is seen by Horujy as radically dissected. Such a cut is "the initial methodological position of the philosopher, and its division is the final outcome (metaphysical and anthropological)."[17] By adopting this strategy, Descartes reaches a "holistic epistemical perspective [of vision] and a way of knowing, that oriented to the objectives of useful world elaboration."[18] According to Horujy, "consciousness of Descartes's man deprived of integral manifestations [describing the very essence of being a man], it is neither a religious consciousness, nor a loving one; it is also not a consciousness in the experience of being-towards-death, and so on."[19] The Russian philosopher wrote that, in the teachings of Descartes in general, "in his picture of reality, there is no man: as there is no clear image of a man as a man, the whole man in the fullness of his content, structure and properties."[20] Descartes's hypothetical person as a whole is deprived of his own internal content.

The Secularism of Descartes in the Anthropological Aspect

The subject of Descartes is not yet a person, but only a certain autonomous reality, the substance, the only constant feature of which is a cognitive activity. According to Horujy, metaphysics is understood by Descartes primarily as the science of the principles of knowledge, and not as a discourse on God, life and the world. An ontology is present here *implicite*, but it is not here *explicite*. As Horujy states, "Descartes does not deny the existence of things divine, but he eliminates them from the horizon of knowledge and, in essence, from consciousness, transferring [it] to the theology, and carefully fenced off from the latter, arranged for it a kind of a splendid isolation or an honorable ghetto."[21] An area where the man of Descartes—as a thinker and as an independent actor—can manifest itself most fully, "the scene of his independence and self-sufficiency was basically relations with the outside world."[22] Thus, there was a reorientation of priorities and goals of the person from the religious sphere to cognitive and economic activity.

16. Ibid., 82.
17. Ibid., 81.
18. Ibid.
19. Ibid., 84.
20. Ibid., 106.
21. Ibid., 67.
22. Ibid.

A good illustration of the secular character of the anthropology of Descartes is his interpretation of the passions. In asceticism, passions are considered to be an obstacle to reaching God himself, such a way is understood as a goal and a calling of a man. In turn, in Descartes "a strategy of implementation of human nature disappears, *ergo* the task of the total overcoming, the eradication of passions in general as such also disappears." According to Horujy, "in austerity passion are considered as religious ontological and psychological phenomenon; in deistic secular paradigm of Descartes purely psychological aspect [of passion] remains, and thus the ethical assessment of the phenomenon is changing diametrically."[23]

The Man of Kant

According to Horujy, "Kant takes the next major step along the path of structural de-anthropologization, removing the subject from the center to the margins and giving his own discourse the structure of the systematic self-organizing unity of predicates."[24] The role of the subject of ethics significantly increases in Kantian philosophy, and ethics itself receives the status of the main sphere of individual self-realization. Horujy believes that Kant holds "full deconstruction of the subject of knowledge"[25] In the field of pure knowledge, the cognitive act, according to Kant, is justified by ontological (transcendental) knowledge. Thus, as Horujy rightly observes, "the ontology can be considered to be the basis for the epistemology of Kant."[26] In turn, the philosopher considers religion to be the rationale for the ethical sphere, a kind of practical ontology. Thus, the subject field and the purpose of religion have a primarily ethical justification in transcendental philosophy. According to the Russian philosopher, the concept of religious subject in Kant's view is completely absorbed by the concept of the subject of ethics, the concept of God here becomes a part of the ethical discourse. If Descartes's God was needed as a guarantor of objectivity and truthfulness of knowledge, in Kant's system, God provides unconditional moral law.

Despite the fact that Kant does not approve of the Cartesian form of dualism, integral anthropological manifestations are absent in his philosophy, just as in Descartes's. Existential predicates, reducible to love and death, as to the two fundamental realities of human existence, in the philosophy of Kant lose, according to Russian philosophy, their fundamental importance.

23. Ibid., 78.
24. Ibid., 153.
25. Ibid.
26. Ibid.

So, love is understood here as a subsidiary aspect of the debt, as a love for the law as such. In turn, the field of interpersonal relations in Kant's view is absent because of the subjective structure of his philosophy. With regard to the phenomena of a religious life, they are reduced in the critical philosophy to the ethical field, thus losing the nature of integral anthropological manifestations.

The Secularism of Kant in the Anthropological Aspect

According to Horujy, in Kant's system secularization becomes even more radical than it was in the Cartesian dualistic model. Firstly, Kant transforms ontology so that the latter is no longer competing with epistemology, turning into some justification for the latter. Secondly, religion is no longer competing with ethics as with some secular strategy of self-realization, striving for moral perfection, "religion [as Kant puts it] turns into justifying ethics, and all aspects and manifestations of religion cannot be comprised in that function, in the basis of practical reason, and are denied as delusions."[27] According to Horujy, "Kant secularized religion," turning it "from alternative secularized world into one of the functions of its setup."[28] As Horujy puts it, the anthropological sense of the secular paradigm that found favor in the philosophy of Kant, is "an ontology and transcendation fully absorbed [here] in ordinary knowledge, religion and religious life [absorbed] in ethics—there is nowhere and no need to leave the world, to escape from it."[29]

To show the anthropological consequences of the gradual secularization of European philosophical discourse, Horujy examines correlations of a human being to the boundary of the horizon of its existence, to the Anthropological Border.[30] The term describes the space of all human manifestations, in which fundamental changes in the way of its existence take place. The Anthropological Border is created, among others, by the phenomena of religious life, the essence of which is "to implement the aspirations (ascent) of the person to ontological Other, to another horizon of Being, with the finale, conceivable as the transformation [of human being]

27. Ibid., 158.
28. Ibid., 161–62.
29. Ibid.
30. A more detailed explanation of the concept of borders in the context of Anthropological synergetic anthropology Horujy reader will find in: Horujy, *Practices of the Self and Spiritual Practices*; Stöckl, "A New Anthropology," or Turowski, "The Symphonic Unity of Traditions."

to the Other or transcending, actual ontological transformation."[31] In an anthropological sense, secularization is, respectively, "the rejection of strategy or paradigm of meta-anthropological ascent-transcending."[32] In the secular consciousness, the world's border disappears, and with it disappears the Anthropological Border. The adoption of the secular cultural and civilizational paradigm "means the removal from the constitution of human being the relation to the Anthropological Border."[33]

Secular Heritage and the Anthropological Mission of Post-Secularism

The inevitable consequence of the domination of the classical anthropological model was secularization. Wherein, however, "a secular reason has not been able to create neither a fully justifiable system of political ethics nor complete secular reason of fundamental human rights such as the right to life."[34] The tragic events that took place in September 11, 2001 in New York were "understood as a direct and irrefutable proof of the collapse and the destructive policies of complete secularization that resulted in unappeasable confrontation."[35] From that moment post-secularism became a notable trend in social and political thought although, it seems to us, it has not found an adequate theoretical justification in the framework of philosophical anthropology yet. Jürgen Habermas, assessing the possibility of returning the religious discourse to the public discussion, notes that "the monotheistic traditions possess the language with such a semantic potential that has not yet been exhausted and can detect advantage over secular tradition in terms of ability to explain the world and to shape the identity."[36] In this context, the strategy of building a new anthropology as proposed by Horujy and using a spiritual tradition as its conceptual framework and paradigmatic base, can certainly be an important milestone in the deepening of post-secular discourse. Thus, this discourse can be extrapolated not only on social and political philosophy, as Habermas wrote, but also implemented in the area of philosophical anthropology.

Horujy proposes to implement new principles of building relations between philosophical anthropology and of the anthropology that is

31. Khoruzhiy, *Fonar' Diogena*, 68.
32. Ibid.
33. Ibid., 91.
34. Khoruzhiy, "Postsekulyarizm i antropologiya," 6.
35. Ibid., 3.
36. Habermas, "Exkurs," 131.

contained implicite in the Christian spiritual tradition. Thus, the result of the anthropological quest of Horujy could be the creation of an effective theoretical tool for the "formation of the new, post-secular type of relations between secular and religious spheres in the world and society."[37] Besides, his anthropological approach creates a new interfaith discourse, not only on the plane of social life "where the dialogue remains superficial, it does not create a convergence of participants, does not produce significant effects or impact on the internal motivation of participants, [on the] motives of their actions."[38] It is about the development of a clear and generally accepted basic concepts in anthropological dimensions—on that deeper level, on which, according to Horujy, the structure of human personality and identity are formed. This inveteracy in basic anthropological structures distinguishes Horujy's offer from other post-secular proposals, growing out of postmodernist and post-structuralistic ideologies, throwing away all valuable hierarchies, and only through the latter allowing the presence of religion in public discourse.

But Horujy sets even more important goals than the creation of an anthropological basis for a new episteme of humanities, a theoretical foundation for inter-religious dialogue or dialogue between secular and religious. The Russian philosopher takes on the mission "of the anthropological corrections, harmonization and improvement."[39] According to Horujy, the evolution of anthropological thought of the Renaissance through Modern era, the Enlightenment, Modernism and Postmodernism—is "the process of steady reduction of human, degradation of his personality structure, the destruction of his identity—a process that will inevitably approach and already closely approached the prospect of the leaving of a Man."[40] According to the Russian philosopher, the ideology of "limitless human" postulated in the Renaissance that found its theoretical expression in the writings of Descartes and Kant, leads to "the erosion and decay of person's identity, also implies a weakening of responsibility and coordination in dealing with environmental reality and, consequently, a decrease in the safety of these relationships."[41] In the context of our civilization aimed at the endless technological progress, "it must inevitably lead to dangerous blunders, miscalculations, and to an increase in the number and destructiveness of

---

37. Khoruzhiy, "Postsekulyarizm," 1.
38. Ibid., 3.
39. Ibid., 21.
40. Ibid., 20.
41. Ibid., 17.

man-made and partly environmental disasters."⁴² Horujy notes that "if a person refuses to manage his Border, it begins to deal with him itself. If consciousness denies the existence of borders—thus, it opens the way, it gives the freedom of action to the unconscious."⁴³ Summing up his analysis of the classical anthropological model, Horujy asks: "what may be the answer to the declared boundlessness of human and his mind, if not madness? What could be the answer to practically proved [*prakticheski dokazannoye*], imposed as a duty immortality, if not a suicide?"⁴⁴

According to Horujy, such current trends as the gradual cyborgization of a person, attempts at radical restructuring at the level of the genetic code and transhumanism are certain anthropological strategies aimed at "the disappearance of a man, at his death, [that] differ only in the methods of its offensive."⁴⁵ All of them are growing out of the waning classical model of a man that for so long dominated the European consciousness.⁴⁶ All of them "are summed into one large master trend of contemporary anthropological reality, which can be called a trend of Leaving."⁴⁷ Taking our actual situation as a deep anthropological crisis, Horujy looks for ways "of de-reducting of human identity, restoring the integrity of personality structures."⁴⁸ His strategy, built on a new anthropology, is intended to help in the "overcoming of anthropological risks as a means of correcting the global anthropological situation."⁴⁹

---

42. Ibid.

43. Ibid.

44. Ibid.

45. Ibid., 18.

46. For transhumanism, reducing a person serving in a computer file, it is regarded as "*sui generis* ultra-Cartesianism, shall communicate to the Cartesian dichotomy to the absolute limit: *res cogitans* is entirely preserved, meanwhile, as the *res extensa* as wholly subject to elimination," Khoruzhiy, *Fonar' Diogena*, 83–84.

47. Khoruzhiy, "Postsekulyarizm," 18.

48. Ibid.

49. Ibid., 21.

Bibliography

Habermas, Jürgen. "Exkurs: Transzendenz von innen, Transzendenz ins Diesseits." In *Texte und Kontexte*, 127–56. Frankfurt am Main: Suhrkamp, 1992.
Horujy, Sergey S. *Practices of the Self and Spiritual Practices: Michel Foucault and Eastern Christian Discourse*. Translated by Boris Jakim. Grand Rapids, MI: Eerdmans, 2015.
Khoruzhiy, Sergey S. *Fonar' Diogena. Kriticheskaya retrospektiva evropeyskoy antropologii*. Moscow: Institut sv. Fomy, 2010.
———. *Lektsii po vvedeniyu v Sinergiynuyu antropologiyu*. A series of lectures delivered at the Tomsk University, September, 2007. Online: http://http://synergia-isa.ru/?page_id=4301#H.
———. "Novaya antropologiya kak nauka nauk o cheloveke." Lecture delivered at the Pontifical University of John Paul II in Krakow, March 14, 2013. Online: http://synergia-isa.ru/wp-content/uploads/2013/05/horuzhy_talk_krakov_3_2013.pdf.
———. "Postsekulyarizm i antropologiya." Online: http://synergia-isa.ru/wp-content/uploads/2014/02/hor_postsecularizm_i_anthropology.pdf.
———. "Proyekt sinergiynoy antropologii: Dukhovnaya praktika kak osnovaniye dlya novoy kontseptsii cheloveka." Lecture delivered at the Pontifical University of John Paul II in Krakow, March 13, 2013. Online: http://synergia-isa.ru/wp-content/uploads/2013/05/horuzhy_talk_krakov_1_2013.pdf.
Stöckl, Kristina. "A New Anthropology: Sergej S. Khoružij's Search for an Alternative to the Cartesian Subject in *Očerki sinergijnoj antropologii*." *Studies in East European Thought* 59 (2007) 237–45.
Turowski, Roman. "The Symphonic Unity of Traditions: Sergey Horujy's Synergetic Anthropology and the Interpretation of History." In *Apology of Culture. Religion and Culture in Russian Thought*, edited by Artur Mrówczyński-Van Allen, Teresa Obolevitch and Paweł Rojek, 187–96. Eugene, OR: Pickwick Publications, 2015.

19

Christian Philosophical Mysticism in the Poetry of "Leningrad's Underground" as a Challenge to Soviet Secularism

Zhanna Sizova

The emergence of what is now called "the culture of Leningrad's underground" was motivated by the resistance and refusal of norms and values in the Soviet society in the last quarter of the twentieth century that were dictated by militant atheism and, as a result, unrestrained secularism. The cumulative symbol of the underground stands here for, so to speak, a parallel cultural medium, a different system of creativity which aimed abandoning the official ideology for the sake of spiritual freedom. The primary task of such an "underground" was to make a link between religion and culture, that is to create *perichoresis* between the sense of the Divine and human creativity, such as poetry, visual arts, music etc. The stress on these activities was made because all of them were based on personal aspirations and experiences which were not implemented in the social fabric. In this sense, being personal, the whole ethos of such an "underground" was mystical, for its aim was to change the perception of reality and see the world through the eyes of the transcendent. Poetry was a pivotal activity in this sense because it aimed to reflect the high and trans-worldly reality in words. And these words and the very form of speech had to be different not only linguistically, but philosophically. In this way the tendency of the underground of the late seventies and eighties was historically similar to the ideas of the pre-revolutionary Russian philosophers who advocated a synthesis of religion and culture, although in a different form and different context.

We emphasize in this paper the actual place of the acting spirit of new creativity and new philosophy under the symbol of Saint Petersburg (Leningrad). This is done on purpose for, unlike Moscow's "school of underground" leaning towards *avant-garde*, the whole ethos of Saint Petersburg's perception of reality and new philosophy was closely related to the actual physical space of events and persons who were in the foundation and development of the sense of presence God in the midst of the cultural capital of Russia. It is not an accident that religious and philosophical poetry was created in Petersburg, where "houses and streets, parks, squares and rubbish collections gradually, during three centuries, have been saturated by some trans-spatial sense, converting into the unsent letters, untold internal monologues, and historical artifacts which have not reached descendants." Behind Petersburg's landscapes "one can feel a constant sense-forming pressure, some trans-temporal movement of some creative and organising [*sic*] will."[1]

In this paper we undertake a study of the foundations of the synthesis of Christian ideas and poetry, which resisted and opposed the surrounding antireligious pathos of life in Soviet Russia. We concentrate on three particular names, Viktor Krivulin,[2] Leonind Aranzon[3] and Alexandr Mironov,[4] poets, who can be generically referred to the so called "second culture" of the Bronze Age of Russian literature. Indirectly, the poetry implied here becomes an advocate of some ideas from the Russian pre-revolutionary philosophy. One must mention that at the end of the seventies and in eighties many non-official, sometimes secret, philosophical societies were formed with the aim of studying the religious philosophy of the beginning of the twentieth century. Interestingly enough, the initiative for doing this had its origin among poets, writes and artists. A special "*kruzhkovyy* dialect" (as related to the narrow circle of participants) as a form of speech and thought, was created. Lexically, this dialect appealed to the language of Scripture, as well as to characteristic usage of religious and philosophical terminology by Nikolai Berdyaev, Sergey Bulgakov, Pavel Florensky, Semen Frank, Vasily

---

1. Krivulin, *Koncert po zayavkam*, 89.

2. Viktor Borisovich Krivulin (1944–2001) was a Russian poet, prose writer, an outstanding figure in the independent literature and culture publishing (*samizdat*), a theorist of the "non-official" culture.

3. Leonid Lvovich Aranzon (1939–1970) was a Russian poet, developing a poetics of Boris Pasternak and Osip Mandelstam. Was influential among poets of the "second culture." Practically all his publications are posthumous.

4. Alexandr Nikolaevich Mironov (1948–2010) was a Russian poet, a bright representative of the "Leningrad *avant-garde*." Most of his poetry was published as samizdat. The first official publication took place in 1985 in the collective volume *Krug* ("Circle"). His works were published in Russian literature journals in nineties.

Rozanov and others. It is through this language that the appropriation of literature, art of the past, present and future was formed. In this context one can refer to Fyodor Dostoevsky, who made an explicit link between philosophy and poetry, claiming that "philosophy is that same poetry, only in the highest degree." Then it is not surprising that such a study of religious ideas and philosophy had a serious impact on poetry as such, that poetry which has been acting and evolving despite of all secular delimiters of the then mundane life. What can be accentuated first of all, is that the poetry of the "second culture" exercised an intuitive, mystical knowledge (as a direct cognition) of the essence of things. This knowledge cannot be achieved through discursive faculty, but can only be ascended to through a direct grasp of a symbol, that direct grasp which comprises imagination and seizing upon the intrinsic truthfulness and mutability of things in the world. Sometimes, one can read through the lines of the poets, that they were guided by Divine Revelation, whose adjustment to the language of poetry and art required an extra effort and creativity, transcending the boundaries of that which has been available around in the secular social medium.

Logos in the Poetry of Viktor Krivulin as Resistance to Ordinariness

By analyzing the poetic works of Viktor Krivulin, one can trace the spiritual transformation from Soviet materialism and "fringed bloody freedom" to religion and spiritual freedom. The poet pins down the fact that a human life which is empty, torn apart and devoid of God pours out like sand from the "sting of the urban tube" onto the concrete pavement of nothing, into the "inhuman masses of the state." There is an eschatological motive which is manifest in every rhyme of the poet when he speaks about the reality which surrounds him. Reality for Krivulin is the apocalypse of the mundane and ordinary. The edge of the Earth as its end, the abyss of the human life, for a citizen of a big city, who is squeezed by the stones of skyscrapers, is not out there, but it is here and near: "the edge of the earth is not overseas, it is at every bus stop!" The broken man writhes with pain in the pose of an embryo in the urban landscape. This landscape of deserted factories and construction sites is monotonous and dull to the extent that the eyes are filled by despair and solitude: "around all is dark and cold, whenever swollen eyes are doomed to see it." Krivulin accentuates the emptiness and non-sense of life without God, when all existential anxieties related to life and death, as well as to the facticity of existence, are not addressed, so that the horror fills all its gaps. Krivulin writes: "the only warmth the atheistic life acquires is the horror." Here the poet brings up a perennial philosophical issue of the basic human anxieties, which were, for example, articulated by N. Berdyaev in the context of suffering as the natural human condition:

> Man is a suffering being because he is a divided being, one who lives both in the phenomenal world and in the noumenal. Man is an appearance, a creature of nature and subject to the laws of this world. At the same time man is also a "thing-in-itself," a spiritual being, free from the power of this world.[5]

Human consciousness fights spiritual chaos and synthesizes the life of the soul. But it has a suffering modality of splitting man in its own synthesis, although man attempts to use consciousness in order to relive himself of the suffering.

In a similar vein, the poetry of Krivulin becomes the lyrics of a spiritual catastrophe, a précis of that which could be described as the dehumanized being. In this sense, poetry becomes seen as personal everyday dying for the ordinary pleasures available to the Soviet man. Krivulin sees the ways of overcoming and exiting from the emptiness and horror of the dehumanizing suffering in the very act of pain, through its capacity to be a focus point of comprehending everything around. But this pain transcends itself by sending man to the Divine contemplation: "Every pain is the present of the heavenly valleys, where flock of the hills turns silver in worry"[6] or "Any sorrow's unable to be in itself, any tree of the cry emerges from a choir of grove."[7] Here the poet claims as if it is enough to fall and rot: one needs this asceticism in order to acquire a special spiritual vision. The overcoming of the ordinary and mundane through physical pain saturates the being of a human by another experience in order to fly away from the trivial and monotonic, to transform the latter and transfigure it in the poetical language. The misery of flesh and the burden of ailment (Krivulin was a victim of polio and limited in his capacity to move freely) is transfigured in his verses as a special lightness as being a premise and cause of the overcoming of the physical condition. By exercising his gift of spiritual discernment with respect to the flux of reality around him, Krivulin transcends the mundane and extracts from it that which is usually concealed.

One can say that Krivulin's poetry is logo-centric where "logos" is understood as "word's revelation" that attracts and incorporates in itself all other explicating projecting and prophesying meanings. However, this

---

5. Berdyaev, *The Beginning and the End*, 80.

6. Krivulin, *Kompozitsii*, 34.

7. Ibid.

logos is an anthropomorphic exhibition of God-manhood. Logos is great and above reality; it represents an essence of being that is more proximate with respect to the poet: "Logos breathes expanding,"[8] "Logos transcending the limits of reason in a mundane affair,"[9] "Being embraced by the Logos as brother."[10] On the other hand, logos is the human word, the world of pain and silence (as an apophatic word), that is, a "native muteness gift in the heavens of underground." During the most difficult times man-logos (in the series *Requiem* devoted to Krivulin's son who died young) stands before God as a blind hearer of words: "And those are not guilty, and these are still not right, and all of us—we shadows of the words."[11]

Krivulin's Logos assumes the fullness of sincerity in its speech. However, being sincere, he could be subjective, for, according to him, the exploration of the world can only be possible through the subjective discernment of philosophical and metaphysical ideas. (Krivulin believed that any agnosticism in poetry as non-productive, and any stoic denial of the other reality is also deadly for poetry). He also doubted the expression "spiritual poetry"; he said once in an interview: "one can use the word 'god' in a poetic verse, but there will be no God in it if metaphysical thinking is missing." In some cases Krivoulin's logos manifests itself as a kind of a textual decipher, full of Christian and cultural connotations: logos is a link towards mystical knowledge. One can claim that a new poetical language, as multi-variational sign-decipher emerges in Krivulin's poetry. This is the difficult and metaphorical Logos-word, appearing in the era of no faith, dead ends and moral capitulation, the ultimate height of the intuitive knowledge and Divine revelation: "Logos as Golden section, where in every corner and every atom: an awe . . . a straightening out . . . an illumination."[12]

The Sense of Beauty and Earthly Paradise as Theophany: the Case of Leonid Aronzon

Leonid Aronzon was not only outside official literature but, unlike Krivulin, he had no interest in any social problems whatsoever. The term "second culture" was brought into being after his death. The poetry of Aronzon is a neatly made and performed language of *states*, and its philosophical foundation is related to the idea of beauty: "My God, it's so beautiful! Every time,

---

8. Ibid., 48.
9. Krivulin, *Zhurnal Topka*, 17.
10. Krivulin, *Kompozitsii*, 66.
11. Krivulin, *Koncert po zayavkam*, 31.
12. Ibid., 78.

as if anew. There is no gap in beauty, one wants to look away, but no where to, there's no way?"[13] Being an antithesis to this, there is another verse: "I look, but there's no beautiful around, it's only near quiet and joy." Beauty, according to Aronzon, is not dependent on man's judgement; man can miss it and not to see it at all, but man can understand it as being continuous, eternal, all-encompassing, and that it lets us know of itself through silence and tranquillity. The idea of beauty found its response in many Russian religious philosophers, including Vladimir Soloviev, Pavel Florensky and Vladimir Lossky. The sense of beauty invokes the problem of the sense of life, life's priorities and its goals. Beauty is the "object" of unconditional contemplation. This refers us back to Soloviev who spoke of beauty as an idea that "embodied in the world prior to the human spirit, and its embodiment is no less real and much more significant (in the cosmogonic sense) than those material elements in which it embodies itself."[14]

Beauty in Aronzon has two dimensions: in the image of nature and in the idea of the earthly paradise. Key words in his poetry are: heavens, plants, lakes, trees, birds and insects. His texts look like they are formed of flowers. Wherever the poet is located in space, this space is filled in with the natural landscape. Even big cities and capitals are full of fox paths. A mystical landscape is present in very unexpected urban places. Thus, for example, in his notes one reads: "we were passing by the river Neva along the marvelous landscapes."[15] Its reliefs were formed of hills and peaks. These hills and peaks are metaphors of the earthly way of life. Their beauty and majesty articulate insignificance of man: "Every one is light and little, that one who has reached the peak."[16] The hills symbolize fertility and abundance: "the hill is poured out by the lava of flowers." On the one hand ,the poet feels himself a tiny segment of nature, its particle. On the other hand he speaks that man is that creation which is equal to nature. Thus he identifies himself with the garden: "By why I cannot be a wet garden under the lantern?" or "What a butterfly we are ourselves." Aronzon's insight in beauty makes him close to Florensky for whom beauty is an attribute of the Divine: "God is Supreme Beauty, through participation in Which everything becomes beautiful."[17] In this vein Aronzon writes: "I'll have to take notes after God if nobody else does this."[18] In this way the poet begins to describe the earthly paradise.

13. Aronzon, *Izbrannoye*, 1.213.
14. Solovyov, "Beauty in Nature," 38.
15. Aronzon, *Izbrannoye*, 2.294.
16. Ibid., 352.
17. Florensky, *Pillar and Ground of the Truth*, 413.
18. Aranzon, *Izbrannoye*, 2.301.

By filling his landscapes by various aesthetical insects, butterflies and birds, the poet immerses together with the reader in the Eden on earth. However, such a depiction of earthly paradise as the beauty of nature is not idyllic in the sense that it does not expel from a subject of such a contemplation thoughts about death and resurrection. The poet is sure that in spite of all hardship in the earthly life he will enter the paradise as an absolute divine beauty: "Towards the paradise, to which I was admitted in advance, I flew in dreams." Man itself, in Aronzon's poetry becomes similar to a flower. The dying of the man-flower does not distort the flux of events of the beautiful. For the poet beauty is the incarnation and eruption of the flow of flowers with their souls-butterflies hovering over them. Here is another existential mystery is expressed by him, that is of birth.

Nature for Aronzon is the Garden of Paradise before the Fall. The earthly garden as such has its archetype in the primordial Garden that includes the primordial man Adam. The Garden of Paradise and landscape coincide in a unified creation. The beauty of the earthly being is reconciled with the idea of the Divine Paradise. And Paradise is not a utopia but one of the manifestations of the Divine Grace. That Grace that is the very Incarnation: "I had a chance to see the scintillation of the Divine eyes. I know that we are inside the heavens, but these same heavens are inside us."[19]

The "Dark Freedom" of Folly in Poetry of Alexandr Mironov

One of the key issues of philosophy is freedom. Nikolai Berdyaev in his *The Metaphysical Problem of Freedom* considers two types of freedom: rational and irrational freedom.[20] The freedom based on reason is identified by him with truth and virtue, aspired to the determinism of the good. In contrast to this, irrational freedom is unpredictable and is prone to anarchy and self-annihilation. One cannot be sure that such a freedom can save the good. The rational freedom is the freedom of God, but not man. This freedom denies a possibility of choice and leads to the certain conditioning of life. The irrational, "dark" freedom is associated with freedom of man related to his voluntary arbitrariness and the lack of reasonability in actions. In this sense the poetry of the Leningrad underground is an attempt to overcome "dark freedom" by exploiting this freedom. In this context one can claim that the most characteristic figures who was creative in this direction was

---

19. Ibid., 200.
20. Berdyaev, "The Metaphysical Problem of Freedom."

Alexandr Mironov, one of the most dramatic and provocative poets of the "Leningrad's school."

Mironov contemplates the materiality of the world, its being in flesh, with a heightened sensitivity. This materiality appears before him as a chorus of people with red-blooded faces and "hot kisses in the party-style." Man is enslaved by the secular, he is chained to that which does not have God inside. But even if God is around, man is enslaved by the flesh. Correspondingly, freedom for Mironov is beyond his physical body and earthly life, it is not material: "And non-living body, as the constancy temple, is flowing along the eternal stream of life."[21]

Unlike a philosopher, who can use direct propositions, the linguistic equipment of a poet-mystic uses indirect and mediated form of speech. In poetry using direct speech, the I of the author coincides with the I of the lyrical hero. In mystical poetry the lyrical hero is irrational and tormented, he is in constant conflict with his "I-ness," so that his I is not equal to the I of a lyrical hero. There is a paradox here that the more profound is this conflict of the internal lack of freedom, the more rapid its spiritual development leading to true freedom. The way Mironov exercises this conflict of being released from the "dark freedom" is his personal position of being "simple," of "craziness" as a voluntary refusal of one's rationality for the sake of the true vision of God. In Russian this phenomenon is denoted by the term "*yurodstvo*" ("the folly"). *Yurodstvo* here is the manifestation of the weakness and vulnerability of the spiritual dimension of the human reason. *Yurodstvo* here is the apophatic definition and the way of deconstructing not only of secular thought as such, but, contrary to the latter, is a carrier of rational freedom. Mironov's *yurodstvo* is in the middle between secularism as life without God and "refined faith" in him. He uses different ways to express this *yurodstvo*. For example, he uses the category of "laughter": "My laughter, my angel, windy angel, my God—my laughter, that one denying me myself."[22] Sometimes *yurodstovo* manifests itself as a paradoxical breakdown of the sense: "When the Virgin was gently asked as to why she enters Paradise without any prayer, responded she to an angel: today I have no luck for my sausage went rotten."[23] Similar to this: "There is a candle lit for the Mother of God, and a sparrow a tightly-stuffed fat consumes."

Many contemporaries of Mironov found his poetry blasphemous and dirty, offending the image of the Creator. Indeed, the literary hero of the non-repentant sinner is one of the central in poetry of Mironov. His hero

---

21. Mironov, *Izbrannoye*, 49.
22. Ibid., 32.
23. Ibid., 42.

is sinking into temptation. He uses his "dark freedom" and leads the reader into temptation, throws stones in God, so that after this, one finds in his verses: "And God spits upon the poet, that one who is hotter that the iron."[24]

Mironov deconstructs "virtuous" consciousness of his reader through cruelty and shock. He brings the reader through the sufferings not of the literally underground hell, but the earthly hell, and not like Dante who was detached from it, but as a participant of the horrific bacchanalia. Mironov uses the dark freedom of *yurodstvo* in order to create a clash with the ephemeral grace that feeds on sin. Going through exposure, self-emptying and sarcastic laughter, the poet asks: "the blessed, where to run away any more?"[25] His reason seeks for the "pure suffering" by understanding the scale of impurity of his thoughts. Going through the millstones of "dark freedom," the fervor of the "impure spirit" consuming the heart, the poet begs God to place him into the "pure good of knowledge." Thus to bring him close to the absolute light and rest, by understanding at the same time that the light of the absolute freedom and the tranquillity of the earthly life are illusory and transient.

Conclusions

We have considered three different types of a poetico-mystical response to the secular culture and vision of the world without God. Unlike any philosophical attempt for the synthesis of religion and culture for the social purposes, the case studies in this paper have a rather personal and sometimes even anti-social tendency through the appeal to the underlying sense of life for every particular person. In this sense, the most proximate philosophical current associated with this paper is religious existentialism dealing with humanity not on the level on sociology and anthropology, but ethics and soteriology. One can argue that this is a certain way out from the secular, although on a limited and individualistic level. However poetry, being involved in the unconcealment of being (Heidegger) brings the human mind beyond the boundaries of the social and points towards truth in its absolute sense.

---

24. Ibid., 67.
25. Ibid., 21.

Bibliography

Aronzon, Leonid. *Izbrannoye*. 2 vols. Saint Petersburg: Izdatel'stvo Ivana Limbakha, 2006.
Berdyaev, Nikolai. *The Beginning and the End*. Translated by R. M. French. New York: Harper Torchbook, 1957.
———. "The Metaphysical Problem of Freedom." Translated by Fr. S. Janos. Online: http://www.berdyaev.com/berdiaev/berd_lib/1928_329.html.
Florensky, Pavel. *The Pillar and Ground of the Truth: An Essay in Orthodox Theodicy in Twelve Letters*. Translated by Boris Jakim. Princeton: Princeton University Press, 2004.
Krivulin, Viktor. *Kompozitsii*. Moscow: Argo-Risk, 2009.
———. *Koncert po Zayavkam*. Saint Petersburg: Petropolis, 1993.
———. *Zhurnal Topka*. Saint Petersburg, 1989.
Mironov, Aleksandr. *Izbrannoye. Stikhi i Poeziya*. Saint Petersburg: Inapress, 2002.
Solovyov, Vladimir. "Beauty in Nature." Translated by Vladimir Wozniuk, 29–66. In *The Heart of Reality. Essays on Beauty, Love and Ethics*. Notre Dame: University of Notre Dame Press, 2003.

www.ingramcontent.com/pod-product-compliance
Lightning Source LLC
Chambersburg PA
CBHW070240230426
43664CB00014B/2369